First World War
and Army of Occupation
War Diary
France, Belgium and Germany

50 DIVISION
Divisional Troops
Divisional Signal Company
16 April 1915 - 30 April 1919

WO95/2822

The Naval & Military Press Ltd
www.nmarchive.com
Published in association with The National Archives

Published by

The Naval & Military Press Ltd

Unit 10 Ridgewood Industrial Park,

Uckfield, East Sussex,

TN22 5QE England

Tel: +44 (0) 1825 749494

www.naval-military-press.com

www.nmarchive.com

This diary has been reprinted in facsimile from the original. Any imperfections are inevitably reproduced and the quality may fall short of modern type and cartographic standards.

© **Crown Copyright**
Images reproduced by permission of The National Archives, London, England, 2015.

Contents

Document type	Place/Title	Date From	Date To
Heading	50th Division 50th (Northumbrian) Signal Company R.E. Apr 1918-Apr 1919		
Heading	50th Division 50th (Northumbrian) Signal Coy R.E Vols. 1.2.3.4.5&6 April To Sep 15		
Heading	War Diary Of Northumbrian Divisional Signal Co R.E. From 16th April 1915 To 30th April 1915 Vol I		
War Diary	New Castle On Tyne	16/04/1915	16/04/1915
War Diary	Southampton	16/04/1915	16/04/1915
War Diary	Havre	17/04/1915	18/04/1915
War Diary	Hazebrouck	19/04/1915	20/04/1915
War Diary	Steenvoorde	21/04/1915	30/04/1915
Heading	War Diary Of Northumbrian Divisional Signal Company R.E. 1st May 1915 To 31st May 1915 Volume II		
War Diary	Steenvoorde	01/05/1915	11/05/1915
War Diary	Poperinghe	12/05/1915	25/05/1915
War Diary	Watou	25/05/1915	31/05/1915
War Diary	L 19 B	31/05/1915	31/05/1915
Heading	War Diary Of 50th (Northumbrian) Divisional Signal Company R.E 1st June 1915 To 30th June 1915 Volume III		
War Diary	L 19 B	01/06/1915	04/06/1915
War Diary	G21C	04/06/1915	23/06/1915
War Diary	St Jans Cappel	24/06/1915	30/06/1915
Heading	War Diary Of 50th (Northumbrian) Divisional Signal Company R.E 1st July 1915 To 31st July 1915 Vol IV		
War Diary	St Jans Cappel	01/07/1915	21/07/1915
War Diary	Armentieres	22/07/1915	31/07/1915
Heading	War Diary Of 50th (Northumbrian) Divisional Signal Coy R.E 1st August 1915-31st August 1915 Volume V		
War Diary	Armentieres	01/08/1915	31/08/1915
Heading	War Diary Of 50th (Northumbrian) Divisional Signal Coy R.E.1st September 1915-30th September 1915 Volume VI		
War Diary	Armentieres	01/09/1915	30/09/1915
Heading	War Diary Of 50th (Northumbrian) Divisional Signal Coy R.E From 1/10/15 To 31/10/15 Vol VII		
War Diary	Armentieres	01/10/1915	31/10/1915
Heading	War Diary Of 50th (Northumbrian) Divisional Signal Coy R.E From 1/11/15 To 30/11/15 Vol. VIII		
War Diary	Armentieres	01/11/1915	12/11/1915
War Diary	Merris	13/11/1915	30/11/1915
Heading	50th Divn. Signal Co. R.E Dec Vol IX		
War Diary	Merris	01/12/1915	21/12/1915
War Diary	Hoograaf	22/12/1915	31/12/1915
Heading	50th Div Sig Co Jan Vol		
War Diary	Hoograaf	07/01/1916	28/03/1916
War Diary		03/04/1916	12/04/1916
War Diary	Westoutre	22/04/1916	25/04/1916
War Diary	Fletre	28/04/1916	27/05/1916

War Diary	Westoutre	30/05/1916	29/07/1916
Heading	War Diary 50th Divisional Signal Co. R.E July 1916 Volume No.16		
Heading	War Diary Of 50th (Northumbrian) Divl. Signal Coy R.E From 1/8/16-31/8/16 Volume 17		
War Diary	Westoutre	05/08/1916	09/08/1916
War Diary	Fletre	10/08/1916	11/08/1916
War Diary	Bernaville	11/08/1916	15/08/1916
War Diary	Vignacourt	16/08/1916	16/08/1916
War Diary	Montigny	17/08/1916	28/08/1916
Heading	50th Divisional Engineers 50th. Northumbrian Div. Signal Coy. R.E September 1916		
Heading	War Diary Of 50th (Northumbrian) Divisional Signal Company Royal Engineers September 1916 Volume No XVIII		
War Diary	Montigny	10/09/1916	10/09/1916
War Diary	E Of Millencourt	10/09/1916	14/09/1916
War Diary	Railway Copse	15/09/1916	30/09/1916
Diagram etc	Diagram		
Map	Map		
Diagram etc	Diagram		
Heading	War Diary Of 50th (Northumbrian) Divisional Signal Company R.E Volume XIX		
War Diary	Railway Copse	01/10/1916	03/10/1916
War Diary	E Of Millencourt	04/10/1916	25/10/1916
War Diary	Fricourt Farm	25/10/1916	27/10/1916
War Diary	Fricourt Farm	03/10/1916	24/10/1916
Miscellaneous	50th Division Signal Communication.	30/10/1916	30/10/1916
Miscellaneous	Divisional Telephone Communication		
Diagram etc	Diagram Of Forward Communications		
Diagram etc	Diagram Of Forward Communications LM To LMR		
Map	Route Plan Of Communications		
Heading	War Diary Of 50th (Northumbrian) Divisional Signal Company R.E Volume No. XX		
War Diary	Fricourt Farm	03/10/1916	04/11/1916
War Diary	Fricourt Farm	03/10/1916	19/11/1916
War Diary	Albert	20/11/1916	29/11/1916
Heading	War Diary Of 50th Divisional Signal Company R.E Volume XXI		
War Diary	Albert	01/12/1916	01/12/1916
War Diary	Baizieux	02/12/1916	30/12/1916
Heading	War Diary Of 50th (Northumbrian) Divisional Signal Company R.E Volume No. XXII		
War Diary	Baisieux	01/01/1917	01/01/1917
War Diary	Fricourt Farm	03/01/1917	28/01/1917
War Diary	Ribemont	29/01/1917	30/01/1917
War Diary	Fricourt Farm	03/01/1917	24/01/1917
Diagram etc	Diagram		
Heading	War Diary Of 50th (Northumbrian) Divisional Signal Company R.E. Volume XXIII		
War Diary	Ribemont	04/02/1917	13/02/1917
War Diary	P.C Gabrielle	13/02/1917	01/03/1917
War Diary	Ribemont	01/02/1917	13/02/1917
Heading	War Diary Of 50th (Northumbrian) Div. Signal Coy. R.E. Volume XXIV		
War Diary	P.C Gabrielle	02/03/1917	09/03/1917

War Diary	Mericourt Sur Somme	10/03/1917	31/03/1917
War Diary	Molliens Au Bois	31/03/1917	31/03/1917
War Diary	Mericourt-Sur-Somme	26/03/1917	30/03/1917
Miscellaneous	50th Division Communication Information.		
Diagram etc	Diagram		
Map	Route Plan Of Communications		
Diagram etc	Diagram		
Heading	War Diary Of 50th (Northumbrian) Divisional Signal Co R.E. Volume XXV April 1917		
War Diary	Beauval	03/04/1917	03/04/1917
War Diary	Bouquemaison	04/04/1917	04/04/1917
War Diary	Ramecourt	07/04/1917	07/04/1917
War Diary	Roellecourt	08/04/1917	08/04/1917
War Diary	Le. Couroy	10/04/1917	10/04/1917
War Diary	Berneville	11/04/1917	12/04/1917
War Diary	Arras	22/04/1917	22/04/1917
War Diary	N7d4.4	23/04/1917	26/04/1917
War Diary	Couturelle	27/04/1917	27/04/1917
Miscellaneous	50th Division Communications	21/04/1917	21/04/1917
Heading	War Diary Of 50th (Northumbrian) Divisional Signal Company R.E. Volume XXVI May 1917		
War Diary	Couturelle	02/05/1917	02/05/1917
War Diary	Neuville Vitasse	04/05/1917	04/05/1917
War Diary	Couturelle	05/05/1917	19/05/1917
War Diary	Beaumetz Les Loges	20/05/1917	23/05/1917
War Diary	Couin	24/05/1917	30/05/1917
Heading	War Diary Of 50th (Northumbrian) Divisional Signal Company, Royal Engineers Volume XXVII June 1917		
War Diary	Couin	01/06/1917	18/06/1917
War Diary	Boisleux-St-Marc	18/06/1917	18/06/1917
War Diary	Boisleux-St-Marc (s17a9.4)	24/06/1917	26/06/1917
War Diary	Boisleux-St-Marc	26/06/1917	26/06/1917
War Diary	Boisleux-St-Marc (s17a9.4)	18/06/1917	30/06/1917
Heading	War Diary Of 50th (Northumbrian) Divisional Signal Company, Royal Engineers, Volume XXVIII July 1917		
War Diary	Boisleux St Marc S17a9.4	01/07/1917	03/07/1917
War Diary	Boisleux St Marc	04/07/1917	28/07/1917
Miscellaneous	Work Done On Infantry Lines Between Divisional Headquarters And Brigades		
Miscellaneous	Work Done On Artillery Communication	31/07/1917	31/07/1917
Miscellaneous	Divisional Signal School		
Miscellaneous	Communications Infantry		
Miscellaneous	Communications Infantry Brigades		
Miscellaneous	List Of Subscribers		
Miscellaneous	Communications Artillery		
Miscellaneous	Visual System		
Miscellaneous	Wireless Power Buzzer & Amplifier		
Miscellaneous	Despatch Rider Letter Service		
Miscellaneous	Runner System		
Miscellaneous	System of Labelling		
Miscellaneous	Report On German Buries In Divisional Area		
Miscellaneous	Visual Signalling		
Heading	War Diary Of 50th (Northumbrian) Divisional Signal Company R.E. Volume XXIX August 1917		
War Diary	Boisleux St. Marc	05/08/1917	30/08/1917

Heading	War Diary Of 50th (Northumbrian) Divisional Signal Company R.E. Volume XXX September 1917		
War Diary	Boisleux St. Marc	06/09/1917	30/09/1917
Heading	50th Signal Coy Oct 1917		
Heading	War Diary Of 50th Divisional Signal Company R.E. Volume XXXI October 1917		
War Diary	Near Boisleux-St-Marc (Ref Map 1/100000 Sheet 11 Lens)	04/10/1917	06/10/1917
War Diary	Achiet-Le-Petit Ref. Map 1/100000 Sheet 11 Lens)	16/10/1917	18/10/1917
War Diary	Lederzeele Ref Map 1/100000 Sheet 5a. Hazebrouck	18/10/1917	20/10/1917
War Diary	Proven Ref Map 1/100000 Sheet 5a Hazebrouck	21/10/1917	24/10/1917
War Diary	Elverdinghe Chateau (Refs Maps 1/40000 Sheets 20 And 28)	24/10/1917	31/10/1917
Miscellaneous	Communications		
Diagram etc	Runner System		
Miscellaneous	Despatch Rider Letter Service		
Miscellaneous	Report On German Buries In Divisional Area		
Miscellaneous	Communications		
Diagram etc	Runner System		
Miscellaneous	Despatch Rider Letter Service		
Miscellaneous	Report On German Buries In Divisional Area		
Miscellaneous	Report On Communications During Operations		
Diagram etc	Diagram		
Heading	3 Copies Circuit Diagram (New) 2 For War Diary		
Diagram etc	Diagram		
Miscellaneous	War Diary 2 Copy		
Heading	50 D Signal Vol 31		
Heading	War Diary Of 50th (Northumbrian) Divisional Signal Company Royal Engineers Volume XXXII Nov. 1917		
Heading	War Diary Of 50th Divisional Signal Company Royal Engineers Volume XXXII November 1917		
War Diary	Elverdinghe	02/11/1917	10/11/1917
War Diary	Eperlecques	12/11/1917	28/11/1917
Heading	War Diary Of 50th (Northumbrian) Divisional Signal Co, R.E. Volume No XXXIII December 1917		
War Diary	Eperlecques	02/12/1917	12/12/1917
War Diary	Ref. Map. Sheet 28. 1/40,000	13/12/1917	13/12/1917
War Diary	Ypres	16/12/1917	16/12/1917
War Diary	Ref. Map Sheet 28 1/40,000.	17/12/1917	25/12/1917
War Diary	Ypres	25/12/1917	25/12/1917
War Diary	Ref. Map. Sheet 28 1/40,000	25/12/1917	25/12/1917
War Diary	Ypres	29/12/1917	29/12/1917
Heading	Signal Coy. 50 Div Jan 18		
Heading	War Diary Of 50th (Northumbrian) Divisional Signal Company, Royal Engineers, Volume XXXIV January 1918		
War Diary	Ypres	02/01/1918	03/01/1918
War Diary	Ref, Map Sheets 27 & 28 1/40,000.	04/01/1918	06/01/1918
War Diary	Steenevoorde Ref. Map. Sheet Hazebrouck 5a 1/100,000.	16/01/1918	19/01/1918
War Diary	Wizernes Ref. Map. Sheets 27 & 28 1/40,000	27/01/1918	30/01/1918
Miscellaneous	Telegraphic And Telephonic Communications		
Diagram etc	Diagram Of Communications		
Miscellaneous	Diagram Of Communications		
Heading	Signals 50d Feb 18		

Heading	War Diary Of 50th (Northumbrian) Divisional Signal Company, Royal Engineers Volume XXXV February 1918		
War Diary	Ypres Ref. Map. Sheet 28 1/40,000	02/02/1918	07/02/1918
War Diary	Ypres Ref. 1/10,000 Trench Map Sheet 28 N.E. 1 Zonnebeke	09/02/1918	11/02/1918
War Diary	Ypres	14/02/1918	23/02/1918
Miscellaneous	Return Of Cable Salved By 50th. Divl. Signal Co. R.E.	20/02/1918	20/02/1918
Miscellaneous	Details Of Communications 50th Division. Telegraphic And Telephone Communication		
Miscellaneous	50th Division Position Calls		
Miscellaneous	Despatch Rider Letter Service 50th Division		
Heading	50th Northumbrian Division. 50th Divisional Signal Company R.E. March 1918		
Heading	War Diary Of 50th (Northumbrian) Divisional Signal Company R.E. Volume No. 36 March 1918		
War Diary	Wizernes	01/03/1918	08/03/1918
War Diary	Moreuil	09/03/1918	09/03/1918
War Diary	Harbonnieres	11/03/1918	20/03/1918
War Diary	Beaumetz	21/03/1918	21/03/1918
War Diary	Le Mesnil	22/03/1918	22/03/1918
War Diary	Villers Carbonnel	23/03/1918	23/03/1918
War Diary	Foucaucourt	23/03/1918	26/03/1918
War Diary	Marcelcave Villers Bretonneux	27/03/1918	27/03/1918
War Diary	Villers Bretonneux Hangard Sourdon	27/03/1918	28/03/1918
War Diary	Boves Sains En Amienois	29/03/1918	30/03/1918
War Diary	Sains En Amienois	30/03/1918	30/03/1918
Heading	50th Divisional Engineers 50th (Northumbrian) Divisional Signal Company R.E. April 1918		
Heading	War Diary of 50th (Nbn) Divisional Signal Company, Royal Engineers, For Month Of April 1918, Volume XXXVII		
War Diary	Douriez	01/04/1918	03/04/1918
War Diary	Robecq	04/04/1918	07/04/1918
War Diary	Rebecq Ref. Map Sheets 36 & 36a 1/40,000	07/04/1918	08/04/1918
War Diary	Merville	09/04/1918	11/04/1918
War Diary	La Motte	12/04/1918	12/04/1918
War Diary	J.3.d.9.7. West Of La Motte	13/04/1918	15/04/1918
War Diary	Rocquetoire	16/04/1918	19/04/1918
War Diary	Aire	20/04/1918	26/04/1918
War Diary	Aire Fere-En-Tardenois Ref. Map Soissons 1/100,000	26/04/1918	30/04/1918
Heading	War Diary Of 50th (Northumbrian) Divisional Signal Company Royal Engineers, Volume XXXVIII May 1918		
War Diary	Arcis-Le-Ponsart	01/05/1918	05/05/1918
War Diary	Beaurieux Romain Breuil S/Vesle Branscourt Faverolle Cuisles Igny Le Jard Le Bruil Vert La Gravelle	05/05/1918	31/05/1918
Miscellaneous	50 Divisional Signal Company RE. Circuits In Use At Beaurieux	27/05/1918	27/05/1918
Miscellaneous	Casualties 27.5.18	27/05/1918	27/05/1918
Heading	War Diary Of 50th (Northumbrian) Divisional Signal Company Royal Engineers. Volume. XXXIX June 1918		
War Diary	Vert-La-Gravelle (Marne)	01/06/1918	08/06/1918
War Diary	Montgivroux Chateau to (Mondement)	09/06/1918	17/06/1918
War Diary	La Nove	17/06/1918	30/06/1918

Diagram etc	50th Divl. Communications Artillery Lines To Brigades		
Diagram etc	Diagram		
Diagram etc	Left Infantry Bde		
Diagram etc	Right Infantry Bde		
Diagram etc	50th Divl Communications Visual Induction Sets and Wireless Buried Cable and Poled Routes Desp. Rider and Runner		
Diagram etc	Diagram		
Miscellaneous	50 D Signal		
Diagram etc	50th Divl. Communications Infantry Lines To Brigades		
Diagram etc	Diagram		
Heading	War Diary Of 50th (Northumbrian) Divisional Signal Company Royal Engineers Volume XL July 1918		
War Diary	La Nove (Marne)	01/07/1918	03/07/1918
War Diary	Huppy	04/07/1918	11/07/1918
War Diary	Martin Eglise L Of C	12/07/1918	31/07/1918
Heading	War Diary Of 50th (Northumbrian) Divisional Signal Company Royal Engineers Volume LI August 1918		
War Diary	Martin Eglise	01/08/1918	31/08/1918
Diagram etc	Route Diagram		
Diagram etc	Diagram		
Heading	50 D Signals App to Vol. 33 Dec		
Diagram etc	Route Diagram		
Diagram etc	Diagram		
Diagram etc	Diagram Of Forward Communications		
Miscellaneous			
Heading	War Diary Of 50th (Northumbrian) Divisional Signal Company Royal Engineers Volume XLII September 1918		
War Diary	Martin Eglise	01/09/1918	12/09/1918
War Diary	Lucheux	13/09/1918	25/09/1918
War Diary	Montigny	26/09/1918	28/09/1918
War Diary	Combles	28/09/1918	29/09/1918
Diagram etc	50th Divl. Communications Artillery Groups		
Heading	War Diary Of 50th (Northumbrian) Divisional Signal Company R.E. Volume XLIII October 1918		
War Diary	Combles	01/10/1918	11/10/1918
War Diary	Le Trou Aux Soldats	12/10/1918	31/10/1918
War Diary	Le Cateau	20/10/1918	31/10/1918
Miscellaneous	Appendix I		
Miscellaneous	Appendix 2		
Diagram etc	Diagram Shewing Communications As Handed Over To 25th Divl. Signal Coy. R.E.		
Miscellaneous	50th. Division Instructions No.3	16/10/1918	16/10/1918
Diagram etc	Diagram		
Miscellaneous	50th. Division Instructions No.5 Series "E"	02/11/1918	02/11/1918
Diagram etc	50th Division Existing Communications-Diagram 1a		
Diagram etc	50th Division Communications-Diagram 2a		
Miscellaneous			
Diagram etc	Communications 50th Divisional		
Diagram etc	Diagram 7		
Miscellaneous	Wireless Communications		
Heading	War Diary Of 50th (Northumbrian) Division Signal Company R.E. Volume XLIV November 1918		
War Diary	La Cateau	01/11/1918	01/11/1918
War Diary	La Fayt	02/11/1918	08/11/1918

War Diary	Dourlers	09/11/1918	30/11/1918
Heading	War Diary Of 50th (Northumbrian) Divisional Signal Company R.E. Volume XLV December 1918		
War Diary	Dourlers Map Sheet Valenciennes 1/100000	01/12/1918	17/12/1918
War Diary	Le Quesnoy Map Sheet Valenciennes 1/1000000	18/12/1918	31/12/1918
Map	Map		
Miscellaneous	Message		
Diagram etc	Route Diagram		
Diagram etc	Circuit Diagram		
Diagram etc	Communications 150th Infantry Bde. Taisnieres Area		
Miscellaneous	Herewith Route Diagram	04/12/1918	04/12/1918
Heading	War Diary Of 50th (Northumbrian) Division Signal Company R.E. Volume XLVI January 1919		
War Diary	Le Quesnoy (France)	01/01/1919	31/01/1919
Heading	War Diary Of 50th (Northumbrian) Division Signal Company R.E. Volume XLVII February 1919		
War Diary	Le Quesnoy (France) Map Valenciennes 1/100000	01/02/1919	28/02/1919
Heading	War Diary Of 50th (Northumbrian) Division Signal Company R.E. Volume XLVIII March 1919		
War Diary	Le Quesnoy (France) Map Valenciennes 1/100,000	01/05/1919	31/05/1919
War Diary	Le Quesnoy (France)	01/03/1919	31/03/1919
Miscellaneous	50th Division G	13/03/1919	13/03/1919
Heading	War Diary Of 50th (Northb'n) Div'l Signal Coy. R.E. for Month of April 1919 Volume XLIX		
War Diary	Le Quesnoy (France)	01/04/1919	30/04/1919

50TH DIVISION

50TH (NORTHUMBRIAN) SIGNAL COMPANY R.E.,
APR 1915-APR 1919.

On His Majesty's Service.

50th Division

5th (Northumbrian) Signal Coy RE.

Vols. 1. 2. 3. 4. 5 & 6.

April to Sep. 15

Confidential

War Diary
of
Northumbrian Divisional Signal Co R.E.

From 16th April 1915 To 30th April 1915

Vol I.

Paper - Vol 1

WAR DIARY
of Northumbrian Divisional Signal Co. R.E.
INTELLIGENCE SUMMARY.
Army Form C. 2118.

(Erase heading not required.)

Instructions regarding War Diaries and Intelligence Summaries are contained in F.S. Regs., Part II. and the Staff Manual respectively. Title pages will be prepared in manuscript.

Hour, Date, Place	Summary of Events and Information	Remarks and references to Appendices
3.45 am 16th April 1915 Tweedmouth	Head Quarters of N.D. Sig. Coy. left Necastleupon-Tyne for British Expeditionary Force – the entrainment of the horses & the unloading of the train was partly carried out. The weather was fair throughout	
4.30 pm to Southampton	Arrived at Southampton. Detrained & horses on lines S/S assistance left Southampton at 7:30 pm. The lack of moving the horses aboard etc. from the train to S/S. The ship was fair carried out accordingly a hitch. The weather was fair throughout.	
11.0 am 17th April 1915 Havre	Disembarks at Havre & proceeded to Camp No 5. Where men & horses were rested & requirements etc generally attended to. Several wires & equipment indispensably missing were obtained from the Ord. Dept not to be obtained in England. Distance Dyke at Havre. The weather was fair throughout.	
6.0 pm 18th April 1915 Havre	Left Camp No 5 at 6.0 pm & marched to "Point H." Havre Station. Train left Havre at 11.30 pm. The weather was fair throughout.	
7.30 pm 19th April 1915 Hazebrouck	Arrived at HAZEBROUCK. Detrained and S joined H.Q. Northumbrian Division at Royal Engineers Park Huts. Horses in a field adjoining the Railway Station at HAZEBROUCK and picketed by the officers put up at the Officers Rest House "Close by". The weather was fair throughout.	Hot Rest HAZEBROUCK 5A BELGIUM 1:40,000
6.30 am 20th April 1915 HAZEBROUCK	March from HAZEBROUCK at 6.30 am and arrived at STEENVOORDE at 10.30 am. Divisional HQ Northumbrian Division established in the Town Hall at STEENVOORDE. Telegraph Communication opened with the 28th Army HQ at HAZEBROUCK, N.D. INFANTRY BDE at OUDESTRAETE and the NORTH'D INFANTRY BDE at WINNEZEELE	

Page 2 Vol 1

Army Form C. 2118.

WAR DIARY
of North'd Div'l Signal Co R.E.
INTELLIGENCE SUMMARY.
(Erase heading not required.)

Instructions regarding War Diaries and Intelligence Summaries are contained in F.S. Regs., Part II. and the Staff Manual respectively. Title pages will be prepared in manuscript.

Hour, Date, Place	Summary of Events and Information	Remarks and references to Appendices
6.0 am 21st April 1915 STEENVOORDE.	Signal office working and testing satisfactorily. No. 1 Section out in a fatigue party. R&L. Nos. 2 & 3 to office and general care to taken of our horses and harness and guns etc. Men's arms & equipment are kept in good order. Weather fine.	Map ref HAZEBROUCK 5-A BELGIUM 1:100,000
6.0 am 22nd April 1915 do	Situation the same as 21st April.	
Noon 23rd April 1915 do	Weather continues to be fine. Owing to the enemy using gas and forcing the line back in YPRES salient all Brigades of the Northumbrian Div. are warned & be ready to support. Call lines to Brigades redd in.	
8.0 pm 24th April 1915 do	Headquarters North'd Div. still at STEENVOORDE. Weather fine. Nothing special to report.	
8.0 pm 25th April 1915 do	Situation unchanged. The Brigades are still away from the Divisional H.Q. having taken up places at the defence of General Reserve. Heavy firing is reported from YPRES, 8 miles to fro but little had been otherwise overnight.	

(73989) W4141—463. 400,000. 9/14. H.&J.Ltd. Forms/C./2118/10.

Pas 3. Vol 1

Army Form C. 2118.

WAR DIARY
or ~~Intelligence Summary~~ Signal Co RE
INTELLIGENCE SUMMARY.
(Erase heading not required.)

Instructions regarding War Diaries and Intelligence Summaries are contained in F.S. Regs., Part II and the Staff Manual respectively. Title pages will be prepared in manuscript.

Hour, Date, Place		Summary of Events and Information	Remarks and references to Appendices
10am 26th April 1915	STEENVOORDE	O.C. No 4 Section reports the following casualties in his section on the 25th April 1915. Killed :- 1802 L/cpl. H. Green, 1901 Corporal H. Johns, 1817 Sapper W.L. Armstrong. Wounded:- 1909 Sapper G. Round and 1516 Sapper T. Howard. Capt. Duffy (4CDR) (who was attached to No 4 Section) lost his motor cycle damaged by shrapnel. He also continued to labrador communication with CRA to Railhead STEENVOORDE & ST LAURENT.	HQrs Ref. HAZEBROUCK 5ª BELGIUM. 1:100,000 [signature]
7.30 pm	do		[signature]
7.0 pm 27 April 1915	do	Weather fine, very cold. Lieut Y, CRA division from ST LAURENT to WINNEZEELE (through at 6.30pm) Lahore division was brought into the area between No 4th Div + 1st Army at 6.35pm also brought in the area between No 4th Div + 1st Army.	[signature]
10 am 28th April 1915	do	Weather fine. Very quiet season. Nothing special to report except that the LAHORE Division was transferred from our Signal Com to the 1st Army.	[signature]
11.0 am 29th April 1915	do	Weather fine. Quiet in our area. Following casualties in No 2 Section assistant :- Killed - Lieut T.L. Bainbridge (Commander) Wounded. 1950 Saffer R. White : 1979 Sapper A.E. BENNETT 1945 Sapper F. SHORT. 1931 Sapper H.W. BROWN and 1946 Sapper N. STOREY. These casualties occurred on the 25th April 1915.	[signature]

(73989) W4141—463. 400,000. 9/14. H.&J.Ltd. Forms/C. 2118/10.

Page 4. Vol 1

WAR DIARY
of North Midland Divisional Signal Co. R.E.

INTELLIGENCE SUMMARY

Army Form C. 2118.

(Erase heading not required.)

Hour, Date, Place	Summary of Events and Information	Remarks and references to Appendices
Midnight 24 April 1915 STEENVOORDE	Was the following further casualties received from O.C. No 1st Section :- No. 2007 [struck through] Sapper J. KING. 1819 Sapper J. MARSHALL. Both these casualties occurred on the 25th April 1915. During the whole period there was no great care was taken to see that these men were not actually on the fighting line own type had to clean & otherwise General attention being paid to the coming Arms & equipment.	

Ins of Handwriting for April 1915

Confidential

War Diary

of

Northumbrian Divisional Signal Company RE

1st May 1915 to 31st May 1915

Volume II

WAR DIARY
or ~~Intelligence Summary~~ 7th N. Midland Divisional Signal Co. R.E. Page 1 (Vol 2)

Army Form C. 2118.

(Erase heading not required.)

Hour, Date, Place	Summary of Events and Information	Remarks and references to Appendices
Midnight 1st May '15 STEENVOORDE	Weather fine all day. With the exception of carrying out the usual routine orders, necessary horses, vehicles equipment, going, instructions as to bad conditions in action on the affected lines. Conferences & tests generally there is nothing to report of interest. Lieut J.S.W. STONE, R.E. sent by O.C. Signals 4 Army to replace Lieut T.L. BAINBRIDGE, killed in the 25th April 1915.	
Midnight 2nd May '15 do	Same as 1st May –	
Midnight 3rd May '15 do	Weather fine – O.C. No 3 Section reports the following Casualties:— Wounded: 1700 2nd Corporal F. FAIRFIELD. 1679 Sapper R. MAIN. 1824 Sapper P. HARDMAN. 1679 Sapper R. WILLIAMS. 1706 Driver G.A. DAVIDSON – These Casualties occurred on the 28th April 1915 – On this day the Infantry Brigades with No 2 3 & 4 Sections of this Co. left their lines & moved to new lines at STEENVOORDE.	Map of HAZEBROUCK 5A BELGIUM 1:100,000

WAR DIARY
OF No 1 Hand (and) Divisional Signal Co H.Q. Part 2 (Vol 2)
INTELLIGENCE SUMMARY.

Army Form C. 2118.

(Erase heading not required.)

Instructions regarding War Diaries and Intelligence Summaries are contained in F.S. Regs., Part II. and the Staff Manual respectively. Title pages will be prepared in manuscript.

Hour, Date, Place	Summary of Events and Information	Remarks and references to Appendices
Noon 4th May '15 STEENWOORDE	Vibrator lines laid to the Brigades which are billeted in the STEENWOORDE area - It was that Continue to be lines are working satisfactorily and easy that trouble is heard at about 10 a.m. the damage which the Brigade between supplied whilst they are away from the Company.	Map of HAZEBROUCK 5-A BELGIUM. 1:100,000
6 p.m. do	The weather is over cast & rain is threatened.	
Midnight do	Several showers since 6.0 p.m.	
do 5th May 1915	Weather has been fine all day. The ordinary routine work has been carried on throughout the day - Nothing further to note.	
10 a.m. 6th May 1915	Weather fine - a telephone line was laid from the G.S. Office to the Grenadier Battn. 800 yards away at 10.0 a.m. today.	
	At 9-0 p.m. direct telephonic communication was established between our Signal office & the H.Q. of the 2nd Army at Dranoe - CASSEL. This work was carried out by a working party from the 2nd Army Signals.	
9.30 am 7th May 1915	The Telegraph line from No 1, 2nd Army H.Q. is forward to be in contact German dispatches from both ends. It first received at 10.0 am in the morning the telephone was used to 2nd Army consequently the telegrams	
Midnight do	weather has been fine all day. nothing further to report	

WAR DIARY or INTELLIGENCE SUMMARY

Army Form C. 2118.

Page 3 (Vol 2)

50th (Northumbrian Divisional Signal Co. R.E.)

Hour, Date, Place	Summary of Events and Information	Remarks and references to Appendices
10.0pm 8th May 1915 STEENVOORDE	Weather fair. Ordinary report sent forward as usual. Nothing special to report except that we have received orders to proceed from G.S. that H.Q. may move shortly.	Map of HAZEBROUCK 5A BELGIUM 1:100,000
9.0am 9th May 1915 do	Headqrs. arrange to establish Report Centre at POPERINGHE at 5.0pm. This is duly carried out & a signal office in found in a house near the BREWERY just at the entrance of the town. Opened at 5.0pm. In the meantime the Signal Office is kept open at STEENVOORDE and the telegram from & to POPERINGHE are transmitted. There is nothing special to note — Everything is working well.	
midnight do do	do	
11.0am 10th May 1915 do	Weather fine. Everything is working smoothly from a signal point of view. The Brigades with their Signal Sections are in the vicinity of BRANDHOEK and we are in communication with them via the FIFTH CORPS and other Divisions. We have satisfactory communication with all the Brigades — There is nothing special to report. Our old Brigade Lines at STEENVOORDE are all being worked up by No 1 Section Detachments.	
midnight do do	do	
midnight 11th May 1915 do	The weather continues to be fine — O.C. Signal Co. visited Brigades today & inspected their equipment etc.	

WAR DIARY
of ~~~~~~~ Divisional Signal Co. R.E. INTELLIGENCE SUMMARY.

Army Form C. 2118.

Page 4. (Vol 2)

(Erase heading not required.)

Hour, Date, Place	Summary of Events and Information	Remarks and references to Appendices
10.0pm 12th May 1915. POPERINGHE.	The whole of the Division moved up from STEENVOORDE to POPERINGHE at noon today & the office at the Cattle Place was closed & set travel into action at -. We are in Lined with the 28th INFANTRY BRIGADES Heavy Gunfire & L.Guns -	Map ref HAZEBROUCK 5.A. BELGIUM. 1:100,000
9.0am 13th May 1915. do	The weather today has been wet. Brigade Lines have all been overhauled & kept in best order in places. The following changes have been notified by G.H.Q. today: -	
" "	Northumbrian Division - to be known as - 50th DIVISION NORTHUMBERLAND BRIGADE " " " 149th BRIGADE YORK and DURHAM BRIGADE " " " 150th BRIGADE D.L.I. BRIGADE " " " 151st BRIGADE	
" "	The Brigade Sections were all visited by O.C. Signal Co. and Lines etc inspected.	
10.0pm 14th May 1915. POPERINGHE.	The weather is Still wet. Heavy rain practically all day has prevailed. We have estimated no trouble with our lines but with the bay they have devoted to supplying horse & mule lines to mounted troops etc -	
8.0am 15 May 1915. POPERINGHE.	Weather fine - Nothing special to report - All Telegraph & Telephone Lines working satisfactorily.	

Army Form C. 2118.

Pgs 5. (Vol 2)

WAR DIARY
of 77th Divisional Signal Co R.E.

INTELLIGENCE SUMMARY.

(Erase heading not required.)

Instructions regarding War Diaries and Intelligence Summaries are contained in F.S. Regs., Part II. and the Staff Manual respectively. Title pages will be prepared in manuscript.

Hour, Date, Place	Summary of Events and Information	Remarks and references to Appendices
9 am 16th May 1915 POPERINGHE	9th DLI, & 151st Bde attached 2nd Division, 9th DLI some brigade, attached to Cavalry Force	g.a. Map ref HAZEBROUCK 5A BELGIUM N.33.b.10
Noon do. do.	151st Bde Tlgphs transferred to H5A & 6.	g.a.
3 pm do. do.	151st Bde now under Cavalry Corps, also 2nd Northn Shell Co. R.E. Telegraphic communication established to 151st Bde.	g.a. YPRES 1/40000 BELGIUM Sheet 28
Midnight do. do.	Weather fine all day.	g.a.
9 am 17th May 1915 POPERINGHE	All lines working well. O.C. 4th Northn (Sigs.) Bde R.F.A. reports that Sapr Duddin was hurt by fall from his horse and was evacuated on 23rd April 1915. 9th (North'n) Bde R.F.A. moved to H10A.	} g.a.
6 pm do. do.	Fault on C.R.A. line	
do. do. do.	151st Bde line owing to shell fire.	
9 pm do. do.	C.R.A. and 151st Bde lines working again	
Midnight do. do.	Weather fine.	

WAR DIARY

of 50th (Northumbrian) Divisional Signal Co. R.E.
Vol. II   Page 6

INTELLIGENCE SUMMARY
(Erase heading not required.)

Army Form C. 2118

Place	Date	Hour	Summary of Events and Information	Remarks and references to Appendices
POPERINGHE	18/5/15	9 am	2nd Lt Stone R.E. admitted to Hospital suffering from dysentery. Lines working well except 151st Bde. which was again broken by shellfire.	Map Reference YPRES / BELGIUM / 1/40,000 Sheet 28.
		Noon	All lines working well. O.C. inspected Brigade Sections and Lines.	} g.a.
		Midnight	Weather very wet all day.	
do.	19/5/15	9 am	Nothing to report.	} g.a.
		Midnight	Weather very wet all day.	
do.	20/5/15	9 am	Lines working well. Nothing to report	} g.a.
		Midnight	Weather fine all day	
do.	21/5/15		Nothing to report	
do.	22/5/15	9 am	'Q' Branch G.S. moved to WATOU and telegraphic communication established with them.	} g.a.
		3 pm	Driver Bowman, E.H. returned to duty from Hospital. All lines working well. Weather fine all day.	

WAR DIARY
50th (Northumbrian) Divisional Signal Co. R.E.
Vol. II Page 7
INTELLIGENCE SUMMARY
(Erase heading not required.)

Army Form C. 2118

Instructions regarding War Diaries and Intelligence Summaries are contained in F. S. Regs., Part II. and the Staff Manual respectively. Title Pages will be prepared in manuscript.

Place	Date	Hour	Summary of Events and Information	Remarks and references to Appendices
				Map Reference YPRES BELGIUM 1/40000 Sheet 28.
POPERINGHE	23/5/15		Nothing to report.	g.a.
do.	24/5/15		do.	g.a.
do.	25/5/15	9 am	All lines working well.	
		4 pm	Divl. Hdqrs. moved to WATOU. Signal Office at POPERINGHE closed.	
WATOU	do.	4 pm	Signal Office opened in shed of schoolyard. Wagon lines in farm about quarter of a mile away. Communicating with all Brigades. E.R.A. to established. Light draught horse destroyed by O.C. Mobile Veterinary Section. Weather fine all day.	g.a.
		Midnight		
do.	26/5/15	3 pm	Sapr. Stewart H. rejoined from Hospital.	g.a.
do.	27/5/15	9 am	O.C. visited Brigade Sections.	
		6 pm	2nd Corpl. Dixon W. and Sapper Wharton B. sent to 5th Corps for instruction in Pigeon service work. Weather fine.	g.a.
do.	28/5/15		Nothing to report.	g.a.

WAR DIARY
or
INTELLIGENCE SUMMARY

of 50th (Northumbrian) Divl Signal Co. R.E.

Vol. II Page 8.

Army Form C. 2118

Place	Date	Hour	Summary of Events and Information	Remarks and references to Appendices
				Map Reference
				YPRES
				BELGIUM
				1/40000
				Sheet 28
WATOU	29/5/15		Nothing to report.	g.a.
do.	30/5/15		do	g.a.
do.	31/5/15	4 pm	Local lines taken in. Divisional Headquarters moved to L.19.B just north of ABEELE. Signal Office at WATOU closed.	
L.19 B	do.	4 pm	Signal Office opened in wooden hut near farm. Wagon lines in field g.a. near by. Lines working well. Weather fine all day.	

End of Volume II
Graham Adam
T/A.

Confidential

War Diary

of

50ᵗʰ (Northumbrian) Divisional Signal Company R.E.

1ˢᵗ June 1915 to 30ᵗʰ June 1915

Volume III

WAR DIARY
50th (Northumbrian) Divisional Signal Company R.E.
INTELLIGENCE SUMMARY
Vol. III Page 1

Army Form C. 2118

Instructions regarding War Diaries and Intelligence Summaries are contained in F.S. Regs., Part II. and the Staff Manual respectively. Title Pages will be prepared in manuscript.

(Erase heading not required.)

Place	Date	Hour	Summary of Events and Information	Remarks and references to Appendices
L.19.B.	1 6/15		Nothing to report.	Map Reference YPRES BELGIUM 1/40000 Sheet 28 g.a.
do.	2 6/15		do.	g.a.
do.	3 6/15		O.C. visited Brigade Sections. Decided that Divisional Headquarters lie at farm in G.21.C. when Division moved forward to take over part of line and that Battle Hdqrs be at KRUISTRAATE in H.18.D.2.1. Two lines laid from H.18.D.2.1 to point where railway crosses road at I.20.A.3.4.	g.a.
do.	4 6/15	9am	Cpl. Turnbull, J. admitted to Hospital.	g.a.
		noon	Divl. Hdqrs moved to G.21.C. Signal Office closed.	
G.21.C	do.	noon	Signal Office opened, with communication to 5 Bde (Hdqrs and Advanced Report Centre) Divisions, Battle Hdqrs on three Corps lines on three Corps lines, C.R.A., C.R.E. &c. Weather fine.	g.a.

WAR DIARY

of 50th (Northumbrian) Divisional Signal Co. R.E.

Volume III Page 2

INTELLIGENCE SUMMARY

Place	Date	Hour	Summary of Events and Information	Remarks and references to Appendices
G 21 C	5/6/15	6 am	Line laid from KRUISTRAATE to ECOLE DE BIENFAISANCE in 19 C for 150th Bde.	Map Reference YPRES BELGIUM 1 / 40000 Sheet 28
		10 am	Local lines laid round POPERINGHE taken up.	
		6 pm	Second line laid from KRUISTRAATE to ECOLE DE BIENFAISANCE, last being laid in water of moat outside southern ramparts of YPRES. Both lines broken by shell fire before completion of shelling second one.	S.A.
		Midnight	Second line completed.	S.A.
do.	6/6/15	5 am	Lines laid yesterday repaired and tested.	
		10 am	Route surveyed for buried cable between KRUISTRAATE and ECOLE.	
		3 pm	Two lines laid over surveyed route pending digging of trench.	
		4 pm	Divisional Cyclists commenced digging trench at 6.20 SE and till 1.30 am 7/15.	S.A.
			Cable buried as far as trench cut.	
do.	7/6/15	8 am	Lines working well.	
		8.30 am	L/Cpl Anderson R. joined for duty vice Cpl. Bates L. transferred to "L" Signal Co.	
		4 pm	Communication opened with 5 Corps Report Centre.	
			O.C. instructed Brigade Sections working at able trench mentioned above.	S.A.
		8.30 pm	Divisional Cyclists working.	
do.	8/6/15	8 am	Thunderstorm. T.R. J.S.W. Stone R.E. rejoined for duty from Hospital.	
		8.30 pm	Divisional Cyclists working at able trench.	S.A.

WAR DIARY

of 50 (Northumbrian) Divisional Signal Co. R.E.

Volume III Page 3

INTELLIGENCE SUMMARY

Army Form C. 2118

Instructions regarding War Diaries and Intelligence Summaries are contained in F. S. Regs., Part II. and the Staff Manual respectively. Title Pages will be prepared in manuscript.

(Erase heading not required.)

Place	Date	Hour	Summary of Events and Information	Remarks and references to Appendices
G 21 C	9/6/15	8 am	Thunderstorm	Map Reference YPRES BELGIUM 1 40,000 Sheet 28
		8.30pm	Divisional Cyclists working on Cable Trench. Nothing to report. g.a.	
do	10/6/15	5 am	Thunderstorm	
			Lines between KRUISTRAATE and ECOLE strengthened	
		11 am	O.C. visited 7th Inf. Bde. in south ramparts at YPRES with a view to taking over lines.	
		8.30pm	Divisional Cyclists working on Cable Trench. g.a.	
do	11/6/15	9 am	Very heavy rain.	
		2.30pm	1149 7th Inf. Bde. took over 7th Inf. Bde. HQrs. in YPRES. Test station established in LITTLE GREY HOME IN THE WEST Dug-out on YPRES-MESSINES road just south of LILLE GATE. All lines brought into LGHW and these were now laid to 1Hq & Bde from Test Station.	
			Lines working well.	
		8.30pm	Divisional Cyclists complete Cable Trench. g.a.	
do	12/6/15	9 am	Weather fine.	
			Lines between KRUISTRAATE and ECOLE frequently broken by shellfire and repaired. Work went on alternative lines and so delay lessened.	
		3 pm	O.C. visited Brigd. factions.	
			S.& No 2 section Infantry Brigade Neiging Sapper Turnbull, J. wounded 11.75 and Drum Brodie, A. killed 12.15.	
		11 pm	Very heavy cannonade — Thanks to numerous alternative lines, no delay occurred in spite of frequent breaks during enemy retaliation. g.a.	

WAR DIARY

of 50th (Northumbrian) Divisional Signal Co. R.E.

INTELLIGENCE SUMMARY

Volume III. Page 1st.

Place	Date	Hour	Summary of Events and Information	Remarks and references to Appendices
				Map Reference
				YPRES
				BELGIUM
				1/40000
				Sheet 28
G.21.C.	13/6/15	8 am	Weather fine. Lines working well.	
		9.30 am	First Church Parade since landing in France.	
		noon	Col. Hildebrand, O.C. Signals 2nd Army visited Signal Office.	g.a.
		2.30 pm	O.C. visited Brigade Sections.	g.a.
do.	14/6/15	8 am	Weather fine. O.C. No 2. Section reported No.1952 Sr. X Rutter wounded 13/6/15	
		2 pm	Nothing to report.	g.a.
do.	15/6/15	8 am	Weather fine. Communications good.	
		4 pm	Telegraphists, linemen and instruments (draw) sent to KRUISTRAATE.	
		11.30 pm	Advanced 2nd HQrs opened at KRUISTRAATE	
		Midnight	All lines working well. Very heavy cannonade. Y lines attack. Y lines frequently broken, but no delay.	
do.	16/6/15	2.30 am	Attack at HOOGE began. Very heavy cannonade till 11 am.	g.a.
		8 am	Weather fine. Several lines repaired and improved.	
		5 pm	Advanced Div HQrs closed at KRUISTRAATE.	g.a.

WAR DIARY

of 50th (Northumbrian) Divl Signal Co. R.E.

Volume III Page 5

INTELLIGENCE SUMMARY

Army Form C. 2118

Place	Date	Hour	Summary of Events and Information	Remarks and references to Appendices
G 21 C	17/6/15	8 am	Weather fine. Lines refixed and improved.	Map Reference YPRES BELGIUM 1/40,000 Sheet 28
		5 pm	Advanced Divl HdQrs closed at KRUISTRAATE.	g.a.
do.	18/6/15		Nothing to report.	g.a.
do.	19/6/15		do.	g.a.
do.	20/6/15		do.	g.a.
do.	21/6/15		Two detachments exchanged with two of 46th Divn at St Jean Bapt M31C with whom Division is to exchange. General work of transfer.	g.a.
do.	22/6/15		do yesterday.	g.a.
do.	23/6/15		Divl HdQrs moved to ST JANS CAPPEL M 31 C.	g.a.
ST JANS CAPPEL	24/6/15		Tracing and improving all lines. O.C. visited Brigade Stations.	g.a.
do	25/6/15		Improving lines	g.a.
do	26/6/15		do	g.a.
do	27/6/15	11 am	Conference of Signal Officers.	g.a.

WAR DIARY

50th (Northumbrian) Divisional Signal Co. RE
Volume III Page 6

INTELLIGENCE SUMMARY

(Erase heading not required.)

Army Form C. 2118

Place	Date	Hour	Summary of Events and Information	Remarks and references to Appendices
ST JANS CAPPEL	28/6/15		Improving lines	Map Reference YPRES BELGIUM 1/40000 Sheet 28
do.	29/6/15		Nothing to report.	
do.	30/6/15		do.	
			do.	
			End of Volume III	
			Graham Adam Lt.	

Confidential.

War Diary

of

50th (Northumbrian) Divisional Signal Company R.E.

1st July 1915 to 31st July 1915

VOL IV

WAR DIARY

50 (Northumbrian) Divisional Signal Co. R.E.

INTELLIGENCE SUMMARY

Vol IV

Army Form C. 2118

(Erase heading not required.)

Place	Date	Hour	Summary of Events and Information	Remarks and references to Appendices
ST JANS CAPPEL	1 7/15		Weather fine. Maintaining and improving lines. O.C visited Bde sections.	g.a.
do.	2 7/15		do.	g.a.
do.	3 7/15		do.	g.a.
do.	4 7/15		do.	g.a.
do	5 7/15		do. Trouble on Canadian Division	g.a.
			and 149 Inf. Bde line which was removed.	
do.	6 7/15		Weather showery. Maintaining and improving lines.	g.a.
do.	7 7/15		Weather fine. do. Line to 151st Inf Bde	g.a.
			broken by shell fire and repaired.	
do.	8 7/15		Weather fine. Maintaining and improving lines. O.C visited and inspected Bde sections	g.a.
do.	9 7/15		do.	g.a.
do	10 7/15		do.	g.a.
do	11 7/15		do. O.C visited and inspected Bde sections	g.a.

WAR DIARY

of 50th (Northern) Divisional Signal Company R.E.

INTELLIGENCE SUMMARY

Army Form C. 2118

Place	Date	Hour	Summary of Events and Information	Remarks and references to Appendices
ST. JANS CAPPEL	12/7/15		Weather fine. Maintaining and improving lines. O.C visited Bde Sections	g.a.
do	13/7/15		do.	g.a.
do	14/7/15		do.	g.a.
do	15/7/15		do. Capt Lincoln went on leave	g.a.
do	16/7/15		do.	g.a.
do	17/7/15		do.	g.a.
do	18/7/15		do. O.C visited 27th Divn Signals as to lines available for us when move to Armentieres takes place	g.a.
do	19/7/15		do. O.C. at ARMENTIERES	g.a.
do	20/7/15		do. in ECOLE PROFESSIONELLE	g.a.
do	21/7/15		Office at ST JANS CAPPEL closed and office in ARMENTIERES opened at 10 a.m. Horse lines at PONT DE NIEPPE. Working to 149 (LEFT) and 151 (RIGHT) Inf. Bde. on forward front of lines used to II Corps. lines having been run to meet these near Railway Station. Lines laid to three Artillery Bdes. from C.R.A. Telegs in Rue Sadi Carnot. Capt Lincoln returned from leave. Resting Bde at PONT DE NIEPPE put on telephone also G office a office and ADMS.	g.a.
ARMENTIERES	22/7/15			g.a.

WAR DIARY

or

INTELLIGENCE SUMMARY

(Erase heading not required.)

Army Form C. 2118

50 (Northumbrian) Divisional Signal Company R.E.

Instructions regarding War Diaries and Intelligence Summaries are contained in F. S. Regs., Part II. and the Staff Manual respectively. Title Pages will be prepared in manuscript.

Place	Date	Hour	Summary of Events and Information	Remarks and references to Appendices
ARMENTIERES	23/7/15		G.O.C's house, II Corps, Army Workshops, C.R.A. and C.R.E. hut on telephone. Working superimposed to II Corps and on ground about overhead lines for Lungo circuits to B.H.Q. First Bde. 27 Division hut of Artillery in communication with C.R.A. also 16th Heavy Bde. R.G.A. Switchboard.	g.a.
do.	24/7/15		Officers Billet and D.A.D.O.S. at NIEPPE put on telephone and latter extended to take in Divisional Tram. Improving lines generally.	g.a.
do.	25/7/15		Line to 12th Division on our left put in by II Corps. Line to Flying Corps and C.R.A of 12th and 1st Canadian Divisions put to C.R.A.	g.a.
do.	26/7/15		Improving lines generally. Pigeon Loft put on telephone. Lt. Adam prospecting at Maine and other places for route for cables through Drains.	g.a.
do.	27/7/15		Drain Route for cables surveyed and arrangements made for laying two lines to each of the two Brigades. Improving lines. O.C. visited and inspected Both Sections.	g.a.
do.	28/7/15		Improving lines and opening up lines coming into office	g.a.
do.	29/7/15		Lt. Adam commenced laying cables in drains, beginning at ECOLE. Good progress made.	g.a.
do.	30/7/15		Drain party brought to a stop near RUE DES PROMENADES owing to depth of mud in drain. Various expedients tried to get through but all efforts unavailing.	g.a.
do.	31/7/15		Drain route diverted in Rue de LILLE and lines brought through cellars of house where Left Bde. is billeted, through the garden and out into drain again in PLACE VICTOR HUGO	g.a.

Confidential

War Diary

of

50th (Northumbrian) Divisional Signal Coy. R.E.

1st August 1915 — 31st August 1915

Volume V.

WAR DIARY
of 50 (Northumbrian) Divisional Signal Company R.E.
INTELLIGENCE SUMMARY VOL V

Army Form C. 2118

Instructions regarding War Diaries and Intelligence Summaries are contained in F.S. Regs., Part II. and the Staff Manual respectively. Title Pages will be prepared in manuscript.

(Erase heading not required.)

Place	Date	Hour	Summary of Events and Information	Remarks and references to Appendices
ARMENTIERES	1. 8/15		Actual laying of Drain lines completed – two to Left Brigade two to Railway near Right B'de from ECOLE and two from Left B'de to Gas Works. Burying of lines from railway to Right B'de. Bomplated. O.C. visited B'de Sections. Infantry lines.	G.A.
do.	2. 8/15		Burying of lines from drain near Gas Works through Gas Works yard and school yard completed and all lines tested and labelled as important points. Another line from 151st B'de to 1/2 Durhams brought into office. O.C. visited 151st B'de French lines.	G.A.
do	3. 8/15		Maintaining lines. Putting Seven lines on wooden brackets.	G.A.
do	4. 8/15		do.	G.A.
do.	5. 8/15		do. Drain lines to Rt. and Left B'de. hut on telephone switchboard and Sounders worked satisfactorily. Capt. Lincoln left to take up duties as Instructor to Signal Units of New Armies.	G.A.
do	6. 8/15		Earth faults on Drain lines to Rt B'de eventually found to be a fault in the cable itself, a joint made by the manufacturers and allied having been found through under the insulation.	G.A.
do.	7. 8/15		Maintaining lines. Lt. J.A.S. Tillard R.E. joined for duty, and Capt. Lincoln from II Corps Signals	G.A.

WAR DIARY
or
INTELLIGENCE SUMMARY

(Erase heading not required.)

Army Form C. 2118

Instructions regarding War Diaries and Intelligence Summaries are contained in F. S. Regs., Part II. and the Staff Manual respectively. Title Pages will be prepared in manuscript.

Place	Date	Hour	Summary of Events and Information	Remarks and references to Appendices
Armentières	8.8.15		Improving & straightening lines. Weather fine.	good
"	9.8.15		Improving & straightening lines and leads to Signal office. Weather dull but very stuffy.	good
"	10.8.15		At though a time from R.A. Hdqrs to the 50th D.A.C. Remainder of men straightening lines.	good
"	11.8.15		Reeling up stores lines & improving existing ones. Weather fine.	good
"	12.8.15		Work on lines as before. O.C. went out to left brigade section in the afternoon & inspected the trench lines & which are being improved.	good
"	13.8.15		As for previous days. Weather good.	good
"	14.8.15		Work as before. In the afternoon the O.C. went out to choose the route for a buried line to A.D. Left Bde. Hdqrs.	good
"	15.8.15		Church Parade in the morning. Remainder was followed by a outlet Rendezvous. Remainder of day work as before. Out on Outpost Helgrave	good

Army Form C. 2118

WAR DIARY
or
INTELLIGENCE SUMMARY
(Erase heading not required.)

Instructions regarding War Diaries and Intelligence Summaries are contained in F. S. Regs., Part II. and the Staff Manual respectively. Title Pages will be prepared in manuscript.

Place	Date	Hour	Summary of Events and Information	Remarks and references to Appendices
ARMENTIERES	16.8.15		Started digging in the cable from Divisional Headquarters to left brigade battle headquarters. The line starts in a sewer for 1 mile, then overhead power cable 1 mile, but down for 1 mile & go for 1 mile, & finally ½ mile buried in the river. Two huts were drunk done & as we got the river bank taint & most of the burying had with to done in daylight we were stopped just before the end by a violent thunderstorm.	
"	17.8.15		Finished the buried cable in the morning so far as possible & then did the testing at night; the Divisional Exchange did the digging.	
"	18.8.15		Told the buried cable, a tired out more line. Buried leads into the cellar of Divisional advanced headquarters also had a blind line between the headquarters & 4th How Brigade. so much of an emergency line from CRA to 4th How Brigade, as HOUPLINES line had killed stilled this afternoon & the main line was half cut.	
"	19.8.15			

WAR DIARY or INTELLIGENCE SUMMARY

Army Form C. 2118

Instructions regarding War Diaries and Intelligence Summaries are contained in F. S. Regs., Part II. and the Staff Manual respectively. Title Pages will be prepared in manuscript.

Place	Date	Hour	Summary of Events and Information	Remarks and references to Appendices
ARMENTIERES	20.8.15		Laid a line to the C.R.A. to the emergency line to the 3rd & 4th Brigades. Permanent line improving communication.	
"	21.8.15		Laid a telephone circuit in addition from the Right Brigade to the Boyhan. Had fault improving the sound lines, which are not too good, chiefly owing to the easy strain quality of D 5. cable — now remedied. Improving communication (sound); also a fault to left square of the R.A. lines.	
"	22.8.15		Laid a line from 5th How. Bty. to the Left Bde. and we notes of existing lines.	
"	23.8.15		The 14th Anti Aircraft Section came under us today	
"	24.8.15		we laid two two lines from the office; one to an existing telephone line to them; the other to an overhead bypass line connecting them which to all the gun position.	

WAR DIARY or INTELLIGENCE SUMMARY

(Erase heading not required.)

Army Form C. 2118

Place	Date	Hour	Summary of Events and Information	Remarks and references to Appendices
ARMENTIERES	25.8.15		Improving communications. Lt Adams went on leave.	
"	26.8.15		Improving communications.	
"	27.8.15		Had parts digging a kind a happy lines between advanced [Hdqrs.] & 1st R.A. Bde [Hdqrs.] & 27th Divisional Horse Brigade and the railway; to now within the divisions zone & to take [Hdqrs.] & the C.R.A. to [Hdqrs.] of 1st Bde.	
"	28.8.15		Improving communications, & preparing advanced [Hdqrs].	
"	29.8.15		Improving same.	
"	30.8.15		Most of day spent in running faults on most of the bad telephone lines, visited all out wiring at once.	
"	31.8.15		Preparing advanced headquarters, & introducing linesmen in their duties in the event of a move to those [Hdqrs.]	

End of Vol. 5.

Confidential

War Diary

of

50th (Northumbrian) Divisional Signal Coy. R.E.

1st September 1915 — 30th September 1915.

Volume VI.

WAR DIARY
or
INTELLIGENCE SUMMARY
(Erase heading not required.)

Army Form C. 2118

Instructions regarding War Diaries and Intelligence Summaries are contained in F. S. Regs., Part II. and the Staff Manual respectively. Title Pages will be prepared in manuscript.

Place	Date	Hour	Summary of Events and Information	Remarks and references to Appendices
Armentieres	1/9/15		Preparing advanced headquarters. Ran a line along the railway from CRA adv. hdqrs to the 37 Bty. 3rd Bde. also extended the line from RFC to CRA in to his advanced hdqrs.	
"	2/9/15		Party out to dig in an extension from the Power cables on the Right Brigade. In the afternoon further hdqrs of the Right Brigade. ADAM returned from leave. LILLE went out to the Advanced Hdqrs at advanced Hdqrs.	
"	3/9/15		Completed all preparations at advanced hdqrs. & smalltaggled up all lines above ground. Very wet & all day.	
"	4/9/15	9.0am	Received orders to move up to advanced headquarters for a test scheme.	
		9.15	First lorry load of men & instruments went up to advanced Hdqrs.	
		10.16	all lines through working	
		12.30	Adv. report centre closed.	

WAR DIARY or INTELLIGENCE SUMMARY

Army Form C. 2118

Instructions regarding War Diaries and Intelligence Summaries are contained in F. S. Regs., Part II. and the Staff Manual respectively. Title Pages will be prepared in manuscript.

(Erase heading not required.)

Place	Date	Hour	Summary of Events and Information	Remarks and references to Appendices
Armentières ARMENTIERES	4.9.15		The scheme worked very well, the whole went through in good time. The C.R.A. does not like his headquarters as the dugout is too small & too hard to get into. I expect he will come out & demand digs in future.	
"	5.9.15		Major DODDS went on leave.	
"	6.9.15		Inspection of dismounted half of the company after Church Parade by C.O.C.	
"	7.9.15	9.30 am	Improving communications & preparing for C.O.C.'s inspection. Marching order inspection of mounted half of the company at the horselines by the C.O.C. after inspection Lt ADAM 2/Lt Edmunds R.E. (T.C.) account for detachment	
"	8.9.15		Improving cables along the railway & putting them in wooden blocks under the flanges of the rails.	
"	9.9.15		Clearing st huts its signal office; improving cables along the railway. Patrolling all civilian and field cables. In the afternoon officer i/c Brigade 2nd Corps came out & inspected all the lefts in time in the Town.	

WAR DIARY

or

INTELLIGENCE SUMMARY

(Erase heading not required.)

Army Form C. 2118

Place	Date	Hour	Summary of Events and Information	Remarks and references to Appendices
ARMENTIERES	10.9.15		Lt ADAM and a party picking up the ground cables in the Town. Finishing putting cables along the railway in blocks. Training field cable loop lines.	
"	11.9.15		Lt ADAM & a party picking up ground cables.	
"	12.9.15		Major DODDS returns from leave. Picking up ground cables, & laying a line to the new position of the DADOS.	
"	13.9.15		Picking up ground cables, patrolling lines and replacing field cable by "cavic" cable between Signal Coy & Ordnance.	
"	14.9.15		A new bricks for making homesteadings patrolled lines. Changed the telephone to the Divisional Train at their new billet.	
"	15.9.15		A new bricks for homesteadings. Maintenance of lines at adv. hdqrs. totd. & found O.K.	
"	16.9.15		Finished drawing bricks for homesteadings. Maintenance of lines.	

Army Form C. 2118

WAR DIARY
or
INTELLIGENCE SUMMARY
(Erase heading not required.)

Instructions regarding War Diaries and Intelligence Summaries are contained in F. S. Regs., Part II. and the Staff Manual respectively. Title Pages will be prepared in manuscript.

Place	Date	Hour	Summary of Events and Information	Remarks and references to Appendices
Armentières	17.9.15		Replaced 1 mile of pilot cable between railway and 15th Brigade R.A. by arnie airline. Reeled up the pilot cable.	
"	18.9.15		D run wires for housetakings. Maintenance of lines. Drawing wires for housetakings. Maintenance of lines. Party putting lines through to the new office of Right Brigade Hdqrs., & beginning to move to new office at 11 p.m. B.E. Right Brigade Sounds making superimposed at 11 p.m.	
"	19/9/15		Lt. Hillard went on leave. Instruments and fittings at old advanced H.Q. cleared up and withdrawn placed in cellar of present H.Q. Party putting out airline in front of 14th A.A. Section hut which was in swampy ground. Ashes leading all day.	g.a.
"	20/9/15		All lines met required at old Advanced H.Q. taken up except those to II B/4. 12 Drum and 27 Drum. Leading ashes all day — two lineman broken and sent in for repairs to Ordnance.	g.a.
"	21/9/15		Reeled up the airline thrown above, trying making of new line for 14th A.A.C. Brought Canvas and Leading ashes all day. Arranged for purchase of sand. Arranging for battle Headquarters effect by change of position of Right Brigade, change of Front Battle Wayle and E.K.A. Mugu.	g.a.

WAR DIARY
INTELLIGENCE SUMMARY

of the 50th (Northumbrian) Divl. Signal Co. R.E.

Army Form C. 2118

Place	Date	Hour	Summary of Events and Information	Remarks and references to Appendices
Armentières	22/9/15		Found Power cable running between Gas Works and a factory in Rue Nationale near the new Bde. Brigade HdQrs, the Brigade Signal Office via drains partly and buries through gardens. By joining known cable between Gas Works and Chapelle d'Armentières to this new one, safe communication is established from R6 Brigade forward. Sent two new lines from École along Erquinghem Road to pick up two Bn/o lines to our late advanced HdQrs and the 129 Brigade Advanced HdQrs, which are to be used in new arrangement.	g.a.
do.	23/9/15		Running safe lines to present C.R.A. to connect up with Brigades. Joining through and testing part of lines going forward. Laying lines to Railway to pick up certain Artillery lines.	g.a.
do.	24/9/15		Out on faults on one of B/o lines forward, repaired it where it had been broken, evidently by horses. Joined one of B/o lines to Admir'd Right Brigade — one to 12 Division advanced, one to it North. The Bde. R.J.A. and the fourth to their men to Sub. Station at old Bde. HdQrs at Chapelle d'Armentières thence by a known line to USINE DE GAZ and on to Advanced Lft Bde. Joined spare line to old Rt Bde. to one going from Rt Bde. to Asylum and put it on Exchange. Tested all lines at Advanced C.R.A. which have all working well. Bdes moved up to Advanced HdQrs.	g.a.
do.	25/9/15		Very heavy bombardment by our Artillery about 4 a.m. C.R.A. moved to Advanced HdQrs in École. Infantry moved up to Advanced HdQrs. Communications good, both Divisional and Artillery all day. NATIONALE PROFESSIONELLE	g.a.

Army Form C. 2118

WAR DIARY or INTELLIGENCE SUMMARY

(Erase heading not required.)

Instructions regarding War Diaries and Intelligence Summaries are contained in F. S. Regs., Part II. and the Staff Manual respectively. Title Pages will be prepared in manuscript.

Place	Date	Hour	Summary of Events and Information	Remarks and references to Appendices
Armentieres ARMENTIERES	26.9.15		Lt TILLIARD returned from leave, still standing by 2 units of their battle headquarters. CRA's office still to allow at scale of CRA in the officers room at Signal Office. 151st Brigade took over the area of the 36th Bde, & him were run from YEK office to a power station on the N cliff round to the into town him from 1st him to 36th Hdl. These him were worked extempore and to 151st Bde. afts 8 P.M. One him was also run from the CRA's office to the int a line to the 62nd Bde. R.A. 149th Bde. returned from the battle Zigm. In the late afternoon 151st Brigade took over 2 more battalion trenches from the 37th Bde. & a party was sent to help get lines through for him temporarily. It was too late to do much, & he lines were worked to the night by means of the existing overhead between the 36th to 37th Bdes.	
"	27.9.15		150th Bde returned from its battle headquarters in the evening.	

Army Form C. 2118

WAR DIARY
or
INTELLIGENCE SUMMARY
(Erase heading not required.)

Place	Date	Hour	Summary of Events and Information	Remarks and references to Appendices
ARMENTIERES	28.9.15		Party sent to 15th Brigade to dispose of improving communication to the battalion taken over from 37th Bde. C.R.A. returned to his ordinary headquarters.	
"	29.9.15		Liaison out on the line to 2nd Field Company, but unable to find fault. Improving existing communications. 25th divn. cut off from the 15th Bde. telephone, as they were interfering with the working of the line. Work on 2nd Field Company line.	
"	30.9.15		Lt. ADAM went round artillery brigades of 25th division. Work on 2nd Field Company line. Liaison out on all lines. Party tracing out an old line to the 25th division in the evening.	

End of Vol. VI

50th Division

Confidential

War Diary

of

50th (Northumbrian) Divisional Signal Coy. R.E.

From 1/10/15 to 31/10/15

Vol. VII

WAR DIARY
or
INTELLIGENCE SUMMARY
(Erase heading not required.)

Army Form C.

Place	Date	Hour	Summary of Events and Information	Remarks and references to Appendices
ARMENTIERES	1.10.15		Line to 2nd Field Company closed & sent a contact. Direct telephone communication to 25th Division restored, but cut off again in the evening as the line was unworkable. Patrolled all lines.	
"	2.10.15		Improving existing communications. Traced out spare line to 25th division, which had fallen into disuse. Ran 2 lines to Power House opposite cook's yard to get a direct telephone to 25th div. Picked up old Wookely telephone line. Tested line from Y E K to N D (advanced report centre of left brigade).	
"	3.10.15		Maintenance of lines. Preparing horse standings.	
"	4.10.15		Weather wet. Maintenance of lines. Recovering cables from disused lines. Maintenance of Brigade in rest billets. Repairing telephone line to 14th A.A.C.	
"	5.10.15		Weather wet. Repairing horsestandings & maintenance of lines.	
"	6.10.15		Maintenance of lines, & preparing of horse standings. O.C. of 2 T/2 ARD went out to 2nd Corps for a conference.	

Army Form C. 2118

WAR DIARY or INTELLIGENCE SUMMARY

(Erase heading not required.)

Place	Date	Hour	Summary of Events and Information	Remarks and references to Appendices
ARMENTIERES.	7.10.15		Maintenance and patrolling lines. Lᵗ TILLARD out on a counterattack in the morning. Preparing counterattacks. Lᵗ TILLARD went to see the 25ᵗʰ Division about some lines in the afternoon.	
"	8.10.15		A new line brought into use between YEK and ZDL (1st), being the third one of the power cable runners in use. Lead run from power station to YEK, & also 2 existing leads to ZDL joined up, to then give ZDL one of the line forward. Leads in cellar opposite 150ᵗʰ Bde also cleared up & fixed. Maintenance of lines, & returning housestanding & harneshed juncᵗ. Changing CRE's telephone to his new billet across the road. Maintenance of lines, & work on trenches.	
"	9.10.15		& shelling & maintenance of lines. Finding fault on 149ᵗʰ Bde. telephone. Arranging for alterations on AAC line.	
"	10.10.15		Pᵗˢ from BCO assisted by 2 men from YEK & 3 from RA, altering the AAC line, & turning it into 3 lines brought to a central exchange, with a switch.	
"	11.10.15		Laying an emergency wire from CRA to 9B & Bde, who have been taken	

WAR DIARY
or
INTELLIGENCE SUMMARY
(Erase heading not required.)

Army Form C. 2118

Place	Date	Hour	Summary of Events and Information	Remarks and references to Appendices
ARMENTIERES	11.10.15 contd.		over from the 1st. Was leading ═══ line from 3rd Bty. 3rd Bde. into 16th Bde. Lt Adam gone to line temporarily at Horse lines.	
"	12.10.15		2 shelling lines & maintenance of lines. 1 line repaired across the river where it had been broken by a barge. O.C. & Lt TILLARD went in to the 2nd Corps in the afternoon.	
"	13.10.15		2 shelling & maintenance of lines. Lines to Battle Headquarters of 149 & 151st Bdes tested in the morning & found O.K.	
		12.30 P.M.	Yorkshire Hussars on the telephone through B.C.O. Working 151st Bde. 'phone & wonders to Battle Hdqrs, no answer, to Peace Hdqrs.	
		1.30 P.M.	149th Bde. Bnzgr to Peace & Battle Hdqrs. ditto.	
		2.45 P.M.	Line to 151st Battle Hdqrs put through to Pumera Sta.; Peace Hdqrs. cut off. 2.5 # Div. 'phone faulty in their office.	
		3.30 P.M.	T.long & 25th Div. 'phone.	
		5.30 P.M.	Advanced office 149th & 151st Bde. closed. AAC telephone faults.	
"	14.10.15		2 shelling lines & maintenance. Work on dovetails. Running more line across a new gateway on the railway siding. Refining anti-aircraft line.	

WAR DIARY or INTELLIGENCE SUMMARY

Army Form C. 2118

Instructions regarding War Diaries and Intelligence Summaries are contained in F. S. Regs., Part II. and the Staff Manual respectively. Title Pages will be prepared in manuscript.

(Erase heading not required.)

Place	Date	Hour	Summary of Events and Information	Remarks and references to Appendices
ARMENTIERES	15.10.15		Labelling & maintenance. Tracing out new lines on boards & repairing line to 23rd & 25th Div. Inspecting & identifying lines along the canal. O.C. went in to see 2nd Corps.	
"	16.10.15		Labelling & maintenance. Party under 2nd Shewards replacing a cable tie across the river from the Left line by some airline. Spare line to PONT DE NIEPPE also old telephone line to Rt Bde handed over to Trench Howitzer brigade. Major A.D.A.S. came out after lunch.	
"	17.10.15		Labelling & maintenance. Received G.S. wagon from 7th Field Coy. Party out picking up the cable that they replaced yesterday by some airline. Fault on 15/2 Bde. Transport telephone.	
"	18.10.15		Maintenance of lines, & recovering spare cables. Carting wood for hut standings.	
"	19.10.15		Lt TIZARD went round the tracks of the right sector in the morning. Singer car sent into Supply Column for repair. Maintenance of lines & recovering spare cables. Finishing up making transtandings. 2nd Lieuts DOWSON and MCLAUGLIN joined the company.	

WAR DIARY
or
INTELLIGENCE SUMMARY
(Erase heading not required.)

Army Form C. 2118

Place	Date	Hour	Summary of Events and Information	Remarks and references to Appendices
ARMENTIERES	20.10.15		Maintenance and labelling lines. Casting diagram for a road at the Howitzers. O.C. visited the brigade in the morning.	
"	21.10.15		Officers from BCO came out in the morning to see about running a telephone line from HAR to the Anti-Aircraft Section. Lt TIZZARD took him round. Lt EDWARDS went round Centre Brigade trenches. O.C. 21st Sig. Coy. came out in morning to arrange about taking over from the division; he is going to send an officer and 3 or 4 linemen to learn the lines. O/C Sigs BCO and Sig 25th Div. come over in the afternoon for a conference.	
"	22.10.15		Labelling lines & maintenance. Morning spent in drawing a diagram of ideal lines for a division for the benefit of O/C Sigs. 21st Corps. In afternoon diagrams drawn for Sig. 21st Div. Maintenance of lines and ruling up of lines. Linemen from 21st Div. come out to learn our lines, also staff for 21st R.A. who the over tonight. Alterations in R.A. lines. 12 men arrived from Sig. Park depôt	
"	23.10.15			

WAR DIARY
INTELLIGENCE SUMMARY

(Erase heading not required.)

Army Form C. 2118

Place	Date	Hour	Summary of Events and Information	Remarks and references to Appendices
ARMENTIERES	24.10.16		R.A. 21st Div. took over from R.A. 50th Div. the morning. R.A. 50th Div. went into reserve at CAESTRE.	appx
"	25.10.16		Reeling of spare lines & maintenance. Adam about moved the R.A. Signal Office of 21st Div. Cable from PONT DE NIEPPE to 18th Heavy Bde. R.E.A replaced by comic airline. Signal officer from 21st Div. showed round office. 62nd Bde. then over from 149th Bde. in the afternoon. 63rd Bde. comes into town to 3 Rue Bayard in the evening, for attachmt. Fault on 97th R.A. Bde. line.	appx
"	26.10.16		Testing lines & finding fault on 95th R.A. bde. Tending to own from 21st Bde. higher enobring. BCO build line from HAR to Water Billet. Exchange of Anti-Aircraft Section.	appx
"	27.10.16		Maintenance of lines. Tracing out routes of all R.A. lines for purposes of line book.	appx
"	28.10.16		Maintenance and repair of lines. Finishing off showing 21st Div. hummer round lines. Opening up leads to C.R.A's offices & billetings. Fault on Ordnance Line.	appx

Place	Date	Hour	Summary of Events and Information	Remarks and references to Appendices
ARMENTIERES	29.10.15		Maintenance of lines, & repairing at C.R.A. lines. Clearing position for a heavy which shewing serious signs of altering loops in the trenches. Trouble with faults on BCO lines, due to working parties on the line.	
"	30.10.15		Party out under Lt. ADAM noting it spare lines and clearing at C.R.A's Office. Party repairing up the road down to the wheatery and the terminal pole at the railway. Cpl Twentyfolt repairing farm cable on the railway. CHAPELLE road, & interfered with by 23rd div. R.A. Lt EDWARDS building out station to a camp hyllays. O.C. 2nd Sig. Coy. came out in person to tempt about hygiene.	
"	31.10.15		Repairing at R.A. lines, also tidying the road down to the railway. Finding stations for a long range set of the strtic kept by Divs. 23rd DIV. wanted to talk their lateral line to us, so we risked it at TIZZARD front without consulting us, & so cut us off from 25th DIV. We went out & reinstated with Sigs. 23rd & they not going to try & put through again tomorrow. We will send 25th DIV. on spare line if they can find it in their office. END OF VOL. VII	

50th Division

Confidential

War Diary

of

50th (Northumbrian) Divisional Signal Coy. R.E.

From 1/11/15 to 30/11/15

Vol. VIII

WAR DIARY or INTELLIGENCE SUMMARY

(Erase heading not required.)

Army Form C. 2118

Place	Date	Hour	Summary of Events and Information	Remarks and references to Appendices
ARMENTIERES	1/11/15		Long distance daylight lamp test carried out in the morning for the benefit of the G.O.C. The day was very bad, first misty & then raining, & we only got 500" with the whole sign.) & just under 1000" with field glasses. 2 men were out tidying up the road to the railway, & more working at the C.R.A. Another man putting a tee on the line from CRA to the DAC. RFC telephone faulty. 25ᵗʰ & 23ʳᵈ div. lines not yet through. Lᵗ TILLARD went out to see 25ᵗʰ Div in the afternoon about their line.	[signed]
"	2/11/15		Another very wet day; Lᵗ EDWARDS went down to the landing after breakfast & reported the state of the field in trouble, & men were going sick. Line to 25ᵗʰ Div failed in the morning but 'dys'; set out & [mending?] to trace fault. Physical line from CRA to 97ᵗʰ How. Bde. where at by anthill, & also failed emergency line; fault found near culvert at CHAPELLE where line is buried. Party out clearing the RFC line of earth. Lᵗ ADAM not well today & staying in bed. Through to 23ʳᵈ DIV in morning.	[signed]

WAR DIARY or INTELLIGENCE SUMMARY

(Erase heading not required.)

Army Form C. 2118

Place	Date	Hour	Summary of Events and Information	Remarks and references to Appendices
ARMENTIERES	3.11.15		State of trenches still very bad, 1 & 2 more cases of sickness. Weather slightly better today; and men down from trenches to assist at translations. Work today:- Repairing portion of the B.C.O. telephone line; the steps had been swept to the exit. 1 man out to find fault on the 16th Bde. R.A. line. 2 men under Lt EDWARDS running fault on 97th Bde. line who when tested yesterday. Men out on 20th Div. buzzer line. Lt PORTEOUS 81st Div came out in morning, & I showed him the line to Left & Centre Bde. adv. Hqrs. before lunch.) & after lunch line to and CHAPELLE.	
"	4.11.15	6 P.M.	25th Div. buzzer line through. Weather better, dry but misty. Lt EDWARDS repairing line to 97th Bde.	
"	5.11.15		Weather dull & misty. Party tidying up the road towards the railway. Lt TIZZARD went round the brigades after lunch. Lt EDWARDS left for duty at 2nd Army. 18 reinforcements arrived in the evening for duty.	

Army Form C. 2118

WAR DIARY
or
INTELLIGENCE SUMMARY
(Erase heading not required.)

Instructions regarding War Diaries and Intelligence Summaries are contained in F. S. Regs., Part II. and the Staff Manual respectively. Title Pages will be prepared in manuscript.

Place	Date	Hour	Summary of Events and Information	Remarks and references to Appendices
ARMENTIERES	6.11.16		Major DODDS took 2/Lt DOWSON and McLAUGHLIN round the trenches in the morning. Operation from 21st Div. visited the office for instruction. Parties still out tidying up the Rue Jules Lebleu.	
"	7.11.16		Party helping Anti Aircraft Section to utilise some wire that had fallen down owing to the wet, & to lay a new line to Winter Billet. Party out maintaining old line to 25th Div. adv. H.Qrs. Parties on Rue Jules Lebleu as usual.	
"	8.11.16		Parties on 25th Div. line & Rue Jules Lebleu as usual. Remainder of company cleaning up the Camp. O.C. & Lt TILLARD went to MERRIS in the morning to see the lines & accommodation there.	
"	9.11.16		Party out on Rue Jules Lebleu's & also other men seeing that all lines are properly labelled. O.C. 21st Sig. Coy. came out to look round the office. Lt DYEMONT came out in afternoon to look at A.A. lines	

WAR DIARY or INTELLIGENCE SUMMARY

Army Form C. 2118

Instructions regarding War Diaries and Intelligence Summaries are contained in F. S. Regs., Part II. and the Staff Manual respectively. Title Pages will be prepared in manuscript.

Place	Date	Hour	Summary of Events and Information	Remarks and references to Appendices
ARMENTIERES	10.11.15		Parts on Rue Jules Lebleu; others finishing labelling of ditch lines to old R.T.Bde. Fire at boulangerie; 5 kilomes burnt down & all equipment etc. destroyed. Fire began 5.50 P.M., out 6, 6, 15 P.M.	
"	11.11.15		Finishing Rue Jules Lebleu; also ditch line to old R.T.Bde. Board to enquire into fire at boulangerie at 11 A.M. Lt. McLAUGHLIN visited Right Bde. Advance party from 21st Divn. arrived at 10.30 A.M.; sent back an advanced party, 1 N.C.O. & men, by bus on its return; also stores. Handling our materials, changing offices, preparing for move.	
		7.30 P	Went began to 2nd Bde.	
		10 p.m.	Company moved off under Lts. Adam & McLaughlin. Lt Tillard left behind to assist 21st Signals and to remainder of stores at Signal Office and C.O.M.S. Lt. Dawson informing Squadn. duties at Rauf. O.C. proceeded to MERRIS to authorised taking over of new offices, which consisted of Sounder to Army, Vibrator to 149 Bde, 50 SD G. 3rd Wh. Bd. RTGA, and earth return telephone to 150 Bde. Communication with 151st Bde through 2nd Infbde. Armentières shelled; test had several large, any which succeeded in breaking some twenty of the wing wires, all of which were put through at daylight. Lt. Tillard assisting 21 Signals.	J.A.
	11/12/15			

WAR DIARY
or
INTELLIGENCE SUMMARY

(Erase heading not required.)

Army Form C. 2118

Instructions regarding War Diaries and Intelligence Summaries are contained in F. S. Regs., Part II. and the Staff Manual respectively. Title Pages will be prepared in manuscript.

Place	Date	Hour	Summary of Events and Information	Remarks and references to Appendices
MERRIS	13/11/15		Linemen sent out learning and repairing lines from Armentieres. Clearing billets & routine work. Lt Tillard returned 5 p.m. Remainder of stores brought up. Cleaning up lines entering office and general work. Lineman and working party sent to Armentieres to assist 21st Signals and load remainder of stores.	g.a.
do.	14/11/15		Various bells fixed for staff. Aire lines ruled up and work done in straightening of lines entering Signal Office. Church Parade. Lt Tillard and Adam visited 150th and 151st Bdes and 2nd Corps Signals. Arrange to replace 151st Bde lines by corps airline. Lineman learning lines. Weather fine but frosty.	g.a.
do	15/11/15		Corps Airline Detachment under Lts Tillard and Dowson replacing 151st Bde lines by corps airline. 2nd Corps Sounder and Transformer returned. Telephs to 1st Adm billets transferred to Signal Offices' Mess. Spare local lines ruled up. Lt McLaughlin in charge of Exercise Ride.	
do	16/11/15		Extract from London Gazette d/d 12.11.15 "2 Lieutenants to be temporary Captains" - viz. 3. A.S. Tillard R.E. d/t 23.9.15. Capt. Tillard & Lt. Dowson out completing corps airline for 151st Bde. Line completed by 2 p.m., & return to camp by 5 p.m.	

Army Form C. 2118

WAR DIARY
or
INTELLIGENCE SUMMARY

(Erase heading not required.)

Instructions regarding War Diaries and Intelligence Summaries are contained in F. S. Regs., Part II. and the Staff Manual respectively. Title Pages will be prepared in manuscript.

Place	Date	Hour	Summary of Events and Information	Remarks and references to Appendices
METRIS	16/11/15 contd.		Lt McLaughlin in charge of exercise. Maintenance and patrolling of lines.	ggt.
do	17/11/15		Party out repairing wire airline to STAZEELE under Lt ADAM. Short exercise under Lt DOWSON. Preparing fresh housestartings.	ggt.
do	18/11/15		Party of 18 Regular R.E.'s left for Signal Dpot by train at 8 A.M.; they have been replaced by Territorials. Party out on line from STRAZEELE to BORRE. Exercise under Lt McLAUGHLIN. Preparing housestartings.	ggt.
do	19/11/15		Loading for lamp station. Party out on line to STRAZEELE. Preparing housestartings and draught wires. Training lamps to scheme.	ggt.
do	20/11/15		Preparing housestartings. Putting up hut for lamp addition Exercise. Headquarters + 1 section put on new stations. Training in afternoon.	ggt.
do	21/11/15		Church parade + service. Dinners shifted into hut on new buildings.	ggt.

WAR DIARY or INTELLIGENCE SUMMARY

Army Form C. 2118

Place	Date	Hour	Summary of Events and Information	Remarks and references to Appendices
MERRIS	22/11/16		Putting up known dist, & improving standings. R.A. Signalling class turned up (35 men). Sorted them out in morning, & started flag drill in afternoon. 12 good, 8 fair, 20 poor. 5 of our own doing same too.	
"	23/11/15		Report on our repetition at ARMENTIERES sent to 2nd Army. Work on known dist & homesteadings as usual. Exercise & signalling class.	
"	24/11/15		Detachment out on show cable drill, riding drill started, signalling class. Work on known dist. Fault on BCO lines, cleared in morning.	
"	25/11/15		Same as 24th inst.	
"	26/11/15		Same as 24th inst.	
"	27/11/15		Same as 24th, but riding drill stopped owing to state of fields which made trotting & cantering impossible. Court martial on 2nd Cpl. Williamson.	
"	28/11/15		As before, but half day's work, & toy in afternoon. Church parade in morning.	

WAR DIARY
or
INTELLIGENCE SUMMARY
(Erase heading not required.)

Army Form C. 2118

Place	Date	Hour	Summary of Events and Information	Remarks and references to Appendices
METZIS	29/11/15		Wet day. Cable drill and exercise in morning. Signalling class bugger work and lectures. 10 Signallers & 1 M.C. lent to Div. Mtd. Troops for a scheme.	
"	30/11/15		Medical inspection of 2/L W by A.D.M.S. at 9 A.M. 3 M.C's sent to get hurricane lamp supplies for use from MT NOIR. Party out as usual.	

END OF VOL. VII.

50ü dicke Sapone co. Rif.

Data 10/

XX VIII / XI

9496 / 10 bebl

Army Form C. 2118

WAR DIARY
or
INTELLIGENCE SUMMARY
(Erase heading not required.)

Instructions regarding War Diaries and Intelligence Summaries are contained in F. S. Regs., Part II. and the Staff Manual respectively. Title Pages will be prepared in manuscript.

Place	Date	Hour	Summary of Events and Information	Remarks and references to Appendices
MERRIS	1.12.15		L^t. ADAM went on leave in morning. CAPT. TILLARD went to see C.R.A. at CAESTRE in morning. Cable drill and signalling as usual, and exercise work on horsestandings in afternoon. Remaining ½ Coy. inspected by A.D.M.S. at 9 A.M.	
"	2.12.15		Major W.H. DODDS quitted company for duty in England. New commanding officer Capt. DALE R CAPT. TILLARD went to meet the C.R.A. in morning. Signalling as usual, fresh out collecting faggots to house standings. Parts on line to C.R.A.	
	3.12.15		Signalling class as usual at Hd.s Quarters.	
	4.12.15		Signalling class as usual at H.Q.	
	5.12.15		Sunday. Signalling class in morning.	
	6.12.15		Signalling class as usual at H.Q.	
	7.12.15		Signalling Selves as usual at H.Q.	
	8.12.15		Signalling class as usual & horsemen with Camp, shoeing & stickney Leave	
"	15.12.15		Signalling class dismissed, men returned to their batteries. Cavalry H. new horse good [?] M.D. A. Co. Conway 30 6 Bn Sh...	

WAR DIARY
or
INTELLIGENCE SUMMARY

Army Form C. 2118

Place	Date	Hour	Summary of Events and Information	Remarks and references to Appendices
MERRIS	20.10.15		Capt J Lillard & advance party to take over office at HOOGRAAF from 9th Divs Sigs.	
	21.10.15		Signal office closed at MERRIS. 10 am re-opened at HOOGRAAF at 10 am. 9th Divn Sig Coy R.E. left HOOGRAAF for MERRIS 10 am. The field allotted to the Mounted Section of the company is cut up a great deal no practically a sea of mud. Horses are under shelter & the men in bivouacs. Visited Advanced Report centre & decided to remain in the present dugout & not move into the new one. Visited 149th, 150th & 151st Fd. Signal offices & walked over the ground & set the Laying of the buried lines.	
HOOGRAAF	22/75			
	23/3	15/-	Overhauling lines from Advanced Report centre to Bde H.Q.	

Arnold Copp
Commdg 50th Divl Sig Coy R.E.

50th Ave Sing Co

Jam

Vol XT

WAR DIARY
or
INTELLIGENCE SUMMARY
(Erase heading not required.)

Army Form C. 2118

Place	Date	Hour	Summary of Events and Information	Remarks and references to Appendices
HOOGRAAF	7-1-16	—	Three buried cables to 149th Bde completed	
	8-1-16	—	Three new ditch cable lines from No. 9 Lock Canal to 151st Bde completed.	
	9-1-16		New lines to 1st & 3rd Bdes RFA taken into use. Unable to work to ZDL on Saunder. Communication by buzzer only. Working Saunder to ZDL. Ringing telephone also OK.	
	10/1/16		All new buried lines completed	
	13/1/16		All 9 lines to Advanced Report centre damaged by shell fire. Relaid by the Corps linemen	
	15/1/16		All wires connecting Advanced Report Centre with Div. HQ broken by shell fire. Communication maintained to Bdes.	
	16-31/1/16		Nothing but this quietly of communication nothing to report	

M. K. Dale Capt.
Comdg 50th Div. Sig. Cy

WAR DIARY
or
INTELLIGENCE SUMMARY

Army Form C. 2118

Place	Date	Hour	Summary of Events and Information	Remarks and references to Appendices
HOOGRAAF	1-2-16 to 12-2-16		Normal conditions prevailed. Maintenance of lines.	
	13.2.16		Nothing further to report	
	14.2.16		Severe enemy bombardment from 2.30pm till late in the evening when all lines were broken by shell fire, between Advanced Divn Report Centre & Brigades. Communication was only actually cut off for 1 hour 17 minutes. Lines were repaired, one man being wounded & evacuated	
	16.2.16		New twin armoured cable laid between Advanced Report Centre & Left Supply Pole at Zillebeke Lake.	
	25.2.16		Took over two wires from 2nd & Div R.K. Picked up at Dickebuschcheek & led into YEKR. Tested out Led into Right Pole H.Q. Insulation Rx 7. 10° Rx 8. 20° Rx 7. 10° Rx 8. 20°	
	26-29 2.16		Nothing to report	

M Wake Capt
Commdg 50th Div. Sig. Coy R.E.

Army Form C. 2118

WAR DIARY
or
INTELLIGENCE SUMMARY
(Erase heading not required.)

Place	Date	Hour	Summary of Events and Information	Remarks and references to Appendices
HOOGRAAF	8/3/16	—	The 149th Infy Bde handed over the Bde H.Q. & whole of communications from Trench # 3-4 Northwards to 19th Infy Bde.	
	23-4 3-16		The 151st Infy Bde took over the communications from N of Canal — BLUFF — to trench 34.	
	28/3/16	9 am	150 Infy Bde offices closed at OUDERDOM. Brigade proceeded to Canadian Rest Area II being relieved by 1st Canadian Div"	

McHale Capt.
Commdg 50th Div Sig Coy R.E.
31/3/16.

WAR DIARY
or
INTELLIGENCE SUMMARY

(Erase heading not required.)

Army Form C. 2118

Place	Date	Hour	Summary of Events and Information	Remarks and references to Appendices
	3/4/16		50th Divison moved from Hoograaf to Watuiten	Sheet 28 Ypres G 26 c
			149th Fd Coy) In action	
			150th Fd Coy)	
			151st Fd Coy In rest Querdom	
	4/4/16		151st Fd Coy took over left sectn relieving 4th Can Engrs Fd Coy at La Clytte	
	10/4/16		No 1947 Sapper Storey T. Awarded the Distinguished Conduct Medal for Distinguished conduct in the field (No 2 Section)	Authority S of S London Gazette 14.1.16
	12/4/16		No 957 Sapper Wharton M (attached No 4 section) awarded the Military Medal for distinguished conduct in the field	

Army Form C. 2118

WAR DIARY
or
INTELLIGENCE SUMMARY
(Erase heading not required.)

Instructions regarding War Diaries and Intelligence Summaries are contained in F.S. Regs., Part II. and the Staff Manual respectively. Title Pages will be prepared in manuscript.

Place	Date 1916	Hour	Summary of Events and Information	Remarks and references to Appendices
WEST OUTRE	APRIL 22		CAPT C.C. BAGNALL 9th DURH L.I. assumed command of the 50th Signal Co R.E. CAPT W.M. DALE leaving to take command of the 6th Signal Co R.E.	Reference Sheet 27 Belgium & part of France 1:40,000
"	24		On the night of May 22nd/23rd the 8th Infantry Brigade relieved the 151st Infantry Brigade & came under the orders of G.O.C. 50th Division. The 151st Inf Brigade moved to rest area with Bde Headquarters near LE MONT DES CATS (R19 d 6.5) & came under the orders of G.O.C. 3rd Division	
"	25		On the night of May 25th/26th the 9th Infantry Brigade relieved the 149th Inf Brigade. The G.O.C. 149th Infantry Brigade assumed command of KEMMEL DEFENCES on completion of relief. Bde Headquarters at LOCRE. G.O.C. 3rd Division assumed command of the Divisional Front on completion of above relief, & consisting of 8th, 9th & 150th Brigades & 50th Div. Arty. Troops consisting of the G.O.C. 50th Division assumed command of rest area, 3rd Divisional Arty. DIVISIONAL Headquarters 76th, 149th, 130th Inf Bdes, THE CHATEAU, FLETRE.	

Army Form C. 2118

WAR DIARY
or
INTELLIGENCE SUMMARY
(Erase heading not required.)

Instructions regarding War Diaries and Intelligence Summaries are contained in F. S. Regs., Part II. and the Staff Manual respectively. Title Pages will be prepared in manuscript.

Place	Date	Hour	Summary of Events and Information	Remarks and references to Appendices
FLETRE	April 1916 28		On the night of April 28/29th the 76th Inf Brigade relieved the 150th Brigade, the latter moving to rest area with Bde Hd Qrs at THIESHOUK (Q 35 - 24 2)	

Matl Bagnall
Capt. & "Dvd L.I"
Comdg 50th (Nbn) Signal C.R.E.

D

1875 Wt. W593/826 1,000,000 4/15 J.B.C. & A. A.D.S.S./Forms/C. 2118.

WAR DIARY
or
INTELLIGENCE SUMMARY
(Erase heading not required.)

Army Form C. 2118

Signal Coy. Vol 9

50
57

Place	Date 1915	Hour	Summary of Events and Information	Remarks and references to Appendices
FLETRE	MAY 3		35 N.C.Os & men sent from Divisional R.A. to Signal Company for course of instruction in Signalling.	
"	23		General Sir Herbert C.O. Plumer G.C.M.G., K.C.B. presented D.C.M. and Military Medals to N.C.Os & men of the 50th Division. The following N.C.Os & men of the 50th Signal Co. R.E. received awards at the hands of Gen. Plumer. No 1672 Sergt SMITH, R.S. No 3 Section D.C.M. " 1949 Sapper Turnbull T. " 2 " " " 1947 " STOREY T. " 2 " " " 957 " WHARTON H. HdQrs Military Medal	
"	24	3 PM	50th Division became responsible for defence of KEMMEL HILL. V Corps Mounted Troops consisting of V Corps Yeomanry Regt. V Corps Cyclist Battalion & No 3 Motor Machine Gun Battery were placed under the command of 50th Division.	

Army Form C. 2118

WAR DIARY
or
INTELLIGENCE SUMMARY
(Erase heading not required.)

Instructions regarding War Diaries and Intelligence Summaries are contained in F.S. Regs., Part II. and the Staff Manual respectively. Title Pages will be prepared in manuscript.

58

Place	Date 1916	Hour	Summary of Events and Information	Remarks and references to Appendices
FLETRE	MAY 24	3 PM	No. 4 Co. ROYAL MONMOUTH RE also placed (for tactical purposes) under the orders of G.O.C. 50th Division.	50th Div. Operation Order No 35 of May 18nd 1916
		3 PM	LIEUT COL D.A. WAUCHOPE D.S.O. Cmdg V. Corps Mounted Troops relieved the 149th Infantry Brigade, taking over command of KEMMEL DEFENCES.	"
			No. 4 Co. ROYAL MONMOUTH RE were placed under the orders of O.C. V Corps Mounted Troops for defence of KEMMEL HILL	
			During the night of May 24th/25th, the 149th Brigade completed the relief of Centre Sector. The G.O.C. 149 Brigade took over command of Sector from G.O.C. 9th Brigade with Headquarters 800 yards SE of SCHERPENBERG. (Ref: Sheet 28. M18 d4.1).	50th Div. Operation Order No 3 of May 20th 1916.
"	27		On the night of May 27th/28th, the G.O.C. 150th Inf Brigade took over command of Right Brigade Sector from G.O.C. 76th Inf Brigade, Headquarters at LOCRE. G.O.C. 151st Infantry Brigade relieved G.O.C. 8th Inf. Brigade Headquarters at LA CLYTTE. The G.O.C. 50th Division took over command from G.O.C. 3rd Division, with Headquarters at WEST OUTRE	

Army Form C. 2118

59

WAR DIARY
or
INTELLIGENCE SUMMARY

(Erase heading not required.)

Instructions regarding War Diaries and Intelligence Summaries are contained in F. S. Regs., Part II. and the Staff Manual respectively. Title Pages will be prepared in manuscript.

Place	Date 1916	Hour	Summary of Events and Information	Remarks and references to Appendices
WEST OUTRE	May 30		On night May 30/31st C.R.A. 50th Division took over command of Divisional Artillery from C.R.A. 3rd Division. Headquarters WEST OUTRE.	

M H Bryne Ll Captain
Comdg. 50th (North'n) Divisional Signal Company R.E.

1875 Wt. W593/826 1,000,000 4/15 J.B.C. & A. A.D.S.S./Forms/C. 2118.

WAR DIARY or INTELLIGENCE SUMMARY

Army Form C. 2118

Signal Coy
Vol 15

Place	Date 1916	Hour	Summary of Events and Information	Remarks and references to Appendices
WEST OUTRE	JUNE 3		The following Honours & Awards were gazetted.	
			Military Cross — CAPT. C.K. BAGNALL	
			" — " A.G. SHAW	
			Military Medal No 1442 SERGT JENSON N	
			" No 1932 " DODDS R.N.	Authority BAR 3101 dated 21/6/16
			" 1360 CORPL RUSHFORTH	
	6		LIEUT J.V. SHAW joined for duty from 14th CORPS.	
	9		LIEUT L.H. LEWIS L/S. for 2ND ARMY SIGNALS	
	17		The following Honours were gazetted	
			Mentioned in Despatches — LIEUT G. ADAM	
			2/LIEUT A.E. O'DELL	
	19		LIEUT C.J. CADMAN & 2/LIEUT C.W. M. CROLL joined for duty from V CORPS. (left England 12/5/16)	

Army Form C. 2118

WAR DIARY
or
INTELLIGENCE SUMMARY
(Erase heading not required.)

Place	Date	Hour	Summary of Events and Information	Remarks and references to Appendices
WEST OUTRE	JUNE 1916 26		On the night of June 26/27th the 73rd Infantry Brigade relieved the 150th Infantry Brigade. The G.O.C. 150 Inf Brigade remained in Command of the KEMMEL DEFENCES under the orders of the G.O.C. 50th DIVISION. BRIGADE HEADQUARTERS remained in LOCRE	Sheet 28 M16d3.7
"	27		150 Brigade Headquarters moved to farm about 1500 yards S.E. of WEST OUTRE. CAPT. SHAW Cmdg No 3 Section was relieved by LIEUT C CADMAN. CAPT SHAW was attached to Headquarters for special duty in connection with General System of Cable.	

[Signature]
CAPTAIN
Comdg. 50th (North bn.) Divisional Signal Company R.E.

Army Form C. 2118

62

WAR DIARY
or
INTELLIGENCE SUMMARY
(Erase heading not required.)

Instructions regarding War Diaries and Intelligence Summaries are contained in F. S. Regs., Part II. and the Staff Manual respectively. Title Pages will be prepared in manuscript.

Place	Date 1916	Hour	Summary of Events and Information	Remarks and references to Appendices
WEST OUTRE	JULY 1st		During night of July 1st/2nd the 24th DIVISION extended their front Northward to point * N.28.a.5½.3 relieving troops of 149th Infantry Brigade	Sheet 28 France & Belgium. 50th Div Operation Order No 37 of June 30/16
"	3rd		During night of July 3rd/4th the 150th Infantry Brigade relieved the 149th Infantry Brigade in right Sector Trenches T3 to L5 inclusive	
"	8		During night 8th/9th July the 150th Infantry Brigade extended its front Southward taking over trenches from 24th Division as far as the KEMMEL-WYTSCHAETE Road inclusive	50th Div Operation Order No 38 of July 9th 1916
"	15		During night 15/16th July the 149th Infantry Brigade relieved the 151st Infantry Brigade in Left Sector Trenches M1 to O4, the 151st Brigade taking over the accommodation vacated by the 149th Brigade.	50th DIV Operation Order No 39 of July 12th 1916

Army Form C. 2118

63

WAR DIARY
or
INTELLIGENCE SUMMARY
(Erase heading not required.)

Place	Date 1916	Hour	Summary of Events and Information	Remarks and references to Appendices
WEST OUTRE	July 19.		During the night of July 19/20th the 50th Division extended its right southwards as far as French D'ismetrerie. The 151st Infantry Brigade took over from 17th Infantry Brigade of 24th Division French D'ismetrerie to the KEMMEL-WYTSCHAETE Road inclusive with Brigade Headquarters at DRANOUTRE.	50th Division Operation Order No 40 of 19th July 1916
"	21/22		During the night of July 21/22nd the Second Canadian Division prolonged its right southwards as far as the VIERSTRAAT-WYTSCHAETE Road inclusive in relief of 50th Division. The 6th Canadian Infantry Brigade relieved the 149th Infantry Brigade taking over command of the sector at 8 pm on July 22nd	50th Division Operation Order No 41 of July 21st 1916
"	22/23		During the night of July 22nd/23rd the 38th Division prolonged its right southwards as far as junction of trenches 140 and 141 at W 2.1.3 in relief of 20th (Light) Division. The 149th Brigade relieved the 61st Infantry Brigade in Trenches 141 to D4 with Headquarters at T 20.8.4.1 about 1000 yards S.S.E of NEUVE EGLISE	* Sheet 28 FRANCE & BELGIUM

Army Form C. 2118

WAR DIARY
or
INTELLIGENCE SUMMARY
(Erase heading not required.)

Instructions regarding War Diaries and Intelligence Summaries are contained in F.S. Regs., Part II. and the Staff Manual respectively. Title Pages will be prepared in manuscript.

64

Place	Date 1916	Hour	Summary of Events and Information	Remarks and references to Appendices
WEST OUTRE	JULY 22		During the night of July 22nd/23rd prolonged its left Northwards, taking over from the 150th Infantry Brigade the trenches as far as French G4 inclusive	50th Div Operation Order No 42 of July 22nd/1916
"	26		During the night of July 26/27th the 149th Infantry Brigade handed over trenches A1 to C2 both inclusive to 36th (ULSTER) Division, & took over Trenches D5 and D6 from 151st Infantry Brigade.	Operation Order No 43 of 24th July 1916
"	"	7.9 p.m	Infantry Brigade Headquarters together with Artillery Group Headquarters moved as follows:- 149 Brigade to DRANOUTRE 151st " " KEMMEL 150 " " BRULOOZE	50th DIV G X 2312 of July 27th 1916

Signature: *M.W. Bagnall*
CAPTAIN.
Comdg. 50th (North bn.) Divisional Signal Company R.E.

1875 Wt. W593/826 1,000,000 4/15 J.B.C. & A. A.D.S.S./Forms/C. 2118.

ORIGINAL.

WAR DIARY.

50th DIVISIONAL SIGNAL CO. R.E.

JULY. 1916.

VOLUME No. 16.

Vol 17

WAR DIARY OF :-
50th (NORTHUMBRIAN) DIV'L SIGNAL COY R.E.
FROM
1/8/16 — 31/8/16

VOLUME ~~XVIII~~

Army Form C. 2118

WAR DIARY
or
INTELLIGENCE SUMMARY
(Erase heading not required.)

Instructions regarding War Diaries and Intelligence Summaries are contained in F. S. Regs., Part II. and the Staff Manual respectively. Title Pages will be prepared in manuscript.

Place	Date	Hour	Summary of Events and Information	Remarks and references to Appendices
WEST OUTRE	August 1916 AUGUST 5		On the night 5/6th August the 36th (ULSTER) Division extended its left northwards taking over from the 149th Infantry Brigade the line up to DURHAM ROAD inclusive map.	O.O. No 44 My French map.
"	9th		The relief of the 50th (NORTHUMBRIAN) Division was completed during the night of August 9/10th; the division being relieved by the 19th (WESTERN) Division. The 50th Division was concentrated in the Reserve Area & became II Corps reserve. Divisional Headquarters moved to FLETRE	O.O. No 45
FLETRE	10th		The 50th Division (less Divison Supply Column, Ammn Sub Park & Motor Ambulances) was transferred from 3rd Corps to Reserve Army. Entrainment at Bailleul BAILLEUL & GODEWAERSVELDE began about 6 p.m. August 10th.	O.O. No 46
	11th		The Signal Co entrained at BAILLEUL W at 10.28 a.m, detrained at DOULLENS & marched to BERNAVILLE Divisional Headquarters closed at FLETRE at 9 A.M & opened at BERNAVILLE at the same hour.	O.O. 47
BERNAVILLE			Communication by wire to all brigades, supply Column, Railhead & Corps of GHQ advanced The division came under the orders of IX Corps, & became GHQ Reserve in Reserve Army.	

66

Army Form C. 2118

WAR DIARY
or
INTELLIGENCE SUMMARY
(Erase heading not required.)

Place	Date	Hour	Summary of Events and Information	Remarks and references to Appendices
BERNAVILLE	AUGUST 14th		At Midnight on the night of 14/15th August the 50th Division was transferred from GHQ Reserve in Reserve Army to Fourth Army, Third Corps & on 15th	
	15th		August marched from the BERNAVILLE area to area C about VIGNACOURT. Divisional Headquarters being at VIGNACOURT. The Divisional Signal Co. left BERNAVILLE at 3.20 a.m. marching by CANAPLE to VIGNACOURT where it arrived at 6.15 a.m. Communication by wire to 149 & 150 Infantry Brigades, to Xth Corps & 4th Army	O.O. 48 & 49
VIGNACOURT	16th		The Division marched to the area VILLERS BOCAGE – PIERREGOT – MIRVAUX and MOLLIENS AU BOIS with Artillery about MONTIGNY. The Signal Company left VIGNACOURT at 5.30 a.m. & marched to MONTIGNY. Divisional Headquarters at MONTIGNY CHATEAU. Communication by wire to IIIrd Corps but not to Brigades.	O.O. No 50
MONTIGNY	17th		The 50th Division marched to Third Corps Reserve area, the Divisional Artillery remaining on the MONTIGNY aug. Communication by wire to all Brigades.	O.O. No 57

Army Form C. 2118

WAR DIARY
or
INTELLIGENCE SUMMARY
(Erase heading not required.)

Instructions regarding War Diaries and Intelligence Summaries are contained in F.S. Regs., Part II. and the Staff Manual respectively. Title Pages will be prepared in manuscript.

67

Place	Date 1916	Hour	Summary of Events and Information	Remarks and references to Appendices
MONTIGNY	AUGUST 20	6.0 a.m.	50th Divisional Artillery completed relief of 34th Divisional Artillery & came under the orders of Brigadier General E.W. SPEDDING C.M.G., R.A. Headquarters, C.R.A., 2000 yards W. of ALBERT (W.26 c.3.2) LIEUT J.V.N SHAW R.E. with Cable Detachment accompanied HdQrs C.R.A.	O.O. No 52 of 16/8/16. Ref. maps 1/40 000 Sheet 57 D.
"	27-30		Working party sent out to construct ⸺ Air line route for Artillery communication everything forward of BÉCOURT	
"	28	3 p.m.	Presentation of decorations by LT GEN. SIR N. PULTENEY K.C.B., D.S.O. Commanding IIIrd Corps. No 1442 Sergt. JENSON N. & No 1934 Sergt DODDS R.N. received the Military Medal.	

Chas Bagnall
CAPTAIN.
Comdg. 50th (North'n) Divisional Signal Company R.E.

50th. DIVISIONAL ENGINEERS

50th. NORTHUMBRIAN DIV. SIGNAL COY., R. E.

SEPTEMBER 1916.

ORIGINAL.   SECRET.

WAR DIARY

of

50th (Northumbrian) Divisional

Signal Company

ROYAL ENGINEERS.

September, 1916.

Volume No. XVIII.
-aa-

Army Form C. 2118

268

WAR DIARY
or
INTELLIGENCE SUMMARY
(Erase heading not required.)

Instructions regarding War Diaries and Intelligence Summaries are contained in F.S. Regs., Part II. and the Staff Manual respectively. Title Pages will be prepared in manuscript.

Place	Date 1916	Hour	Summary of Events and Information	Remarks and references to Appendices
MONTIGNY	SEPT 10TH	12 NOON	The 50th Division took over the right sector of the 15th Division from SUTHERLAND ARMY inclusive to about S.2.6.6.1. Two Brigades. The 149th Brigade HdQrs ―― in MAMETZ WOOD with 1 Battalion in the front line. The 150th Brigade HdQrs ―― in O.C. Knipewell S.13.8.9, 1 Battalion in the front line. The 151st Brigade in reserve at BECOURT with Headquarters near BECOURT CHATEAU. Divisional Headquarters were established 1200 yds E of MILLENCOURT (Decourt Advanced Headquarters in RAILWAY COPSE X.28.a.9.1 Central) To obtain communication between Division and Advanced Divisional Headquarters the following work was done 12 line route built by Corps from Division to "A" Point Albert exclusive route & 4 pair route through to FRICOURT 12 line route built by Corps from Division to 15th Division & joined to Artillery and other lines built by Divisional Signal Company. 8 line route built by Signal Company from FRICOURT to Advanced Headquarters	50th Division Operation Order No 53 Sept 7th 1916. Reference MAP 1/40,000 Sheets 57d and 62d 4 French Map. See Diagram

Army Form C. 2118

69

WAR DIARY
or
INTELLIGENCE SUMMARY
(Erase heading not required.)

Instructions regarding War Diaries and Intelligence Summaries are contained in F. S. Regs., Part II. and the Staff Manual respectively. Title Pages will be prepared in manuscript.

Place	Date	Hour	Summary of Events and Information	Remarks and references to Appendices
E of MILLENCOURT	September 1916 10th		Alternative cables were also laid, one West & one pair E of Frécourt	
"		11 — 14th	2nd Lt WR STEWART RE (TF) reported for duty from 19th DIV SIGNAL COY RE. The following work was done forward of Advanced Headquarters. An open trench was dug connecting main Headquarters Corps bury to HdQrs and also from MAMETZ WOOD to Mametz bury. This enabled buried wires to be used to MAMETZ WOOD and O.G. line Brigade Head quarters. One pair was also extended to BAZENTIN Quarry. 5,730 men were employed in digging cable trench to BAZENTIN and to ARTILLERY Brigades. Branches were also cut from this trench to Brigades in MAMETZ wood and O.G. line Altogether over 9,700 yards of trench was dug of a depth varying from 3'6" to 6'6". Visited stations were established between Div. Adv. HdQr. & Brigades in O.G. line & Brigades in MAMETZ wood, also between MAMETZ wood and BAZENTIN le PETIT Quarry.	Trouble Plan + diagram attached All work done by Signal Coy marked in red

WAR DIARY or INTELLIGENCE SUMMARY

Army Form C. 2118

Place	Date	Hour	Summary of Events and Information	Remarks and references to Appendices
MILLENCOURT	1916 SEPT 13/14		A wireless set was sent forward from MAMETZ WOOD to BAZENTIN-le-PETIT quarry and another set sent forward by Corps to MAMETZ WOOD. Each of the assaulting brigades was supplied with 12 pigeons. Preliminary work by RIGHT BRIGADE (149 I.B.) - 900 men were supplied by the Brigade to bury cables from BAZENTIN QUARRY to CLARK'S TRENCH forward to the front line. Two working parties of 300 men were considerably disturbed by shell fire. Six pairs of cable were buried, 4 other lines including a ladder laid to the front line & support battalions. Visual was established between MAMETZ WOOD and BAZENTIN quarry & between ARGYLL trench and BETHELL SAP. Preliminary work by LEFT BRIGADE (150 I.B.) 750 men were supplied by the Brigade to bury cable. Ten pairs were buried 2 feet deep under bottom of communication trenches from O.C. Hd Qrs up SCOTCH ALLEY to a test point near 6th Avenue. 2 pairs were continued up Pioneer Alley to the front line, one pair along 6th Avenue & one pair along Intermediate Trench meeting again in Somme Alley and	70

Army Form C. 2118

WAR DIARY
or
INTELLIGENCE SUMMARY
(Erase heading not required.)

Place	Date	Hour	Summary of Events and Information	Remarks and references to Appendices
E of MILLENCOURT	SEPT 1916 11/14		and continuing to the front line. A lateral was also laid along the front line giving each Battalion 3 months back to Brigade. A forward Visual Station was established on the High ground on Pioneer alley about 70th Avenue & was in touch with 3 Battn Hd Qrs & was also ready to obtain communication with Companies as they advanced. An intermediate station was in communication with the forward station & also Brigade Hd Qrs. Visual stations were tied in on the same line. A dug out was built at Bn Adv. Hd Qrs & electric lighting set installed	
"	14"		Headquarters of 50th Division moved forward to Advanced Kiw. Hd Qrs at Railway Copse. Division was disposed with 2 Infantry Brigades in the trench line viz, 149th on right with HdQrs in BAZENTIN-le-PETIT Quarry and 150th Bde on left with HQ in O.G. line. 151st Brigade in reserve with Headquarters in MAMETZ WOOD. The whole of the Divisional Artillery were in action. Casualties Wounded (at duty) LIEUT J. V. SHAW RE.	

WAR DIARY or INTELLIGENCE SUMMARY

Army Form C. 2118

72

Place	Date	Hour	Summary of Events and Information	Remarks and references to Appendices
RAILWAY COPSE	1916 SEPT 15th	6.20	Attack begins. Casualties. No 2736 Sapper Armstrong F. Killed	
"	18		Disposition 151 Brigade Hd Qrs BAZENTIN-le-PETIT Right " 150 " " O.G. Line Left " 149 " " MAMETZ WOOD Support Reserve During the night of Sept. 18/19th the 23rd Division relieved 15th Division on left of 50th Division	
"	19		69th I.B. of 23rd Div. took over from 150th Bde of 50th Division as far E. on M33 & 47. Disposition 151 Brigade in Front Line Hd Qrs Quarry " 149 " in Support Hd Qrs O.G. Line " 150 " " Reserve " " Mametz Wood	
"	20		149 Brigade relieved 151 Brigade. 150th Bde in Support. 151 Brigade in Reserve. 1st Division on Right relieved 47th Division on Right.	

Army Form C. 2118

73

WAR DIARY
or
INTELLIGENCE SUMMARY
(Erase heading not required.)

Instructions regarding War Diaries and Intelligence Summaries are contained in F. S. Regs., Part II. and the Staff Manual respectively. Title Pages will be prepared in manuscript.

Place	Date 1916 Sept.	Hour	Summary of Events and Information	Remarks and references to Appendices
RAILWAY COPSE	22		Dispositions 149 Brigade in front line " 150 " " Support " " 151 " " Div Reserve	
"	23		Casualties Motor Cyclist Corp. Trumbull T. wounded	
"	24		Dispositions. 150 Brigade in front line " 151 " " Support " " 149 " " Div Reserve.	
"	25	12.28	Zero hour for 4th Army attack including VII Corps	
"	28		Dispositions 151 Brigade in front line " 150 " " Support " " 149 " " Div Reserve.	
"	29		149 Brigade moved into support " 150 " " — Back & became Div Reserve	

Army Form C. 2118

74

WAR DIARY
or
INTELLIGENCE SUMMARY
(Erase heading not required.)

Place	Date	Hour	Summary of Events and Information	Remarks and references to Appendices
RAILWAY COPSE	Sept 15/30		Communication between Divisions and Brigades never failed during the operations and it was never found necessary to resort either wireless or visual. This also applied between C.R.A. and Artillery Brigade. Considerable trouble was experienced with cables in open trenches and on the ground when transport and troops moved forward after the first advance. Much useful information received from Aeroplanes by dropped messages. 149 Bde Communication by wire lost on one or two occasions but only for about 20 minutes each time. Visual much used. 150 Bde formed Visual on relay system very useful, i.e. Visual from front line to transmitting station & thence to Brigade by wire or vice versa. French lamps and 50th Division pattern Signalling lamps used. 2.00 Signalling fans were made by the Division and another 3.00 from parts made & furnished by 4th Army for distribution.	

Army Form C. 2118

WAR DIARY
or
INTELLIGENCE SUMMARY
(Erase heading not required.)

Instructions regarding War Diaries and Intelligence Summaries are contained in F. S. Regs., Part II. and the Staff Manual respectively. Title Pages will be prepared in manuscript.

75-

Place	Date	Hour	Summary of Events and Information	Remarks and references to Appendices
RAILWAY COPSE	SEPT 15/16 1916	to finish.	Power buzzer and amplifier were sent up but it was found impossible to pick up messages owing to number of earthed circuits in use. Pigeons were available throughout the operations but owing to time taken out were rarely used. 3 Plans & diagram of Communication attached.	

M.W.Bayurall Capt.
Coy 50th Div. Signal C.R.E.

III

50th D.A. Communications
Sept. 15th 1916

— REFERENCE —

Airline
Twisted D5 to ground
Twisted D5 in open 4'·6" Trench
Quad in open 4'·6" Trench

FJR
50th D.A. HQ

LUH
15th D.A.H.Q.

YEK
(Exch)

ACY
1st Cdn HA

1st Cdn HA

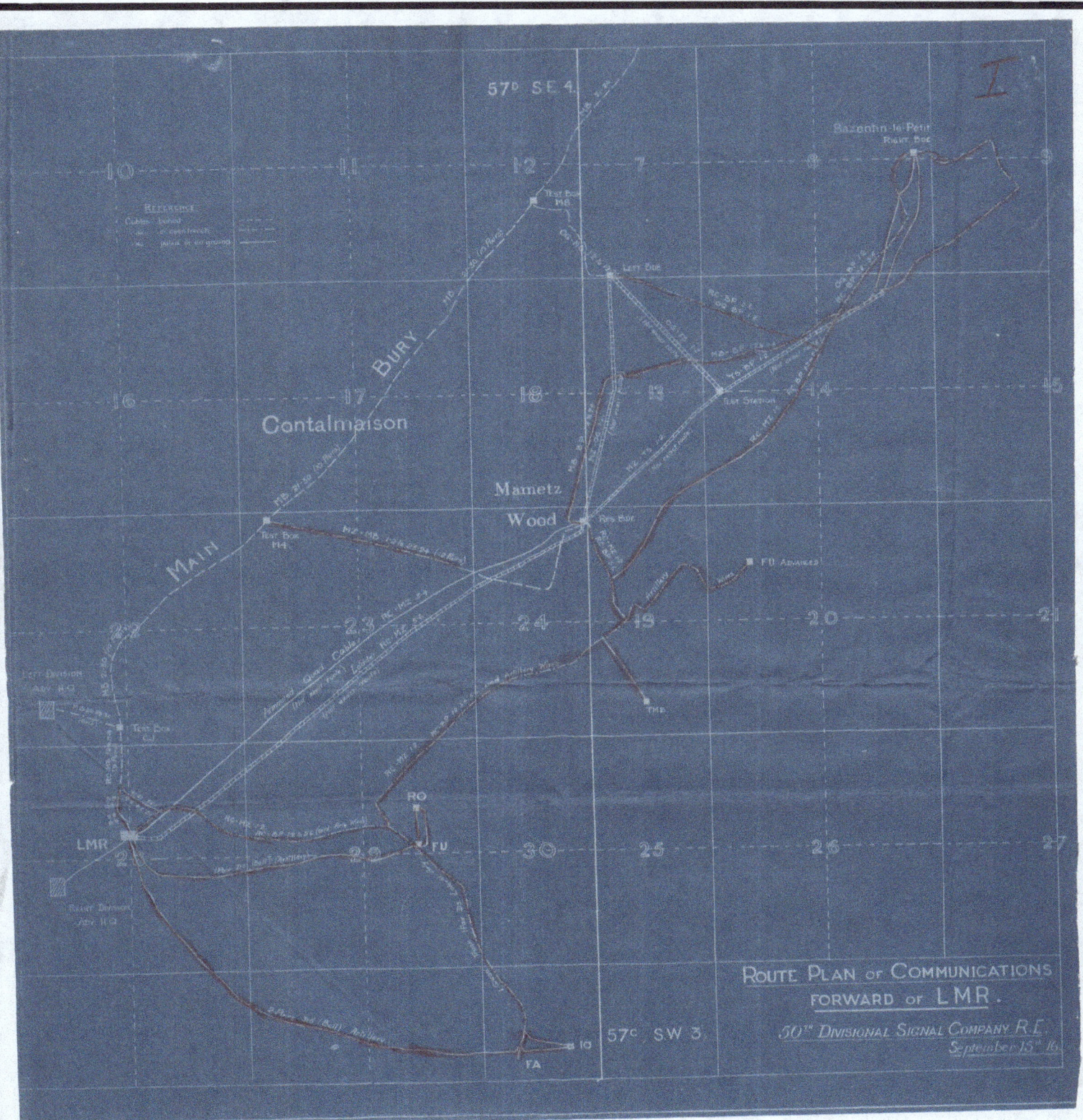

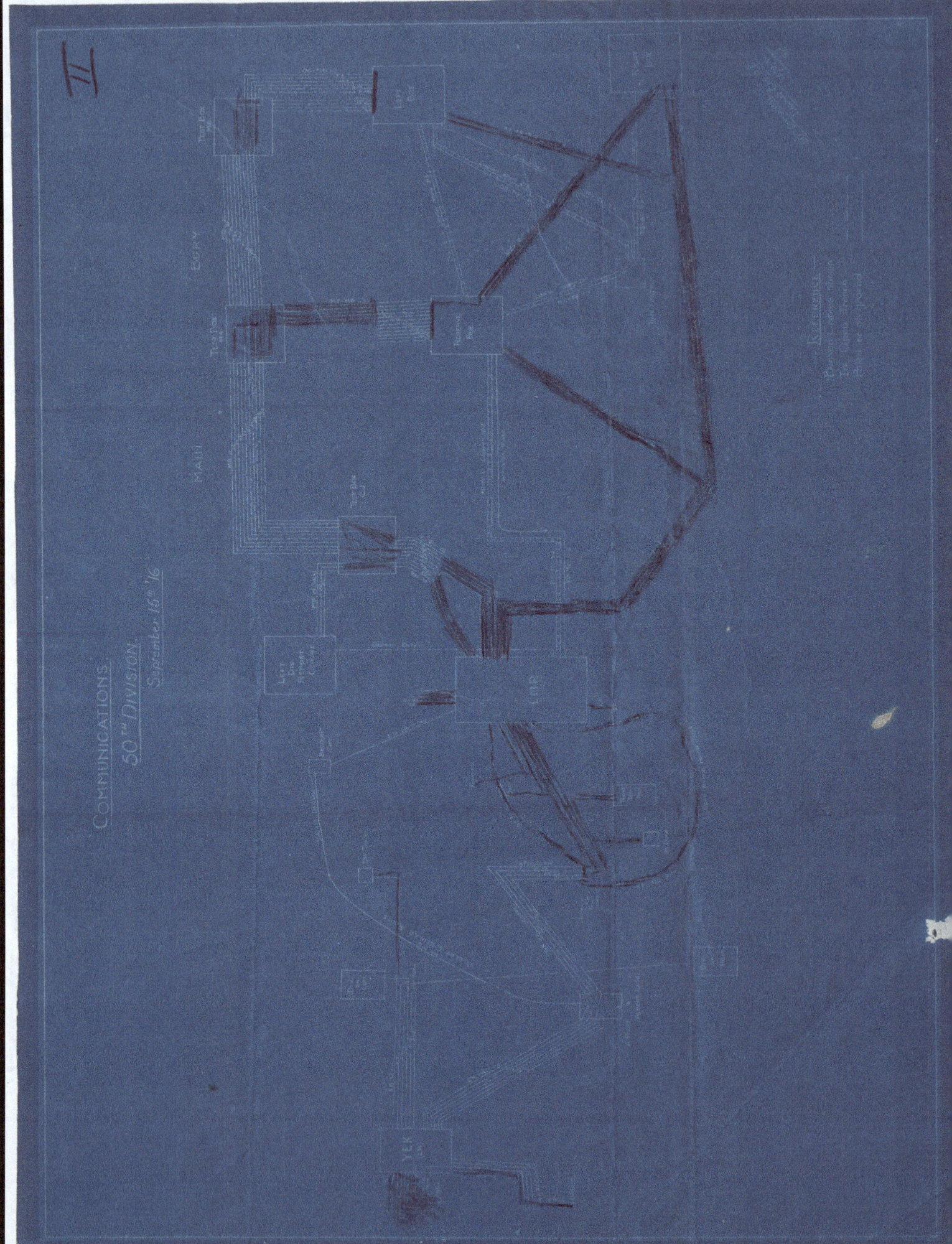

(Original).

S E C R E T.

WAR DIARY

OF

50th (NORTHUMBRIAN) DIVISIONAL
SIGNAL COMPANY R.E.

Volume XIX.

OCTOBER 1916.

WAR DIARY or INTELLIGENCE SUMMARY

Army Form C. 2118

Place	Date 1916	Hour	Summary of Events and Information	Remarks and references to Appendices
RAILWAY COPSE	OCTOBER 1.		The 50th DIVISION attached hundred two lines of trenches between M.22 & 3.4 and M.21 & 8.4.	
"	3		The 50th (NORTHN) DIVISION was relieved by the 23rd DIVISION. Two battalions of Brigade relieved 151st Brigade on support Brigade. During the afternoon & evening the 68th Infantry Brigade relieved the 149th Brigade, the latter moving back to MAMETZ WOOD. The 70th & 113 of 23rd Division moved up to SWANSEA TRENCH - O.C. LINE with Headquarters an O.G. line. At 2pm Command of the Divisional front was passed to G.O.C 23rd Div. 50th DIVISION Headquarters moved to Camp E of MILLENCOURT.	
E of MILLENCOURT	4		149 Brigade moved from to ALBERT and BECOURT	
			150 " " " BAIZIEUX WOOD	
			151 " " " HENENCOURT	
	5		149 Brigade moved to MILLENCOURT. Communication by wire to all Brigades.	
	6/7		23rd DIVISION vacated BAZENTIN & PETIT & O.O. Line Headquarters. These were later occupied by Brigade 50th DIV. R.A. & 1 Brigade Headquarters.	

Army Form C. 2118

WAR DIARY
or
INTELLIGENCE SUMMARY
(Erase heading not required.)

77

Place	Date 1916	Hour	Summary of Events and Information	Remarks and references to Appendices
E of MILLENCOURT	Oct 7		No 1950 2/Cpl WHITE R.R. No 2 Section awarded the Military Medal " 1948 R/Sgt TURNBULL J " " " " " "	
"	17		Capt. L.S. LINDSEY-RENTON 1/14th Bn LONDON REGT (LONDON SCOTTISH) joined for duty as second in command from RESERVE ARMY SIGNAL CO. R.E.	
"	21		No 1699 2/Cpl SMITH H No 3 Section awarded military medal " 1675 " Sapper CAMPBELL G.A " " " " " " 1997 " RYCROFT B.C No 4 " " " " " " 1617 " Sergt. McDONALD A.T " " " " "	
"	23		One Bn Hdq 1 Sec, one Bn 150, 1.13a. moved by motor bus from MILLENCOURT to HENENCOURT & CONTALMAISON & marched to BAZENTIN-L-PETIT for attachment to 9th Division to dig in forward trenches. Cook kitchen 13oth Battalion moved forward in the evening to FIERS LINE 150, 13bb, less 2bn at MAMETZ wood and one bn attached 9th Division moved from BAZIEUX to MILLENCOURT 15"1 Inf Bde (less Corps working parties) moved from HENENCOURT wood to BECOURT.	Operation Order No 58 of October 22nd

Army Form C. 2118

78

WAR DIARY
or
INTELLIGENCE SUMMARY
(Erase heading not required.)

Place	Date 1916	Hour	Summary of Events and Information	Remarks and references to Appendices
E of MILLENCOURT	OCTOBER 24/25		During day 24th and night 24th/25th the 50th Division relieved the 9th Division. 149th Brigade relieved the 26th I. Brigade on right, & 150 I. Brigade relieved the 27th Inf Bde on left.	
FRICOURT FARM	25	9.0 am	Command of Divisional front passed to G.O.C. 50th Division	
		12 midday	151 Bde completed relief of one Brigade of 9th Division. Brigade Headquarters of front-line Brigade in BAZENTIN LE GRAND. Headquarters 50th Division at FRICOURT FARM. Four Brigades RFA 25, 39, 50 & 57, covered 50th Div front. 2 Brigades 50th Div RA cover part of 15th Div front. 5th AUSTRALIAN DIVISION on right, HdQrs at FRICOURT CHATEAU on left, in rear FRICOURT FARM. 15th DIVISION	
	27		No 1801 Sergt T. ROWLANDSON Hd Qrs. awarded Military Medal " 1810 " H HALL No 4 Section " " 870 L/Cpl SADLER H.A. No 1 " " 1.940 Sapper JOHNSTONE J. No 2 "	

Army Form C. 2118

79

WAR DIARY
or
INTELLIGENCE SUMMARY

(Erase heading not required.)

Instructions regarding War Diaries and Intelligence Summaries are contained in F. S. Regs., Part II. and the Staff Manual respectively. Title Pages will be prepared in manuscript.

Place	Date 1918	Hour	Summary of Events and Information	Remarks and references to Appendices
FRICOURT FARM	Oct 3/24		During the time the Division was at rest 3 detachments of the Signal Company were employed improving communications improving etc. etc.	

M.W.Segrave
CAPTAIN,
Comdg. 50th (North'bn.) Divisional Signal Company R.E.

1875 Wt. W593/826 1,000,000 4/15 J.B.C. & A. A.D.S.S./Forms/C. 2118.

SECRET.

50th DIVISION SIGNAL COMMUNICATION.

30th OCTOBER 1916.

1. The following means of Communications will be available for use during the following operations :-

    (a) Telegraph and Telephone.
    (b) Visual.
    (c) Runners.
    (d) Pigeons.
    (e) Wireless.
    (f) Aeroplane.
    (g) Power Buzzer.

2. TELEGRAPHS and TELEPHONE.

The Divisional Advanced Headquarters at BAZENTIN-LE-GRAND WOOD, S.14.d.2.9. is in telephonic communication with all three Infantry Brigades; Divisional O.P. M.28.b.2.6., Divisional Advanced Dressing Station S.8.a.4.6., Divisional A.P.M. S.14.a.4.7., Divisional Advanced Dump S.14.d.2.9., with its Covering Artillery, and with the Divisions on the Right and Left. Direct Telephonic Communication has also been established with the Corps Wireless Station at S.13.b.5.8.

The Right Brigade (149th Infantry Brigade, H.Q. M.35.a.7.5.) is in communication with the Left Brigade (14th Inf. Brigade, H.Q. M.30.c.3.1.) of the 5th Australian Division.

The Left Brigade (150th Inf. Brigade, H.Q.M.22.d.6.2.) is in communication with the Right Brigade (44th Inf. Brigade H.Q. M.33.a.1.9.) of the 15th Division.

3. VISUAL.

Divisional Visual Stations will be established at H.T. (HOOK TRENCH) S.3.a.8.9. and B.G. (BAZENTIN-LE-GRAND) S.15.b.3.6.

Communication between the VISUAL Stations and Divisional Advanced Headquarters will be by telephone.

Brigades will arrange for visual signalling back from the captured trenches.

(2).

4. RUNNERS.

Runner posts will be established at the following points approximately :-

    V.C. (Test Box) .... M.28.d.4.4.
    H.T. (HOOK TRENCH).. S. 3.a.8.9.
    B.P. (THE QUARRY)... S. 8.b.9.2.
        BAZENTIN LE PETIT.

The personnel will be found by the Brigades in the line, who will also maintain four runners each at their own H.Q. for this Post Service for taking messages to V.C.

The 150th Brigade will find 1 N.C.O. and eight men to man V.C. and the 149th Brigade 1 N.C.O. and six men to man H.T.

B.P. will be manned by 1 N.C.O. and three troopers from the Yeomanry, and B.G. (Divisional Rear Visual Station) will have two yeomanry troopers allotted to it.

Runners from Brigades to H.T. and back will run in duplicate, the first man carrying the messages, the 2nd man following fifty yards in the rear.

The Hours of ordinary as against special posts will be issued later.

5. PIGEONS.

Messages sent by Pigeon post will be transmitted by telegraph from the Corps Pigeon Loft.

Special care must be taken that all orders that have been issued about Pigeons are strictly adhered to.

In action Pigeon Post messages are always "PRIORITY".

6. WIRELESS.

The Third Corps WIRELESS Station is at S.13.b.5.8. and is in communication with Divisional Advanced Headquarters.

Of the two Sets allotted to the 50th Division one has been established near the Left Brigade H.Q. (150th Infantry Brigade) at M.22.c.9.1.

The Second Set is near H.Q. Reserve Brigade (151st Infantry Brigade) at S.13.b.2.6.

(3).

7. **AEROPLANES.**

One Aeroplane (Contact patrol Aeroplane) will be up during the attack, and will work for the Infantry as required by Corps.

Means of Communications between this Aeroplane and Battalions, Brigades and Divisional H.Q. will be as follows:-

      (a) Flares.
      (b) Panel Shutters.
      (c) Dropping Messages.

(a) **FLARES.**

These Flares will indicate to the Aeroplane Observer the position reached by our troops.

(b) **PANEL SHUTTERS.**

Panel Shutters will be used by all Battalion H.Qs. and Brigade H.Qs. in the line. They will be placed as near as possible to the H.Qs. concerned.

Messages can be sent to the Aeroplane and replied to by the "KLAXON HORN.

(c) **DROPPING MESSAGES.**

A site for the purpose has been selected at
Orderlies will bring the Messages direct to the Signal Office.

8. **POWER BUZZER.**

A Power Buzzer Set has been installed at M.17.c.3.4. and I.T. at C.E.R. (M.22.d.6.2). Another one has been applied for and if received will be installed in the area of the 149th Infantry Brigade.

SECRET.

DIVISIONAL TELEPHONE COMMUNICATION.

1. Division Advanced H.Q.
   to Divisional Observation Post.   1 pair.

2. Division Advanced H.Q.
   to Right Bde. Battle H.Q.   4 pairs.   1 for Artillery Liaison Officer.

3. Division Advanced H.Q.
   to Left Bde. Battle H.Q.   4 pairs.   - do -

4. Division Advanced H.Q.
   to Reserve Bde. Forward Station.   2 pairs.

5. Division Advanced H.Q.
   to (1) Right Bde. "Q".
      (2) Left Bde. "Q".   B.G.
      (3) Reserve Bde. Battle H.Q.   8 pairs.

6. Division Advanced H.Q.
   to Reserve Bde. "Q".   1 pair.

7. Division Advanced H.Q. to Right Division.   1 pair.

8. Division Advanced H.Q. to Left Division.   1 pair.

9. Right Bde. Battle H.Q. to Left Bde.
                          Battle H.Q.   2 pairs.   (Lateral Communication).

10. Reserve Bde. Forward Station
    to Right and Left Brigade.   1 pair each.

11. Reserve Bde. Forward Station
    To Reserve Bde. Battle H.Q.   2 pairs.

12. Divisional Advanced H.Q. to A.P.M.
    and Advanced Dressing Station.   1 pair.

13. Divisional Advanced H.Q.
    To Divisional Advanced Dump.   1 pair.

MAINTAINANCE.

1. The Division will maintain
   (A) L.M.R. - B.G.
   (B) L.M.R. - B.P.
   (C) B.P.   - H.T.

2. The Right Brigade (149th Inf.Brigade) will maintain
   D.L.R. - V.C.

3. The Left Brigade (150th Inf.Brigade) will maintain
   (A) O.E.R. - V.C.
   (B) B.G.   - H.T.

4. The Reserve Bde. (151st Infantry Brigade) will maintain

    (A) H.T. - V.C.
    (B) V.C. - D.G.O.
    (C) V.C. - L.M.O.

5. The Division and Reserve Brigade (151st Infantry Brigade) ~~(151st Infantry Brigade)~~ will divide maintenance between B.G. - B.P.

6. One Division Lineman will be allotted to each Brigade.

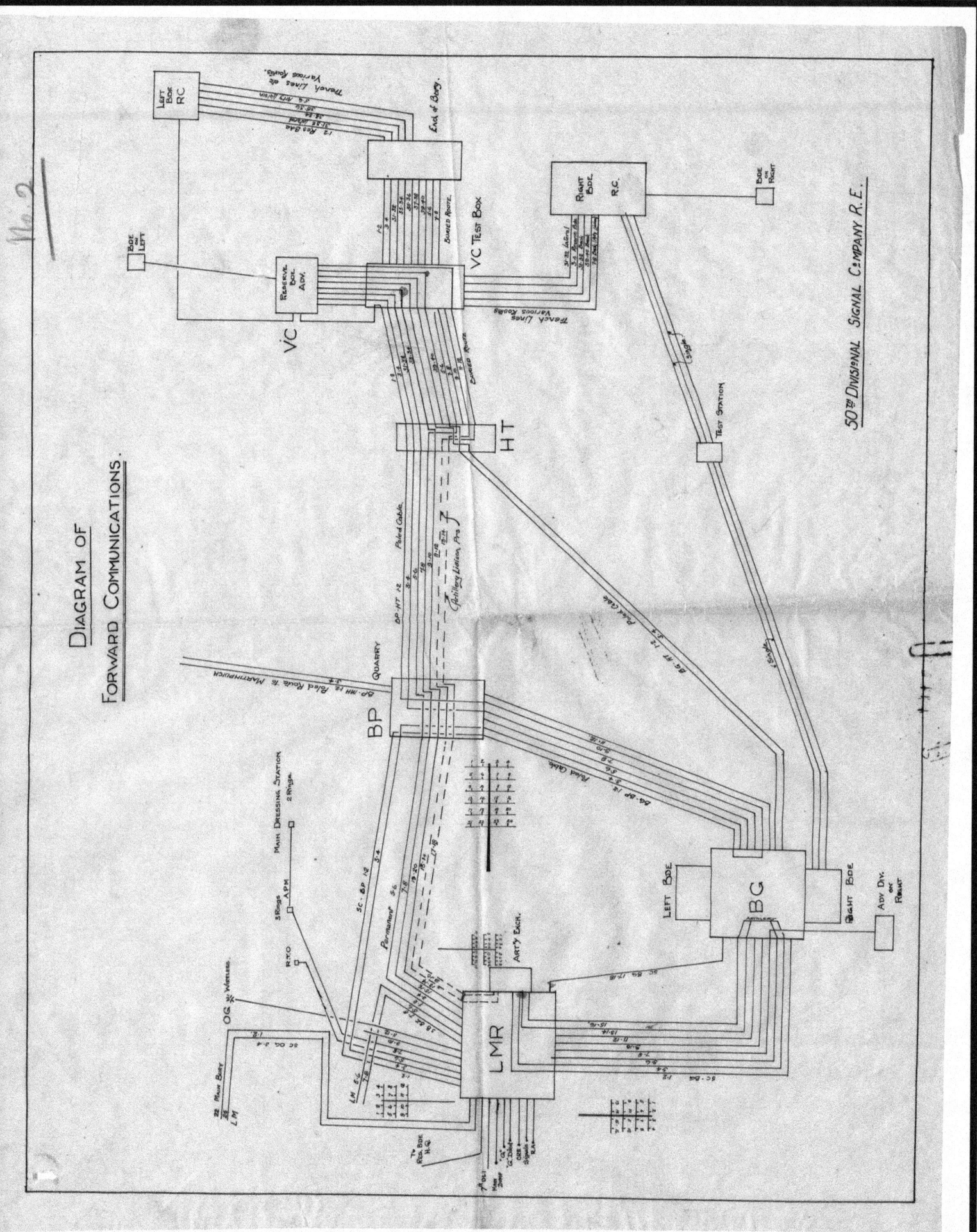

No. 1

DIAGRAM OF COMMUNICATIONS
LM TO LMR.

50th DIVISIONAL SIGNAL COMPANY R.E.

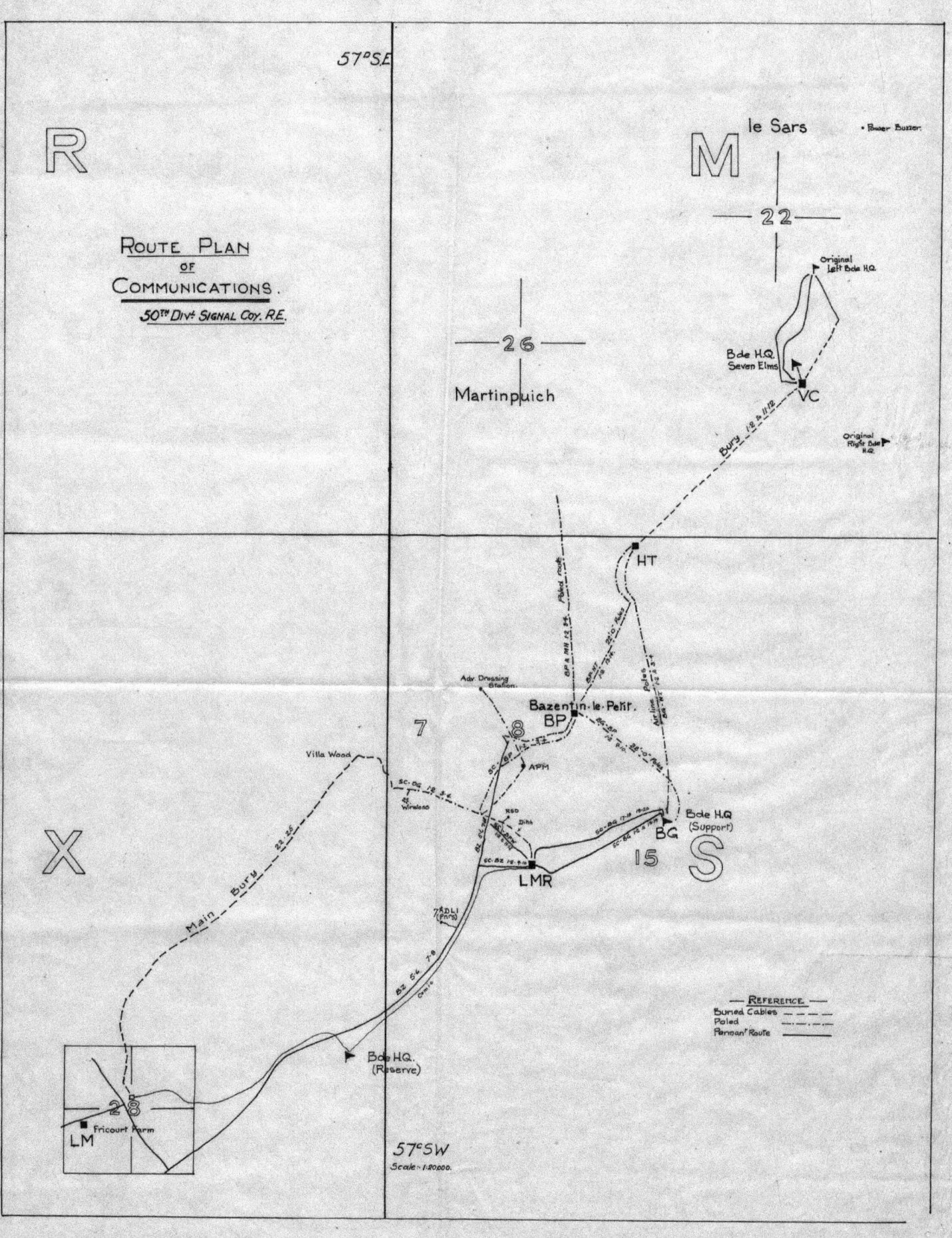

(Original)

S E C R E T.

W A R   D I A R Y

O F

50th (NORTHUMBRIAN) DIVISIONAL SIGNAL COMPANY R.E.

Volume No: XX.

November 1916.

WAR DIARY or INTELLIGENCE SUMMARY

Army Form C. 2118

Place	Date	Hour	Summary of Events and Information	Remarks and references to Appendices
FRICOURT FARM.	Oct 31st to Nov 4 1916		During the time the Division was at rest and up to Nov 4th the following work was done.	
			(a) Pole route erected from BAZENTIN le PETIT Quarry to MARTINPUICH, 22'0" poles, every other pole a double stayed on to sand blocks. 2 pairs of cable BP-MH 1.2 4 3.4	
			(b) A similar route erected from Quarry to end of bury about S 3 a 8.8. 7 pairs of cable numbered BP-HT 1.2 to 13.14	
			(c) A similar route erected from Quarry to Brigade Headquarters at BAZENTIN le GRAND. Six pairs of cable BG-BP 1.2 to 11.12	
			(d) LMR fitted out as advanced Divisional Headquarters. Corps permanent extended by cable to Quarry to pick up cable routes (a) (b) (c)	
			(e) Main bury put through to FRICOURT FARM and extended by cable to edge of BP wood (S14a 4.6) & from there to LMR (2 pairs)	
			(f) 12 line permanent built from LMR to edge of BP wood (S14c 4.6) used for BP Quarry (2 pairs) and extended also by cable to A.P.M, Adv. Dressing Station, wireless & O/p I/c Tramways.	

Army Form C. 2118

WAR DIARY
or
INTELLIGENCE SUMMARY
(Erase heading not required.)

Instructions regarding War Diaries and Intelligence Summaries are contained in F.S. Regs., Part II. and the Staff Manual respectively. Title Pages will be prepared in manuscript.

Place	Date 1916	Hour	Summary of Events and Information	Remarks and references to Appendices
FRICOURT FARM	Oct 3rd to Nov 1st		Station line Permanent to Brigade Headquarters, BAZENTIN le GRAND from L.M.R. completed. One pair foot through to Adv Division Hd Qrs and to Brigades (and to 9th Divisional Artillery, remainder used to Brigades on right); four pairs for the operation of 5" instant communication were as detailed on attached document and front marked 1 & 2 respectively. These were slightly altered owing to only one brigade being in the front line with advanced Headquarters at M22d 6.2	
"	Nov 2		The 151 Brigade commenced relieving 149 & 150 Brigades in front line. During the night of Nov 3/4th the Relief 151st Brigade completed relief of 149 & 150th Brigades completed command of the whole front at 6.0 p.m. The B.G.C. 151st Brigade assumed command of the whole front at 6.0 p.m.	Divisional O.O. No 614 Nov 2nd 1916
"	Nov 3		The 149th Brigade became supporting Brigade with Hd Qrs of Brigade at BAZENTIN le GRAND. The 150th Brigade became reserve Brigade with Hd Qrs of Brigade at X30 a 4.9	

Army Form C. 2118

82

WAR DIARY
or
INTELLIGENCE SUMMARY
(Erase heading not required.)

Instructions regarding War Diaries and Intelligence Summaries are contained in F. S. Regs., Part II. and the Staff Manual respectively. Title Pages will be prepared in manuscript.

Place	Date 1916	Hour	Summary of Events and Information	Remarks and references to Appendices
FRICOURT FARM	Nov 5.	am 8.15	151 Brigade ~~staff~~ moved at Advanced Headquarters. 50th Division 'G' Staff CRE & CRA 9th Division moved to Advanced Headquarters.	50th DIV O.O. No 62 with amendment 50th Div G-Y285/21
		9.10am	The 50th Division of the III Corps & 1st Anzac Corps attacked the GIRD line as far west as the BAPAUME road. The attack was carried out by the 151st Infantry Brigade with two Battalions of the 149 Brigade attached. The objective was taken but during the night after several heavy counter attacks our troops were driven back to their original position. Communication to Advanced Brigade Headquarters was maintained throughout the operations.	
			Lt J. V. Shaw proceeded on leave to U.K.	
"	6		The 150th Brigade relieved the 151 Brigade with Headquarters at BAZENTIN LE GRAND 149 Brigade remained in support. 151 Brigade became reserve Brigade.	

WAR DIARY
or
INTELLIGENCE SUMMARY

(Erase heading not required.)

Army Form C. 2118

83

Place	Date 1916	Hour	Summary of Events and Information	Remarks and references to Appendices
FRICOURT FARM	Nov 11		On the night of Nov 11/12th the 149th Infantry Brigade relieved the 150th Infantry Brigade with advanced Brigade Headquarters at SEVEN ELMS. On completion of Brigade relief 150th Infantry Brigade was in support, the 151st Brigade ~~relieved~~ remaining in divisional reserve. The Divisional Artillery of the 1st Division relieved the 9th Divisional Artillery & came under the orders of G.O.C 50th Division	50th Div O.O. No 64 dated 10th Nov 1916
	12th		The 149 Infantry Brigade attacked that part of the GIRD LINE and BUTTE Trench included in the area M.18.a.3.1 – M.18.a.0.3. M.17.d.3.3. – M.17.a.7.9. Orders were issued that the attack would be continued on the morning of the 13th but were later cancelled owing to difficulty of observation	50th Div O.O's No 66 + 67 dated 12th & 14th Nov respectively.
	13		Fighting on GIRD line still in progress. No 2739 Sapper T WATERMAN No 4 Section awarded the Military Medal " 1634 " G Watson No 6 " wounded	

Army Form C. 2118

WAR DIARY
or
INTELLIGENCE SUMMARY
(Erase heading not required.)

Place	Date 1916	Hour	Summary of Events and Information	Remarks and references to Appendices
FRICOURT FARM	Nov 16		Fighting on GIRD LINE still in progress. Enemy repeated counter attacks our troops pushed back to original jumping off trenches. Communication with Brigade maintained throughout the operations. Communication with front line broken lost periodically. Very valuable information sent back by pigeon.	
	Nov 17		150th Inf. Bde relieved by 1st Inf. Bde and moved to Thipval in BECOURT Bd. Hdqrs and 1 Battn 151st Inf Bde relieved by 3rd Inf. Bde and moved to Millencourt the other remaining at Mametz Wood	Bde O.O. No. 68
	Nov 18 /19		Rt. Half of 149 Bde in line relieved by 1st Inf. Bde and moved to HIGH WOOD. Rt. Half of 149th Inf. Bde relieved at High Wood and by 2nd Inf Bde and moved to Hdqrs in ALBERT. Left Half 149th Inf Bde. relieved by 'A' Bde 148th Divn, and moved to PEAKE WOOD.	
	Nov 19	10.30 am	Hdqrs and Left Half 149th Inf. Bde relieved by 'A' Bde 48th Divn and moved to ALBERT, command passing at 10.30 am Command of area handed over G.O.C. 1st and 48th Divns, Divn taking over Hdqrs at FRICOURT FARM. 50 Bd Hdqrs opened at Villa Kocher, ALBERT at 10.30 am.	

Army Form C. 2118

85

WAR DIARY
or
INTELLIGENCE SUMMARY
(Erase heading not required.)

Place	Date	Hour	Summary of Events and Information	Remarks and references to Appendices
ALBERT	20/11/16		Capt. E.F. Bagnall and Lt. A.V.L. Craddock proceeded on leave to U.K.	
	22/11/16		Lt. E.J. Cadman proceeded on leave to U.K.	
	24/11/16		Capt. J.S. Lindsay-Renton proceeded on leave to U.K.	
	29/11/16		2nd Lt. A.E. Odell proceeded on leave to U.K.	
			Otherwise, there is nothing to report.	

Graham Adam
Lt.
for O.C.
50th (Northbn) Divl Signal Co. R.E.
30th November 1916.

SECRET.

WAR DIARY

OF

50th DIVISIONAL SIGNAL COMPANY R.E.

Volume XXI.

December 1916.

Army Form C. 2118

86

WAR DIARY
or
INTELLIGENCE SUMMARY
(Erase heading not required.)

Instructions regarding War Diaries and Intelligence Summaries are contained in F. S. Regs., Part II. and the Staff Manual respectively. Title Pages will be prepared in manuscript.

Place	Date 1916	Hour	Summary of Events and Information	Remarks and references to Appendices
ALBERT	Dec 1/16	10am	Div Headquarters moved from ALBERT to BAISIEUX CHATEAU	DIV. O.O No 69 Appy No 7
			149 Inf Bde moved from ALBERT to BRESLE, relieved by 44th Inf Bde	
			150 Inf Bde (Hédauville) " BECOURT & WONTAY-BARLEUX area relieved by 46th Inf Bde	
			151 " " " MILLENCOURT & WARLOY " " 45th Inf "	
BAIZIEUX	2"		28 N.C.O's & Gunners of 50th Div RA arrived to attend Course of Signalling 3 Bns " 46th " "	
"	9"		10 Infantry Officers & 12 Infantry N.C.O's arrived to attend short Course of Signalling	
"	20		D.C.M awarded to No 19134 Sergt DODDS, R.N. No 2 Section	
"	23		Signalling Courses completed. Results on the short-time very satisfactory the artillery Signallers showing marked improvement.	

Army Form C. 2118

87

WAR DIARY
or
INTELLIGENCE SUMMARY
(Erase heading not required.)

Place	Date 1916	Hour	Summary of Events and Information	Remarks and references to Appendices
BAIZIEUX	Dec 28		149 Brigade moved from BRESLE to BECOURT & relieved a Brigade of the 48th Div. 151 Brigade moved from WARLOY to ALBERT & relieved a Brigade of the 48th Div.	
"	29th		149 Brigade moved from BECOURT to BAZENTIN & HIGH WOOD & relieved four battalions of 1st & 3rd Inf Brigade. 150 Brigade (2 Battns) moved from CONTAY & BAIZIEUX to BECOURT & relieved the 149 Brigade.	
"	30th		On the night of Dec 30th & 31st the 149th Inf. Brigade moved from BAZENTIN & HIGH WOOD to front system of Trenches (Trenches M17/1 & M17/3) relieving 4 Bns of 1st & 3rd Inf Bdes. On completion of relief the G.O.C. 149 Brigade assumed command of the whole front.	

M.H.Bagnall
Capt
Actg for Bgd GSO2

Original.

SECRET.

WAR DIARY

OF

50th (Northumbrian) Divisional Signal Company R.E.

Volume No: XXll.
****

January 1917.

Army Form C. 2118

88

WAR DIARY
or
INTELLIGENCE SUMMARY
(Erase heading not required.)

Instructions regarding War Diaries and Intelligence Summaries are contained in F. S. Regs., Part II. and the Staff Manual respectively. Title Pages will be prepared in manuscript.

Place	Date 1917	Hour	Summary of Events and Information	Remarks and references to Appendices
BAISIEUX	JAN 1st		On the night of Dec 31st/Jan 1st the 151st Inf Brigade moved from BAZENTIN-le-PETIT to the front line (Right Sector) with Headquarters at S 6 a Central	Trench Maps 57 C
	3	10 am	The G.O.C. 50th Division took over command from 1st Division. Divisional Headquarters moved from BAISIEUX to FRICOURT FARM	50th Div O.O. No 70 of Dec 26. 1916
FRICOURT FARM			2nd LIEUT. A.E. ODELL O.C. No 2 Section awarded Military Cross	
"	4		Capt. F. Crook 5th South Lancs Reg.t attached to 50th Div. Signal Coy for duty	
			Lieut G. ADAM, Lieut J.V. SHAW, Lieut C. CADMAN, M.C No 1685 C.S.M King F and No 1663 2/Cpl W. Thornly mentioned in despatches	
"	5		No. 2706 Sapper H. BROWN killed in action near Envecourt l'Abbaye	

Army Form C. 2118
89

WAR DIARY
or
INTELLIGENCE SUMMARY
(Erase heading not required.)

Instructions regarding War Diaries and Intelligence Summaries are contained in F.S. Regs., Part II. and the Staff Manual respectively. Title Pages will be prepared in manuscript.

Place	Date 1917	Hour	Summary of Events and Information	Remarks and references to Appendices
FRICOURT FARM	JAN 5		During the night of Jan 5/6th the 150th Infantry Brigade relieved the 149th Infantry Brigade in Left Sector	
"	14		Lieut. J.V. SWAN evacuated sick to England	
			No 27411 Sapper A Newton, No 3 Section wounded	
"	15		During the night of Jan 15/16th 149 I.B. relieved 150th Infantry Brigade in Left Sector	
			During the night of Jan 23rd/24th the 150th I.B. relieved the 149th Brigade in the Left Sector	
"	23			
"	25 26		149th Infantry Brigade moved from GAZENTIN le PETIT to ALBERT	
			Lieut. C.J. CADMAN M.C. killed in action near FAUCOURT L'ABBAYE	
			During the night of Jan 26/27th the 151st Infantry Brigade was relieved by a Brigade of the 1st Australian Division. 151st I.B. moved from S 60 Central to Site 5 Camp near BAZENTIN le PETIT	
"	27		151st I.B. moved from Site 5 to BECOURT	

1875 Wt. W593/826 1,000,000 4/15 J.B.C. & A. A.D.S.S./Forms/C. 2118.

Army Form C. 2118

90

WAR DIARY
or
INTELLIGENCE SUMMARY
(Erase heading not required.)

Place	Date 1917 JAN	Hour	Summary of Events and Information	Remarks and references to Appendices
FRICOURT FARM	27		During the night Jan 27/28th the 150th Infantry Brigade moved from COUCHDROT & BAZENTIN-LE-PETIT on completion of relief by a brigade of the 1st AUSTRALIAN DIVISION	
"	28th		150th I.B. moved from BAZENTIN-LE-PETIT to FRICOURT	
"	28th	10am	The 1st AUSTRALIAN DIVISION took over command of the line from G.O.C. 50th DIV. Headquarters 50th Division moved to RIBEMONT. Communication handed over to 1st Australian Division shown on attached diagrams marked I, II & III.	50th DIV A.O. No 95 + 96 of Jan 21st of Jan 24th
RIBEMONT	29th		The 149th Infantry Brigade moved from ALBERT to DERNANCOURT " 151st " " " " " BECOURT to RIBEMONT	
"	30th		" 150th " " " " " FRICOURT CAMP to BUIRE	

Army Form C. 2118

50 D Signals
9.1.22

WAR DIARY
or
INTELLIGENCE SUMMARY
(Erase heading not required.)

Instructions regarding War Diaries and Intelligence Summaries are contained in F. S. Regs., Part II. and the Staff Manual respectively. Title Pages will be prepared in manuscript.

Place	Date	Hour	Summary of Events and Information	Remarks and references to Appendices
FRIEQURT FARM	JAN 3rd to Jan 24th		The following work was done in connection with III Corps buried Cable Scheme.	See diagram No VII attached
			Trench dug 6 feet deep & filled in Point C to W about 700 yards	
			" " " " " " " W to F " 600 "	
			" " " " " " " F forward " 250 "	
			" " " " " " " W to H " 1350 "	
			" " " " " " " H to J " 1250 "	
			" " " " " " " H to G " 1550 "	
			" " " " " " " H to E " 1600 "	
			" " " filled in " P to C " 3000 "	
			" " " " " B to G " 1250 "	
			2 dugouts were built and 4 way cross connection terminal boards fitted at Points B, G, W and H.	
			About 11,500 men were employed.	

M.M. Pegnall
CAPTAIN.
Comdg. 50th (North Um.) Divisional Signal Company R.E.

Diagram
Buried Cable Scheme.
Aug 23rd 1917.

TEST POINT F

TEST POINT Y

TEST POINT H   J

— Route Diagram —

— 50th Divisional Signal Co. R.E. —

TEST POINT B

To Point P

TEST POINT G
LEFT BRIGADE
HQRS

RIGHT BRIGADE
HQRS
E

LM To LMR.

50th Divisional Signal Company R.E.
January 1917.

L.M.R. TO BRIGADES.

50TH DIVISIONAL SIGNAL COMPANY R.E.
JANUARY 1917

ORIGINAL. SECRET.

Vol 23

WAR DIARY

OF

50th (NORTHUMBRIAN) DIVISIONAL SIGNAL COMPANY, R.E.

Volume XXIII.

February, 1917.

Army Form C. 2118

WAR DIARY
or
INTELLIGENCE SUMMARY
(Erase heading not required.)

Instructions regarding War Diaries and Intelligence Summaries are contained in F. S. Regs., Part II. and the Staff Manual respectively. Title Pages will be prepared in manuscript.

92

Place	Date 1917	Hour	Summary of Events and Information	Remarks and references to Appendices
RIBEMONT	FEB. 4th		50th Divisional Artillery less D.A.C. moved from PIERREGOT to FOUILLOY - VAIRE	O.O. No 77 of Feb 1st
"	5th		50th D.A.C. moved from MIRVAUX to VAIRE	O.O. No 80 of Feb 7th
"	8		149th Infantry Brigade Group moved from DERNANCOURT to MERICOURT-sur-SOMME	
"	9th		150th " " " " " BUIRE to MORCOURT	Ref map 1/40,000 Sheet 62c 62d.
"	10th		151st " " " " " RIBEMONT to HAMEL	
"	10th		149 " " " " " MERICOURT sur SOMME to FAY, LES CUISINES – FONTAINE les CAPPY area with Brigade Headquarters at FONTAINE les CAPPY	
"	11th		150 Infantry Brigade moved from MORCOURT to FOUCAUCOURT area with Brigade Headquarters at P.C. MOULIN, FOUCAUCOURT	O.O. No 78 & 80 of Feb 7th
			During the night of Feb 11/12th the 4th N.F. (149 I.B.) relieved one battalion 123rd Regiment, 35th French Division in support at BELLOY	Ref map 1/40,000 Sheet 62c 62d.
"			4th Bat. Yorks & 4th Yorks (150 I.B.) relieved the whole of the front line companies of the 36th French Division belonging to the 15ME & 34 EY 218ER Regiments	

Army Form C. 2118

93

WAR DIARY
or
INTELLIGENCE SUMMARY
(Erase heading not required.)

Instructions regarding War Diaries and Intelligence Summaries are contained in F. S. Regs., Part II. and the Staff Manual respectively. Title Pages will be prepared in manuscript.

Place	Date 1917	Hour	Summary of Events and Information	Remarks and references to Appendices
RIBEMONT	12		Half of the 50th Division Artillery moved from FOUILLOY area to PROYART area	O.O.77 of Feb 10th 1917
"	13		Remainder " " " " " " " "	"
"	12		151st Infantry Brigade moved from HAMEL to PROYART Brigade Headquarters at CHATEAU PROYART During the night of Feb 12/13 the 5th and 7th N.F. (149 I.B.) relieved the companies of the 144th & 249th Regiments on the front line.	O.O.78 & 80 of Feb 7th 1917
			The 6th Yorks (150 I.B.) relieved the support battalion of the 36th French Division in BERNY	Ref: map 1/40,000 Sheet 62c
			On completion of these reliefs the G.O.C. 149th & 150th Infantry Brigades assumed command of the sectors held by the 33rd and 36th French Divisions	
			Headquarters of 149 Infantry Brigade at P.C. BULOW (N25-d 6.4)	" 62c
			" " " " " " SAPE 6 (N9a 9.2)	" 62d
	13		50th Division Headquarters moved from RIBEMONT to P.C. GABRIELLE and PROYART. At 10am the G.O.C. 50th Division assumed command of the new area with Headquarters at P.C. GABRIELLE (M.20 2 2.0)	
"	"		Headquarters 151st Inf. Brigade moved from PROYART to P.C. BICHAT (M.3 1 3 3.8)	

Army Form C. 2118

WAR DIARY
or
INTELLIGENCE SUMMARY
(Erase heading not required.)

Instructions regarding War Diaries and Intelligence Summaries are contained in F.S. Regs., Part II. and the Staff Manual respectively. Title Pages will be prepared in manuscript.

94

Place	Date 1917	Hour	Summary of Events and Information	Remarks and references to Appendices
P.C. GABRIELLE	Feb 13		During the night of 13th/14th February the 149 Infantry Brigade handed over to 2nd Infantry Brigade 1st Division (H.Q. Bois de BOULOGNE) that portion of the line North and exclusive of the ESTRÉES – VILLERS – CARBONNEL road.	O.O. No 79 of 7th Feb 1917 Ref Map 1/40,000 Sheets 62E 62d
"	14		During the night of 14/15th Feb the 149 Brigade extended its right and took over from the 150 Infantry Brigade that portion of the line as far South as the BOIS des ARAS exclusive.	
"	19		During the nights 19/20th & 20/21st Feb the 151st Infantry Brigade relieved the 150th Brigade in the right sector.	O.O No 82 of 17th Feb 1917
"	20			
"	21		At 10 am the G.O.C. 151st Infantry Brigade assumed command of the Right Sector.	
"	26 Feb & 28/1st March		During the nights 26/27th 27/28 Feb and Feb 28th/march 1st the 150th Infantry Brigade relieved the 149th Infantry Brigade on the Left Sector. The G.O.C. 150th Infantry Brigade assumed command of the Left Sector at 10 am 1 March.	O.O No 86 of 24th Feb 1917

Army Form C. 2118

95

WAR DIARY
or
INTELLIGENCE SUMMARY

(Erase heading not required.)

Place	Date	Hour	Summary of Events and Information	Remarks and references to Appendices
RIBEMONT	Feb 1-13		From Feb 1st to 13th the 50th Signal Company was engaged in taking over communications from the French; N.C.O's & men being attached to the 35th French Division for the purpose. Communications were taken over from 7 different French Signal Units viz: 35th French Division - Artillery Unit 36th " " - " 36th " " - Artillery Unit 18th " Corps - " 18th " " - Artillery Army (Forward buried cable exchanges) Owing to the large number of telephone exchanges (about 20) in the area, considerable reorganisation had to be made, most of the exchanges being ultimately closed. The attached diagrams show communications as completed and in use.	

M H Bagnall
CAPTAIN.
Commdg. 50th (North'bn.) Divisional Signal Company R.E.

Vol 24

SECRET

War·Diary
of
50th (Northumbrian) Divl· Signal·Cy· R·E·
Volumn·XXIV

March 1917

Army Form C. 2118.

96

WAR DIARY
or
~~INTELLIGENCE SUMMARY~~
(Erase heading not required.)

Instructions regarding War Diaries and Intelligence Summaries are contained in F. S. Regs., Part II. and the Staff Manual respectively. Title Pages will be prepared in manuscript.

Place	Date	Hour	Summary of Events and Information	Remarks and references to Appendices
P.C. GABRIELLE	MARCH 2		L/Cpl. H. Saddler, 463038, awarded the D.C.M.	
"	1-9		(Martial Snook (Interpreter) awarded the D.C.M.)	
"			Clearing up the Area preparatory to handing over to 59th Div.	
"	9	10.0 AM	149th Infy Bde H.Q. from P.C. BICHAT to WARFUSEE on relief by 178th Infy Bde	O.O. No. 88 of 2nd MARCH 1917
"	"	10.0 AM	150th Infy Bde H.Q. moved from Left Sector Frontline to BAYONVILLERS on relief by 177th Infy Bde	
"	"	10.0 AM	137st Infy Bde H.Q. moved from Right Sector Frontline to MORCOURT on relief by 176th Infy Bde	
"	"	10.0 AM	50th Div: H.Q moved from P.C. GABRIELLE to MERICOURT-SUR-SOMME, on completion	O.O. No. 88 March 2nd 1917
MERICOURT-SUR-SOMME	10th		of relief by 59th Div H.Q.	
"	"		Capt C.L. BAGNALL. M.C. (O.C. 50th SIGNAL COY.) granted leave to U.K.	
"	"		50th Div: became Corps reserve in the MERICOURT-SUR-SOMME	O.O. No. 90 March 5th 1917
"	11th		Lieut. R. STEWART granted leave to U.K.	
"	12th	10.0 AM	50th Div SIGNAL SCHOOL assembled at Camp 6. MERICOURT-SUR-SOMME. (13 officers, 26 other ranks)	
"	29th	2.0 PM	50th Div SIGNAL SCHOOL dispersed.	
"	30th	7.0 AM	H.d.Qrs 9 No 1 Section of 50th Div Signal Company moved to St GRATIEN.	O.O. No 91 of 29th MARCH 1917
"	"		149th Infy Bde H.Q. moved from WARFUSEE to RIVERY.	
"	"		150th Infy Bde H.Q. moved from BAYONVILLERS to CORBIE area.	

Army Form C. 2118

WAR DIARY
or
INTELLIGENCE SUMMARY
(Erase heading not required.)

Place	Date	Hour	Summary of Events and Information	Remarks and references to Appendices
MERICOURT -SUR- SOMME.	31st March	8:30 A.M.	Hqrs. & No.1 Section of 30th Divl. Signal Coy. from ST.GRATIEN to MOLLIENS-AU-BOIS.	{ O.O. No. 91 of March 29th 1917 }
"	"		149th Infy. Bde. H.Q from RIVERY to VILLERS BOCAGE.	
"	"		150th Infy. Bde. H.Q from CORBIE area to MIRVAUX.	
"	"		151st Infy. Bde. H.Q from MORCOURT to TALMAS.	
"	"		50th Divl. H.Q from MERICOURT-SUR-SOMME. to MOLLIENS - AU - BOIS.	
MOLLIENS AU BOIS.			Head Quarters opened at 11.0 AM. Communication established as follows:-	
			4th ARMY ... (Telephone Sounder)	
			5th ARMY.. via. Beauquesne. (Telephone)	
			149th Infy.Bde. ... via 4th Army out. Exchange Villers Bocage. (Telephone)	
"	"	5:0 pm	"O" Cable Section (1 Officer, 3 T.O.R. & 30 horses) joined Division.	
			Record of Artillery move from III Corps Area to III Army Area (XVIII Corps).	
MERICOURT -SUR- SOMME	March 26th		50th Divl. Artillery H.Q. from III Corps Area to FLESSELLES	O.O. 68 (arty.)
"	28th		" " from FLESSELLES to OUTREBOIS	O.O. 69 (arty.)
"	29th		" " from OUTREBOIS to COUTURELLE (III Army Area.)	O.O. 70 (arty.)
"	30th		" " from COUTURELLE to BEAUMETZ.	{ O.O. 71 (arty) }
"	"		50th D.A. loaned temporarily to VII Corps.	

W.R. [signature] Lt for CAPTAIN.
Comdg. 50th (North bn.) Divisional Signal Company R.E.

SECRET.

50th DIVISION COMMUNICATION.

INFORMATION.

Post.	Map Reference.		CALL.
1. Divisional Headquarters	X.28.c.3.8.		L.M.
2. Divisional Advanced Headquarters.	S.14.d.2.9.		L.M.R.
3. Divisional Observation Post.	M.28.d.2.6.		L.M.O.
4. Right Bde.(149th Bde) Battle H.Q.	M.35.a.7.5.		D.L.R.
5. Right Bde.(149th Bde) "Q" H.Q.	S.15.b.3.6.	B.G.	D.L.
6. Left Bde. (150th Bde) Battle H.Q.	M.22.d.6.2.		C.E.R.
7. Left Bde. (150th Bde) "Q" H.Q.	S.15.b.3.6.	B.G.	C.E.
8. Left Bde. (150th Bde) Wireless Station.	M.22.c.9.1.		
9. Left Bde. (150th Bde) Power Buzzer.	M.17.c.3.4.		
10. Left Bde. (150th Bde) I.T.	M.22.d.6.2.		
11. Reserve Brigade (151st Bde) Forward Station.	M.28.d.3.7.		D.G.O.
12. Reserve Bde.(151st Bde) Battle H.Q.	S.15.b.3.6.	B.G.	D.G.R.
13. Reserve Bde.(151st Bde) "Q" H.Q.	X.30.a.4.9.		D.G.
14. Reserve Bde.(151st Bde) Wireless Station	Near S.15.b.3.6.	B.G.	
15. Corps Wireless Station.	S.13.b.5.8.		
16. Divisional MAIN Dump.	S.14.d.2.9.		
17. Divisional Forward Post Station.	M.28.d.4.4.	V.C.	
18. Divisional Central Post Station.	S.3.a.3.9.	H.T.	
19. Division/Rear Post Station.	S.8.b.9.2.	B.P.	
20. Divisional Forward Visual Station.	S.3.a.8.9.	H.T.	H.T.
21. Divisional Rear Visual Station.	S.15.b.3.6.	B.G.	B.G.
22. Divisional Dropping Station.			
23. Divisional Advanced Dressing Station.	S.8.a.4.6.		
24. Division A.P.M.	S.14.a.4.7.		

Circuit Diagram
of
Divisional Communications.
February 1917.

Reference
Telephone
D III Telephone
Telegraph
Artillery lines to Brigades shown in red.
forward of Brigades thus — — — —

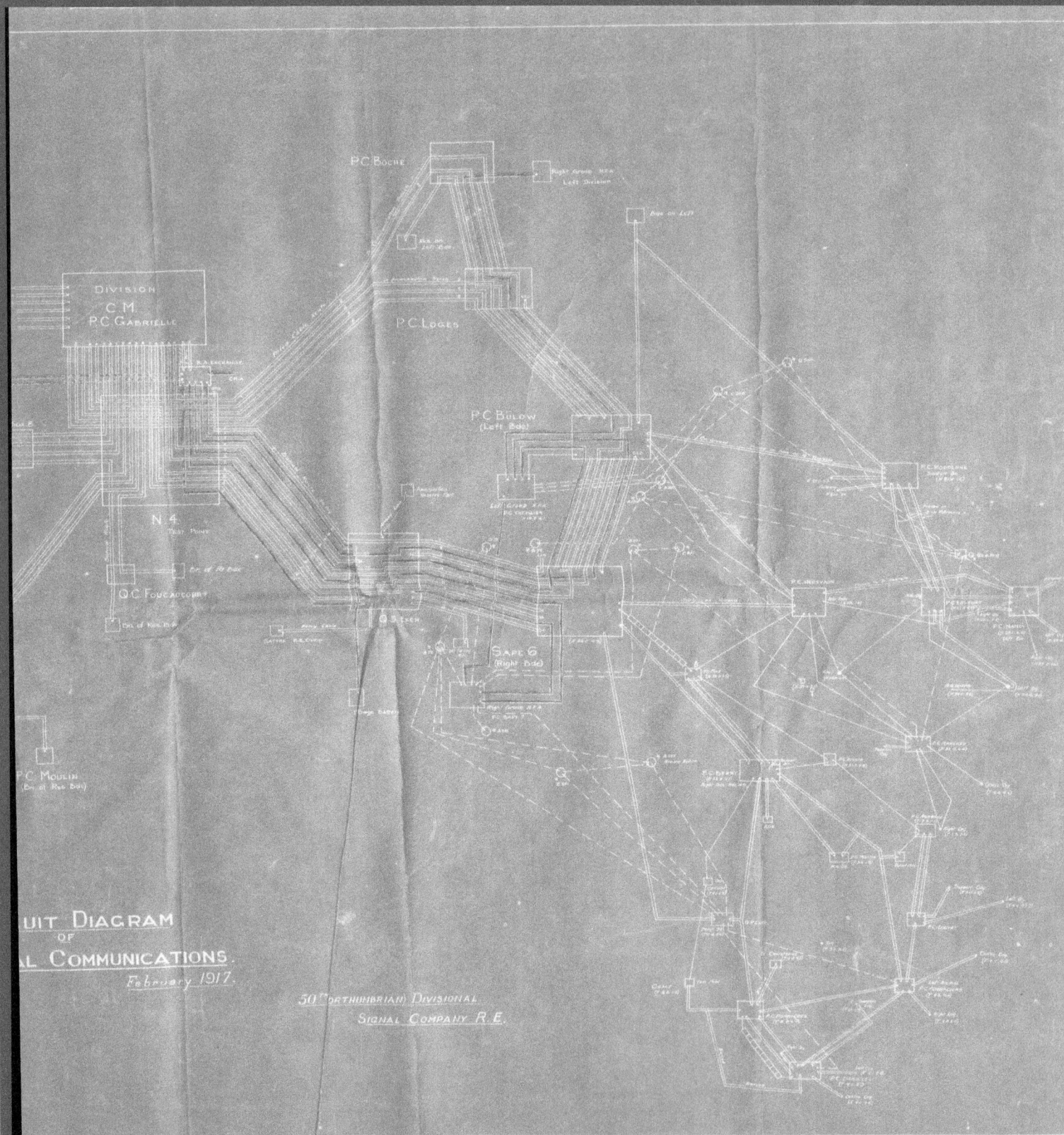

ROUTE PLAN
OF
COMMUNICATIONS.
February 1917.

Reference.—
Maps: 62^d S.W. & 62^d N.W. Scale: 1/10000

Buried Cable shown thus ———
Cable laid in ditch or trench ———
Telephone Exchange ▣
Test Dugout ⊙

ROUTE PLAN
OF
COMMUNICATIONS.
February 1917.

50TH (NORTHUMBRIAN) DIVISIONAL
SIGNAL COMPANY R.E.

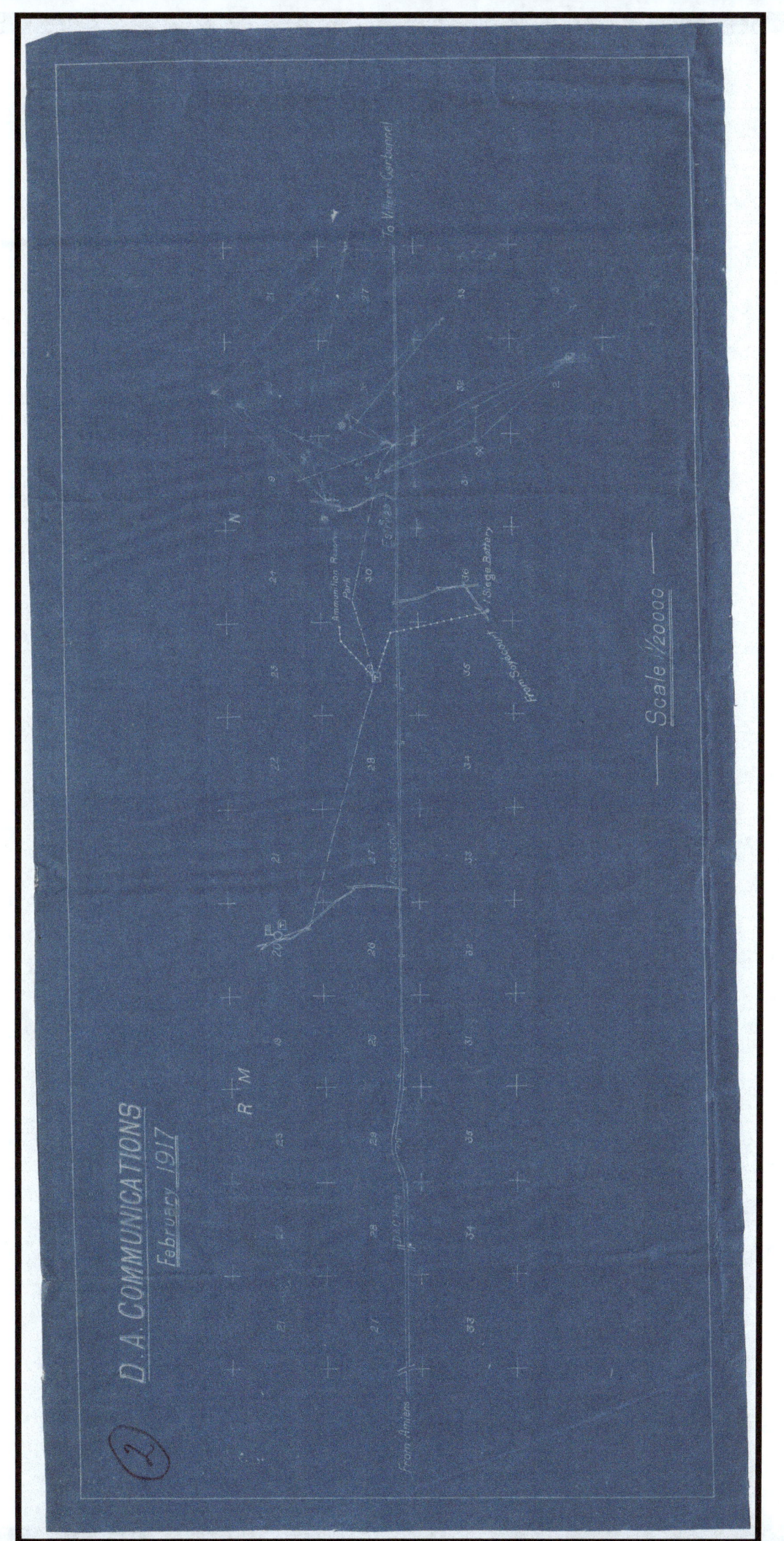

SECRET.

WAR DIARY

of

50th (Northumbrian) Divisional Signal Co, R.E.

Volume XXV.

APRIL, 1917.

Army Form C. 2118

98

WAR DIARY
or
INTELLIGENCE SUMMARY
(Erase heading not required.)

Instructions regarding War Diaries and Intelligence Summaries are contained in F. S. Regs., Part II. and the Staff Manual respectively. Title Pages will be prepared in manuscript.

Place	Date 1917	Hour	Summary of Events and Information	Remarks and references to Appendices
MONCHY AU BOIS / BEAUVAL	APRIL 3rd		151 I.B. Group moved from GEZAINCOURT area to BOUQUEMAISON No 1 area, Bde HdQrs REBREUVE	50th DIV O.O.
			149 " " " " " BEAUVAL " BOUQUEMAISON No 2 " " " BONNIERES	93 dated 1/4/17
			150 " " " " " TALMAS " GEZAINCOURT area " " " GEZAINCOURT	
			50th DIVISIONAL HDQRs Group moved from BEAUVAL to BOUQUEMAISON	
			DIV HdQrs closed at BEAUVAL at 9am and opened at BOUQUEMAISON at the same hour.	
			Telephone Communication was established with XIX Corps. Communication with brigades by D.R.o.	
BOUQUEMAISON	4th		151 I.B. Group moved from BOUQUEMAISON No 1 area to FLERS area. Bde HdQrs at BLANGERMONT	50th DIV O.O.
			149 " " " " " No 2 " " " " " " NUNCQ	93 dated 1/4/17
			150 " " " " GEZAINCOURT area " BOUQUEMAISON " " " " BONNIERES	
			DIV. HDQR " " BOUQUEMAISON " RAMECOURT	
			DIV HdQrs closed at BOUQUEMAISON at 8.30 am and opened at RAMECOURT at 9.30 am	
			Telephone & Telegraphic communication with XIX Corps. Communication with Brigades by D.R.o.	Ref. Map 1/100000 LENS

Army Form C. 2118.

WAR DIARY
or
INTELLIGENCE SUMMARY.
(Erase heading not required.)

Instructions regarding War Diaries and Intelligence Summaries are contained in F. S. Regs., Part II. and the Staff Manual respectively. Title pages will be prepared in manuscript.

Place	Date	Hour	Summary of Events and Information	Remarks and references to Appendices
RAMECOURT	7		Div. Hd Qrs. Group moved from RAMECOURT to ROELLECOURT. Hd Qrs at RAMECOURT closed	O.O. No 94
		at 9 am & opened at ROELLECOURT the same hour	
		151 I.B. Group march from FLERS area to ROELLECOURT area. Gde Hd Qr ROUELLIN - NICOMBEZ dated 4/4/17 & correspondence	
		149 I.B. " " " " " " BUNEVILLE	No 1.
		150 I.B. " " " " " " HOUVIN - HOUVIGNEUL	
		151 I.B. " " " " " " BOUQUEMAISON - HOUVIN - HOUVIGNEUL	
ROELLECOURT	8		DIV Hd Qrs Group moved from ROELLECOURT to LE COUROY. Hd Qrs at ROELLECOURT closed	
		at 9 am and opened at LE COUROY the same hour	O.O. 94
		149 I.B. Group moved from ROELLECOURT AREA to AVESNES area. Bde Hd Qrs at MANIN	dated 4/4/17
		150 I.B. Group moved " " " " " " Bde Hd Qrs at LIGNEREUIL	
		151 I.B. Group " " " " " " Bde Hd Qrs at AMBRINES	
LE COUROY	10		DIV Hd Qrs Group moved from LE COUROY to BERNEVILLE. Hd Qrs at LE COUROY closed at 4 pm	O.O. No. 96
		and opened at BERNEVILLE the same hour	dated 10/4/17
		149 I.B. Group moved from AVESNES AREA to WANQUETIN - HAUTVILLE area. Bde HdQrs at WANQUETIN	
		150 I.B. Group " " " " " to HABARCQ - NOYELLETTE - LATTRE - ST QUENTIN area. Bde Hd Qrs at HARBARCQ	

WAR DIARY or INTELLIGENCE SUMMARY

Army Form C. 2118.
- 100

Place	Date	Hour	Summary of Events and Information	Remarks and references to Appendices
LE COÛROY	10th		151 I.B. Group moved from AVESNES area to AGNEZ-LES-DUISANS-GOUVES-MONTENESCOURT area. Bde. H.Qrs. at AGNEZ-les-DUISANS	2x M.70.96 10/4/17
BERNEVILLE	11th		50th Div. transferred from XVIII Corps to VII Corps.	O.O. No. 97
			149 I.B. Group moved from MAROEUIL, HAUTEVILLE area and relieved 42 I.B.Group in trenches South of TILLOY area.	11/4/17
			151 I.B. Group moved from AGNEZ-LES-DUISANS-GOUVES-MONTENESCOURT area to CAVES in FAUB.	
			RONVILLE, ARRAS. area relieved 43 I.B.	
BERNEVILLE	12		Div. HdQrs Group moved to BERNEVILLE to ARRAS (No.1 RUE L'ABBE HALKIN) Div. HdQrs at BERNEVILLE	
			closed at 4.0 p.m. and opened at ARRAS the same hour.	O.O. No. 98
			150 I.B. Group moved from HARBARCQ-NOYELLETTE-LATTRE-ST QUENTIN area to CAVES in FAUBOURG	aluled
			RONVILLE and came under orders of G.O.C. 14th DIV.	12/4/17
			The 50th Division took over the forward lines of the 14th Division, but in order	
			to connect up to the lines advanced exchange 14 pairs lead L to be laid from Div	
			Headquarters to "C" point on the ARRAS sewer system. This was done by	
			midnight, when the command passed from the G.O.C. 14th Division to G.O.C.	
			50th Division.	Ref maps 1/20,000 LENS sheet 1/40,000 SCARPE valley

WAR DIARY
or
INTELLIGENCE SUMMARY.

(Erase heading not required.)

Army Form C. 2118.

101

Place	Date	Hour	Summary of Events and Information	Remarks and references to Appendices
	APRIL 1917			
ARRAS	22		"C" Staff C.R.A. C.R.E. moved to Advanced Headquarters at N7d4.4	
			No 46311 Sapper CRESSWELL R. wounded, shell Rpr.	O.O 99
N7d.4.4	23		The VIth VIIth Corps continued their advance Eastward	N.o of 20.4.1917 with Corrigenda
			Details of communication shown in Appendix 2 of O.O 99	
			when the Division took over their area 2 lines to Brigade H.Qrs at N7d4.4.	No1.
			The Brigade at N7d.8.4 moved forward to N15d and the former Brigade	Addendum
			being prepared as an advanced Divisional Headquarters.	1, 2, & 3
			Four poled pairs over Land, two two from end of tramway to N7d4.4	Appendix
			and line from artillery test point BT to N7d.4.4, a third pair was	X + Z.
			also laid on first south and split at artillery exchange 22	
			from N7d.4.4 thence to power over land 2 to the ground +	Ref Map
			2 poled to N15d	1:100,000
				LENS SHEET
			As it was thought probable that the Division Hd.Qrs. would	1:40,000
			move to N24c0.5 a laddered cable was laid from N15d. This cable	Sheet 51G
			however was destroyed by the constant barrage and later an	
			armoured cable was run out. The fortunately held and enabled	
			the Brigade to keep communication with a battalion at N24c0.5	

Army Form C. 2118.

WAR DIARY
OF
INTELLIGENCE SUMMARY.
(Erase heading not required.)

102

Place	Date	Hour	Summary of Events and Information	Remarks and references to Appendices
N7 A.4.4	Apl 17 April 23/25		Throughout the operations, communication was maintained with all units. In despite the presence of much there was no delay on O' message. The Signal Coy was complimented by the G.O.C. on their work throughout the operations. No. M63150 Sappr EVERY F. killed in action	
"	24		During the night of April 24/25th the 150th Infantry Brigade was relieved by the 142nd Infantry Brigade and moved to ARRAS	
"	25		The 149th Infantry Brigade moved to HARP about N7.B in relief by 142nd I.B. During the night April 25/26th the 42nd I.D. relieved the 151st I.B. on the front line. The 151 I.B. moved to W. of WANCOURT & became Reserve supporting Brigade.	O.O No.100 of 24/4/17
"	26		The 149 I.B. moved to ARRAS. " 151 I.B. " " " Heap on relief by 141st I.B. & became Reserve Brigade.	
"	26	5:0pm	G.O.C. 50th Div. handed over Command of the area to G.O.C. 14th Div. H.Q.s moved to COUTURELLE	
COUTURELLE	27		The 151 I.B. moved to ARRAS on relief by 43rd I.B.	

WAR DIARY
or
INTELLIGENCE SUMMARY.
(Erase heading not required.)

Army Form C. 2118.

103

Place	Date	Hour	Summary of Events and Information	Remarks and references to Appendices
	1917 April			
COULLEMELLE	26		150 I.B. moved from ARRAS by tactical train to BALLOY area. Bde Hd Qrs GREMAI	"B" indicator
	27		149 I.B. moved from ARRAS by tactical train to POMMERA area.	
			151 " " " " HUMBERCOURT "	
			Communication by wire arranged to 149 & 152 Brigades	

Signed W.H. Bagnall, Major
Cmdg 50 Sig Coy R.E.

Instructions regarding War Diaries and Intelligence Summaries are contained in F. S. Regs., Part II. and the Staff Manual respectively. Title pages will be prepared in manuscript.

50th DIVISION COMMUNICATIONS.
April 1917.

1. The following means of Communication will be available for use during the operations:-
   - (a) Telegraph and Telephone.
   - (b) Visual
   - (c) D.Rs and Runners.
   - (d) Pigeons
   - (e) Wireless Power Buzzer etc.
   - (f) Contact Aeroplane.

2. <u>Telegraph and Telephone.</u>
   The Divl Adv. H.Q. at N.7.d.4.4 will be in communication with the following units.

   VII Corps.
   149. 150. 151 Inf. Bdes.
   Flanking Divisions.
   Covering Artillery.
   Advanced Dressing Station.
   Prisoners' Cage.

   The attacking Brigade will be in communication with the 44th. I.B on its left, and the 90th I.B. on its right.

   During operations the use of Telephone and Telegraph must be cut down to an absolute minimum by Administrative Departments.

3. <u>Visual</u>
   The following Visual Stations will be established:-
   Advd Divl H.Q at N.7.d 4.4.
   Attacking Bde H.Q. N 22 a. 9.6.
   Wancourt Tower (Central Station) N 24 a 1.0.

   The Central Station at Wancourt Tower will maintain communication with attacking Battns, Advd Divl H.Q and Brigade on left (if required) Lamps or Folding Shutter will be used as much as possible at the Central Station and all forward stations.

   Every effort must be made to pick up the enemy's visual signals. Men will be specially detailed for this purpose at Wancourt Tower Central Station. Telegraphists or Visual Signallers must on no account leave their station and companies and other units must arrange for a sufficient supply of orderlies.

4. <u>D.Rs and Runners.</u>
   During operations ordinary D.R.L.S. will be cancelled.

P.T.O

(a) Motor Cyclists will be divided between Div². H.Q and Adv⁴. Div². H.Q. The forward Motor Cyclist post will be on the BEURAINS - NEUVILLE VITASSE Road at M.18. Central: two mounted D.Rˢ will also be stationed at this point to convey messages to Adv⁴. H.Q.

(b) <u>Mounted D.Rˢ</u>
  1. N.C.O and 8 yeomen will be available at Rear Div². H.Q. for mounted D.R. work. Two of these men will be at the Motor Cyclist Post and two at the H.Q. of the attacking Brigade when the situation permits.

(c) <u>Runners</u>
  A system of runners will be organised under Brigade arrangements.

5. <u>Pigeons</u>:-
  Commencing on Zero day the attacking Brigade will have 16 pigeons per day at its disposal.
  Pigeons should accompany the attacking companies, 2 each bat⁹ H.Q. the remainder being kept in reserve at Brigade Adv⁴. H.Q.
  Pigeon messages must indicate the Battalion as well as the Company or Platoon.

6. <u>Wireless</u>:-
  Wireless and Power Buzzers will also be available for use, and full details will be issued later.

7. <u>Contact Aeroplane</u>.
  Communication by Contact Aeroplane is under Corps arrangements.

8. <u>Position of H.Qˢ of units</u>

Division		1. Rue l'Abbé Halluin. Arras.
" Adv⁴.		N. 7 d. 4.4.
Attacking (150) Bde	Cemetery	N. 22 a. 9.6.
" " "	Adv⁴.	~~N.21 c. 0.5~~ N 15 d. 4.4
Support (151) "		~~N. 15 d. 2.4~~ N 14 Central.
Reserve (149) "		N. 7 b. 4.4.
Central Visual Station.	Wancourt Tower	N. 24 d. 1.0.
Div⁹ on Right (30th Div⁹)	nr Rany.	M. 3 c. 1.5
" " "	Adv⁴	M. 18 d. 5.5.
" " Left (15th Div⁹)	17 Rue de la Paix Arras	
" " "	Adv⁴	
Brigade on Right (90th Bde)		N. 13 d. 4.7
" " Left (44th Bde)		N. 14 b. 1.8

Chas Bagnall Major
Comdg. 50th (North⁹ⁿ) Divisional Signal Company R.E.

Original.

SECRET.

WAR DIARY

OF

50th (Northumbrian) Divisional Signal Company, R.E.

Volume XXVI.

May, 1917.

Army Form C. 2118.

104

WAR DIARY
or
INTELLIGENCE SUMMARY.
(Erase heading not required.)

Instructions regarding War Diaries and Intelligence Summaries are contained in F. S. Regs., Part II. and the Staff Manual respectively. Title pages will be prepared in manuscript.

Place	Date 1917	Hour	Summary of Events and Information	Remarks and references to Appendices
COUTURELLE MAY				
	1st		50th Division Ein Artillery moved Eastwards as under:-	
			149 Brigade Group from POMMERA & MONCHIET to SOMASTRE & FONQUEVILLERS	
			Brigade Headquarters established at SOMASTRE	O.O. No 101
			150 Brigade Group from BIENAS and to COIGNEUX-BAYENCOURT	
			Brigade Headquarters at BAYENCOURT	Actual April 30th
			151 Brigade Group with 7th D.I. (less 1 Company) attached from HUMBERCOURT	
			area to POMMIERS – BIENVILLERS au BOIS – BERLES au BOIS.	Reference Map
			Brigade Headquarters at POMMIERS	1/100,000
			Communication to all Brigades by M.C.D.R.	LENS
			Northwards as under:-	Sheet 11
COUTURELLE	2nd		50th Division Ein Artillery moved Northwards as order	
			149th I.B. Group to MERCATEL with HdQrs at MERCATEL	
			150th I.B. " to FICHEUX – BLAIRVILLE & RANSART with Hd Qrs at BLAIRVILLE	
			151st " " " GROSVILLE – BELLACOURT – Y BAILLEULVAL " " " BAILLEULVAL	O.O. No 102
			Advanced Division Headquarters opened at M.18.c.6.4 near NEUVILLE VITASSE at 4pm	dated May 1st
			& closed at COUTURELLE at the same time. D moved to BASSEUX	
			Lines were laid to 14th Division and 18th Division and line to the latter being	

Army Form C. 2118.

105

WAR DIARY
or
INTELLIGENCE SUMMARY.
(Erase heading not required.)

Instructions regarding War Diaries and Intelligence Summaries are contained in F. S. Regs., Part II. and the Staff Manual respectively. Title pages will be prepared in manuscript.

Place	Date 1917	Hour	Summary of Events and Information	Remarks and references to Appendices
COUTURELLE	MAY 2		Being/superimposed enabling direct-litey of communication being maintained with VII Corps	Addendum No 1 to O.O.102
			Communication to 150 Brigade by telephone through VII Corps	
			149 & 151 Brigades by D.R.	
			The office at COUTURELLE was kept open to take work for DADOS all such	
			an officer was spared at BASSEUX to take "Q" work	
NEUVILLE VITASSE	4"		Division marched Southwards as under.	
			149 I.B. Group to SOUASTRE once with headquarters at SOUASTRE	
			150 " " " COIGNEUX " " " BAYENCOURT	Telegram
			151 " " " HUMBERCOURT " " " HUMBERCOURT	G.A. 296/f
			Communication by D.R. to 149 & 150 Brigade, by telephone to 151 Brigade May 4th 1917	
			Division Headquarters opened at COUTURELLE at 4.30 pm & closed at	
			NEUVILLE VITASSE & BASSEUX at the same hour	

Army Form C. 2118.

WAR DIARY
or
INTELLIGENCE SUMMARY.
(Erase heading not required.)

Instructions regarding War Diaries and Intelligence Summaries are contained in F. S. Regs., Part II. and the Staff Manual respectively. Title pages will be prepared in manuscript.

Place	Date	Hour	Summary of Events and Information	Remarks and references to Appendices
COUTURELLE	1917 MAY 5		The E.O.R. Division continued the move to not area	
			149 Bde Group moved FOUNDERS encamped and Headquarters at POMMERA	G.R. 297
			150 " " " HALLOY	" GRENAS 1/May 4th 1917
			Telegraphic & telephonic communication to CORPS & telephone to all brigades	
	16		The undermentioned NCOs & men of No 3 Section 50th Signal Co. RE were awarded the military medal for conspicuous gallantry in the field during the fighting of between April 12th & 26th 1917	
			No 463118 Sergt. JENKINS W	
			" 463066 H/Cpl SCOTT R.E.	
			" 463144 Sapper HOLMES G.E.	
			" 463239 " JONES N	
	17	Noon	30th Division (less Artillery & Cavalry) area transferred to VII Corps and moved on	O.O. No 183
			follows:-	ditto
			149th Bde Group 149th Bde to SOUASTRE area with HdQrs at SOUASTRE	May 15/17
			150 " Group " COIGNEUX " " " " BAYENCOURT.	

WAR DIARY
INTELLIGENCE SUMMARY

Army Form C. 2118.

107

Place	Date 1917 MAY	Hour	Summary of Events and Information	Remarks and references to Appendices
COUTURELLE	18		149 Bde (one Field Coy & Field Ambulance) moved to MOYENVILLE area where it came under	
			33rd Division	O.O.No 103 dated May 15/17
			150 Bde Group moved to DOUCHY and AYETTE area with Headquarters at DOUCHY les AYETTE	Ref map
			151 " " " " MONCHY au BOIS area " " " MONCHY au BOIS	1:100,000
				Sheet 11 LENS
"	19		Divisional Headquarters opened at BEAUMETZ les LOGES at 5.0 pm & closed at COUTURELLE at the same hour.	
			The Signal Company both own BEAUMETZ exchange & communications established as below.	
			To VII Corps Telegraph & Telephone	
			To 149 Bde Telegraph & telephone through 33rd Div Exchange	
			To 150 & 151 " " 21st " "	
BEAUMETZ les LOGES	20		The 33rd Div VIIth Corps carried out an attack on the HINDENBURG LINE	O.O No 104 of May 19th
			The 149 I. Bde were placed temporarily under the orders of the G.O.C. 33rd Division for this operation	Ref map
			The remainder of the 50th Division were in VIIth Corps reserve & ready to move at 6 hours notice.	Sheet 51 & 2 S W H BULLE COURT

Army Form C. 2118.

WAR DIARY
INTELLIGENCE SUMMARY.
(Erase heading not required.)

Instructions regarding War Diaries and Intelligence Summaries are contained in F. S. Regs., Part II. and the Staff Manual respectively. Title pages will be prepared in manuscript.

Place	Date	Hour	Summary of Events and Information	Remarks and references to Appendices
	MAY 1917			
BEAUMETZ to LOGES	19		The following Officer W.O., NCOs & men were Mentioned in dispatches.	
			Lt W. PYEMONT. R.E. Lt Col CRADDOCK 9th DLI	
			No 463128 C.S.M KING. F. No 3 Section	
			No 463118 Sergt JENKINS W No 3 Section	
			" 532239 L/Cpl RATCLIFE P " 4 "	
			" 463209 SAP. STEARMAN J " 4 "	
			" 463077 " BIRSE H " 2 "	
			" 463241 " KIRBY H " 2 "	
"	23		50th Division (Divn Artillery and 149 I.Bde) moved Westward as under	
			150th I.Bde Group to COIGNEUX area with Hd Qrs at BAYENCOURT	Ref Map
			151st " " " ST AMAND area with Hd Qrs SAULTY	1/100,000 Sheet 11
			Division Headquarters opened at COUIN at 4 pm Y closed at BEAUMETZ at the same hour	LENS
COUIN	24th		151 I.Bde Hd Qrs & 2 Battalions moved to SOUASTRE, 2 Battalions remaining at ST AMAND.	G.B 48 of 24th May

Army Form C. 2118.

109

WAR DIARY
or
INTELLIGENCE SUMMARY.
(Erase heading not required.)

Instructions regarding War Diaries and Intelligence Summaries are contained in F. S. Regs., Part II. and the Staff Manual respectively. Title pages will be prepared in manuscript.

Place	Date 1917 MAY	Hour	Summary of Events and Information	Remarks and references to Appendices
COUIN	24		C.R.A. remained at BEAUMETZ les LOGES.	
			Telephonic communication established with 150 & 151 Bdes through PAS exchange.	
			Telegraph & Telephone to Corps XVIII Corps	
"	25		7th Bn DURH L.I. (Pioneers) moved from COULLEMONT to COUIN	G.A.3/2 of May 23rd
"	26		50th Division was transferred from XVIII to VII Corps	
			Communication to VII Corps established through PAS exchange	
"	28		149th Bde came under the orders of 50th Division & moved to MONCHY au BOIS	
			Communication by telephone through 21st Divi exchange at ADINFER	
"	30		7th DLI moved to FONQUEVILLERS	
"	31		7th DLI moved from FONQUEVILLERS to BOYELLES & relieved the Pioneer Bn of the 21st Division.	

[Signed] Chas H. Bagnall Major
Cmdg 50th Signal Coy

Original.

S E C R E T.

W A R   D I A R Y

O F

50th (Northumbrian) Divisional Signal Company, Royal Engineers.

Volume XXVII.

June, 1917.

Army Form C. 2118.

WAR DIARY
or
INTELLIGENCE SUMMARY.
(Erase heading not required.)

Place	Date 1917	Hour	Summary of Events and Information	Remarks and references to Appendices
COUIN	June 1st		Signal Company and Transport inspected by C.R.E.	
COUIN	5th		Lieut Winthrop Payment R.E. (SR) awarded Military Cross	
			The 50th Division relieved the 18th Division (less Artillery in south area) in the left Section of VII Corps front as follows:-	O.O. 106 June 11th 1917
COUIN	15th		150th Infy Bde Group. From COIGNEUX area to Reserve Bde area S.17 to relieve 53rd Infy Bde. 151st Infy Bde Group from SOUASTRE area to Support Brigade Area N25C, N26C, N31a, N32. Vande. to relieve 2 Battns 53rd Infy Bde.	

WAR DIARY
or
INTELLIGENCE SUMMARY.

(Erase heading not required.)

Army Form C. 2118.

Place	Date	Hour	Summary of Events and Information	Remarks and references to Appendices
COUIN	June 15 1917		50th Divisional Signal Coy. Advance hire. moved from COUIN to BOISLEUX-ST-MARC.	
COUIN	16/6/17		151st Infy Bde. from Saffort Res Area to front line left sub sector to relieve 53rd Infy Bde.	
			G.O.C. 151st Infy Bde. assuming Command of Sector on completion of relief.	
COUIN	17th		The 7th D.L.I. Pioneers relieved the 8th Royal Sussex Regt. near HENIN.	
COUIN	17/18		150th Infy Bde. from Reserve Bde area to front line right sub sector to relieve 54th Infy Bde.	
			G.O.C. 150th Infy Bde. assuming command on completion of relief.	

WAR DIARY
or
INTELLIGENCE SUMMARY.
(Erase heading not required.)

Army Form C. 2118.

Place	Date 1917	Hour	Summary of Events and Information	Remarks and references to Appendices
COUIN	June 18th		149th Infy Bde. from MONCHY Area to Reserve Bde Area S.17 to relieve 34th Infy Bde. 50th Division taking over COUIN to S.17a 9.4 (BOISLEUX-ST-MARC). The G.O.C. 50th Division took over command of Left Section. III Corps front at 11 a.m. at which hour Divisional HQrs closed at COUIN.	
BOISLEUX-ST-MARC	18		CRA 50th Division took over command of the Artillery in the area at 11 a.m., with HQ at S.17 a 9.4.	
BOISLEUX-ST-MARC (S.17a 9.4).	24th		The 149th Infy Bde relieved the 151st Infy Bde in the Left Sub Section, the 151st Infy Bde returning to Reserve Bde Area S.17.	BOISLEUX O.O. 108 June 20th 1917

Army Form C. 2118.

WAR DIARY
or
INTELLIGENCE SUMMARY.
(Erase heading not required.)

113

Place	Date 1917	Hour	Summary of Events and Information	Remarks and references to Appendices
BOISLEUX-ST-MARC (S.17.a.9.4).	June 24th		50th Division Signal School assembled at Boisleux-St-Marc.	
BOISLEUX-ST-MARC (S.17.a.9.4)	25/26th		A minor Operation was carried out by 150th Infy Bde by advancing its flank on to the line :- V.13.7.9 — V.13.8.6 (Junction of Wood Trench and Fontaine Trench — Wood Trench) ZERO HOUR 12·30 am A contact patrol examined the situation on the morning of the 26th and dropped an message at S.17.a.9.4 at 5.5 am.	O.O. 109 June 22nd/17
BOISLEUX-ST-MARC	26th		463049 Dvr Hodgson H. wounded in action.	

WAR DIARY
or
INTELLIGENCE SUMMARY.
(Erase heading not required.)

Army Form C. 2118.

Place	Date	Hour	Summary of Events and Information	Remarks and references to Appendices
Boesinghe (S17a.9.4)	1917 June 18/20		Time spent in improving communications. Diagram will be drawn on completion.	

[signature]
Comdg. 50th (North bn.) Divisional Signal Company R.E.

Original.

<u>S E C R E T.</u>

W A R   D I A R Y

O F

50th (Northumbrian) Divisional Signal Company, Royal Engineers.

<u>Volume XXVIII.</u>

<u>July, 1917.</u>

Army Form C. 2118.

WAR DIARY
or
INTELLIGENCE SUMMARY.
(Erase heading not required.)

Instructions regarding War Diaries and Intelligence Summaries are contained in F. S. Regs., Part II. and the Staff Manual respectively. Title pages will be prepared in manuscript.

111

Place	Date 1917	Hour	Summary of Events and Information	Remarks and references to Appendices
BOISLEUX ST MARC	JULY 1st		151 I Brigade less 2 Battalions moved to neighbourhood of HENIN	
S.14.9.4.			149 I Brigade took over portion of the front held by 150th I Brigade.	Ref 1/40,000. map
			On the night of July 1/2nd the 21st Division took over portion of the line as far North as O.31.d.4.4. from 150th Inf Brigade.	Sheet 51B
			150th Infantry Brigade moved to the Reserve Brigade camp S17.	
	2nd		Remaining troops of 151 Inf Brigade moved to neighbourhood of HENIN. On the night of July 2/3rd the 151 Inf Brigade relieved 56th Div in the subsector N. of COJEUL River	
	3		During the night of July 3/4 151st Inf Brigade completed relief of 56th Division command of the front passing to the G.O.C. 151st Brigade. The 9th Divl Artillery came under orders of the G.O.C. 50th Division on completion of above relief. G.O.C. 50th Division took over command of the new area	O.O. No 111 dated June 29th 1917

Army Form C. 2118.

WAR DIARY
or
INTELLIGENCE SUMMARY.
(Erase heading not required.)

Instructions regarding War Diaries and Intelligence Summaries are contained in F. S. Regs., Part II, and the Staff Manual respectively. Title pages will be prepared in manuscript.

Place	Date 1917	Hour	Summary of Events and Information	Remarks and references to Appendices
BOISEUX ST MARC	JULY 4		On July 4th the 150th Infantry Infantry Brigade moved to a camp west of NEUVILLE VITASSE & remained as Reserve Brigade in the new area.	O.O. 111 dated June 29/17
			In connection with change of Front new semi-permanent cable routes had to be built to the Left Brigade & Reserve Brigade. Four extra pairs were built or put through from Div Headquarters to NEUVILLE VITASSE. Diagram & details of Communications are attached.	
	11th		150th Inf Brigade completed relief of 149 Infantry Brigade on the Right Sector of the 50th Divisional Front.	O.O. 112 dated July 6th 1917
	20th		The 149th Inf Brigade completed relief of 151st Infantry Brigade on the V15 & GUEMAPPE Sectors	OO 113 of July 13th 1917

Army Form C. 2118.

WAR DIARY
or
INTELLIGENCE SUMMARY
(Erase heading not required.)

1/3

Place	Date July	Hour	Summary of Events and Information	Remarks and references to Appendices
BOISLEUX ST MARC	28th	6am	The 151st Infantry Brigade completed relief of 150th Infantry Brigade in the Right (CHERISY) sector.	O.O. No 44 of
			On completion of relief 150th Brigade were moved to Reserve billeting area.	July 2nd 1917.
			Documents attached:—	
			I. Resumé of work done on lines & formation of SIGNAL SCHOOL	
			II. Note on Visual Signalling and to bring with view to being available as new Signal Manual.	
			III. Description of proposed Communications including the following plans:	
			(a) Diagram of communications between the Hd Qrs & Brigades.	
			(B) Route plan of Brigade lines.	
			(c) Diagrammatic Map of Wireless, Power Buzzer, Amplifier	
			Pigeon & Visual communications.	
			[signature] Major	

A6915 Wt. W14422/M1160 350,000 12/16 D.D. & L. Forms/C/2118/14.

WORK DONE ON INFANTRY LINES BETWEEN DIVISIONAL HEADQUARTERS AND BRIGADES.

Prior to taking over front from 56th Division, four extra pairs were put through from Divisional Headquarters to new Advanced Division Exchange near Neuville Vitasse. The exchange was also wired and ready to open up at short notice.

In the Sector handed over to the 21st Division arrangements were made to lay 3 7 pair leads through the whole length of the Hindenburg Tunnel. A considerable quantity of 7 pair lead was re-reeled into 220 yard lengths and sent up for that purpose. 450 feet of piping was also sent up to be used in dangerous parts of the tunnel.

This material was ultimately handed over to the 7th Corps Signal Co.,

The following forward work was done:-

```
6 pair Comic built from  N33b3.6 to N27 central.
4   "    "     "     "   N27 central to 'N' Route N21a2.2
6   2    "     "     "   N21a2.2 to 300 yards short of Division
                                      advanced exchange.
6   "  Poled Cable Route to Division Advanced Exchange.
3   2    "     "     "   from  Adv Exchange to N16a0.0
1   "    "     "     "     "   N15d5.2 to N16a0.0
1   "    "     "     "     "   N22d5.6 to N16d3.3
2   "    "     "     "         N21a9.4 to N15d5.2
Armoured Twin laid from        N16a0.0  to N10d0.0
    "     "    "    "          N16d3.3  to N16 d0.0
    "     "    "    "          N22d4.4  to N27d9.1
    "     "    "    "          N33b1.9  to N28d3.4
    "     "    "    "          N33b1.9  to N27 central.
```

Some of the twin has since been recovered.

Semi-permanent routes were also built from New Reserve Brigade Headquarters connecting up all battalions, Div.Bomb Store and Nos 13 and 14 Mobile Workshops.

In addition a large amount of work has been done improving existing communications.

All Camp and local lines were replaced by Semi permanent routes, extra lines being laid.

Details of all communications, wireless, pigeons, runners etc are shewn on attached diagrams.

WORK DONE ON ARTILLERY COMMUNICATIONS.
to 31st JULY 1917.

Four Artillery Groups viz. the 46th, 82nd, 83rd and 250th Brigades R.F.A.? were in the line when the 50th Division relieved the 18th Division at S17a.

Each Group had a line to the Divisional Artillery Exchange and the 83rd Bde had a second line for message work. In addition there were lines to Corps R.A., Corps H.A., 50th Division, 18th D.A.C., 39th H.A.G.? and 18th A.R.P.

The first work done was to get a line for message work to 46th, 82nd and 250th Brigades and this was done by teeing all three in to one of the lines on the armoured quad cable route. A line was obtained to the 50th D.A.C.? and 50th A.R.P., and the D.T.M.O. was put on the message line to 83rd Brigade.

281st Bde R.F.A relieved 46th Bde on the 18/19th taking over the same headquarters and communications.

On June 21st the 162nd Bde R.F.A.? came under the orders of C.R.A., 50th Division, the batteries being distributed among the groups in the line and Headquarters remaining in rest.

During the night of June 23/24th, the 82nd and 83rd Brigades withdrew to their wagon lines and 251st Brigade took over the headquarters of the 82nd Bde and the right of a re-arranged front. The second line to 83rd Bde position was joined through on an existing line to the 36th K.B.Section, and as 18th A.R.P also withdrew, two subscribers remained on the line, viz. D.T.M.O., and 36th K.B.S.

The 281st Brigade withdrew on the night of 25/26th June leaving the two groups, 250th and 251st Brigades covering the Divisional front.

On July 4th [3rd] the Divisional front was altered and extended Northwards. The 50th and 51st Bdes R.F.A. came under the orders of 50th Div C.R.A., Communication with the 50th Bde was obtained by extending an existing line that had temporarily been put on to 251st Exchange and by putting another tee on the omnibus line.

For the 51st Bde a line was obtained on various Corps Permanent and semi-permanent routes to within a mile of their headquarters and cable laid from that point. A line was also laid from the 51st Headquarters to meet the omnibus line near 50th Bde Headquarters.

The 51st Bde was withdrawn on the night of July 5/6th. On the withdrawal of the 51st Bde one of the lines to their position was diverted to the 50th Bde as a line for message work and the other was re-reeled.

A Fullerphone was superimposed on each of the telephone pairs to 250th and 251st BdesR.F.A., but the omnibus line retained as an alternative means of communication. Later, the 251st Bde moved to a position close to the left Infantry Brigade, necessitating an extension to their lines. The telephone pair was extended by poled cable, a tee was put into the message line of the 50th Bde and the Tee from the old Headquarters to the omnibus line picked up.

A Fullerphone was superimposed as before.

A line was laid from the Div Arty Exchange to No 45 K.B.Section and lines obtained to the Div Artillery on either flank.

DIVISIONAL SIGNAL SCHOOL.

A Divisional School was formed on July 5th at Division Headquarters.

Each Battalion sent 20 students, and the Divisional Artillery 40 students, making a total of 280.

Each Battalion supplied a senior and junior N.C.O. to act as Assistant Instructors. The Div.R.A. also supplied two Assistant Instructors.

Each Infantry Brigade also supplied one officer as an Instructor.

The Signal Company supplied a Commandant, Adjutant, Sergt. Major and Q.M.S., All technical Training is also carried out by N.C.O's of the Signal Company.

Under the existing conditions of Trench Warfare, the extra work of running the School has not put an undue strain on the Officers and N.C.O's concerned.

So far about 60 Signallers have passed out as 1st Class Signallers and have also got a sound technical knowledge of matters that come within the range of Battery or Battalion Signallers.

From a fighting point of view it is considered that a Divisional Signal School is more suitable than either an Army or Corps School for the training of Battalion and Battery Signallers.

A Divisional Signal Company usually has several Officers with a considerable knowledge of forward communications, having had experience as Brigade or Battalion Signal Officer, and the main training required is undoubtedly training in maintenance and laying of Cables in Trench Warfare, Visual Signalling and its application in Mobile or Semi-Mobile Warfare.

COMMUNICATIONS.

INFANTRY.

From Divisional Headquarters there are two telephone pairs to each Infantry Brigade, one pair having Sounder superimposed.

Between the Infantry Brigades in the line and Division there are three main routes.

    I   Corps Route along Cojeul valley to point near HENINEL.
    II Armoured Quads along barbed wire of HENIN - WANCOURT LINE.
    III 'AN' Route.

    IV A lateral route runs from 818 at N33b3.6 - Test station N33b1.9 cuts 'II' about N27 central, cuts 'III' about N21a2.2 to Advanced Divisional EXchange, N21a4.4

All lines from Division, including Artillery lines run along one or more of the above routes, and radiate therefrom.

    V   A supplementary line (Corps 'O' Route) provides communication between Advavced exchange and Right and Left Brigades forward, and backwards to Corps Mobile Pigeon Lofts and Reserve Brigade.

Linesmen are stationed as follows:-

DIV. ADV. EXCHANGE. N21a4.4 Four linesmen, 5 Telephones.

    Maintenance. Forward of Adv.Exchange to Left Brigade.
           "   "   "   "   along 'O' Route.
            IV Route to N27 Central.
            III " to 'W' Pole M24d central

An N.C.O., and forward working party are also stationed at this point.

'W' POLE. M24d central, Two linesmen, 1 Telephone.

    Maintenance 'III' to ARRAS)BAPAUME Road.
    Spur to Reserve Brigade and Locals of Reserve Brigade.

'A' TEST POINT. N33b1.9 N.C.O.? 3 linesmen, 2 Telephones.

    Maintenance 'I' forward of NEUVILLE VITASSE - HENIN - ST. LEGER Road.
            'II'   Ditto,   ditto,
            'IV' to N27 Central
            Line from right Brigade to A.D.S. N27d9.1

One Artillery linesman is also stationed at this point.

RIGHT BRIGADE N22d4.4   Two linesmen 1 telephone.

    To assist 'A' with forward portion.

'B' Test Point HENIN T2a3.1   Two linesmen   1 Telephone.

    Maintenance 'I' and 'II' from ARRAS - BAPAUME Road to
            NEUVILLE VITASSE - HENIN - ST. LEGER Road.
            Lines to R.E.Dump and Pioneer Battalion.

COMMUNICATIONS.
INFANTRY BRIGADES.

RIGHT BRIGADE.

There are two pairs to both front line battalions and to support battalion.

All lines forward of Brigade are led into a Test Point at N29b8.3.

Brigade has communication to Flanking Brigades and to covering Artillery. Battalions are also in communication with Flanking Battalions.

In addition there are lines to M.G.Company, forward Wireless Station, Visual Transmitting station, Brigade O.P. Pigeon Lofts and A.D.S., near HENINEL.

All work to battalions is sent over the Fullerphone.

LEFT BRIGADE.

From Brigade Headquarters to Test Point there are 4 pairs. The Test Point is in MARLIERE CAVES N17d2.0 and is manned by 5 Linesmen operators, assisted by the signallers of Company of Support Battalion living in the Caves.

From Marliere there are two pairs to each front line Battalion. Both pairs to right Battalion are tapped into Support Battalion.

In addition there are lines to Reserve Battalion, to M.G. Coy, covering Artillery, and Flanking Brigades. Battalions are in communication laterally and to Flanking Battalions. There is also a line to Brigade Visual Station.

All work to Forward Battalions is sent over the Fullerphone.

RESERVE BRIGADE.

Semi-Permanent Lines were built connecting all Battalions of the Brigade, Div.Bomb Store and Mobile Workshops.

In addition there are lines to Transport of all Brigades, and to M.G.Company.

LIST of SUBSCRIBERS.

50th DIV. EXCHANGE.

   VII Corps, 2 lines.
   Division on right.
   Division on left.
   149 Infantry Bde. 2 lines.
   150 " " 2 "
   151 " " 2 "
   Adv. Div. Exchange.
   Divisional R. A.
   G.S.O.1
   'G' Office.
   'Q' Office.
   A.D.M.S.
   A.D.S. near HENINEL.
   A.D.S. Marliere Caves.
   C.R.E.
      R.E. Dump. HENIN.
      181 Tunneling Company.
      7th Durham L.I. Pioneers.
   SIGNALS. Orderly Room.
           Mess.
           Horse Lines.
           Instrument Repairers and
           Linemen.
           Corps Wireless Station
           Div. Signal School.
           Linemen 'A' Point.
              " 'B' "
              " 'W' Pole.
              " Adv. Exchange.
   Divisional Train.
   Public Call Office.

   Ordnance stores.

Through DIV. ARTILLERY EXCHANGE.

   VII Corps.
   VII Corps Heavy Artillery
   Artillery of Div. on right.
   " " " " left.
   250 Brigade R.F.A.
   251 " "
   50 " "
   Flanking Brigades R.F.A.,
   39th H. A. G.
   50th D. A. C.,
   50th A.R.P.,
   D.T.M.O.,

Through RIGHT INF. BRIGADE

   Units of Brigade.
   Flanking Brigades.
   Pigeon Loft.
   A.D.S near HENINEL.

Through LEFT INF. BRIGADE.

   Units of Brigade.
   Flanking Brigades.
   A.D.S. MARLIERE CAVES.

Through RESERVE INF. BRIGADE.

   Units of Brigade.
   Adv. Div Exchange.
   Div. Bomb Store.
   No 13 & 14 Mobile Workshops.

COMMUNICATIONS.
ARTILLERY.

There are lines to each Artillery Brigade for Ringing telephones. Fullerphones are superimposed on ringing lines to 250th and 251st Brigades.

In addition each Brigade has a line for message work by an alternative route.

The following subscribers are also on the Divisional Artillery Exchange.

VII Corps.	VII Corps Heavy Artillery.
50th Division	Arty of Div on Right
39th H.AAG.	" " " " Left.
Div Amn Column	A. R. P.
D. T. M. O.	No.45 Kite Balloon Section.

RIGHT ARTILLERY BRIGADE.

There are lines to each Battery, Infantry Brigade, Arty Brigades on each flank, Heavy Artillery Group exchange, Kite Balloon Exchange. Two pairs of Batteries are in communication laterally and each battery has a line to at least one O.P. In addition one battery has a line to the left and another battery a line to the right battalion.

Visual Signalling has been arranged between Bde HdQrs and one pair of batteries, and the latter have visual with another pair of batteries.

CENTRE ARTILLERY BRIGADE.

There are lines to each battery, to left Infantry Bde., Right Battalion of Left Inf Bde, Artillery Brigades on either flank and to Kite Balloon Exchange. There are lines from each Battery to the Brigade O.P. and visual communication between Brigade HdQrs and the Brigade O.P.? 'A' & 'D' Batteries and 'A' & 'B' Batteries are in communication laterally.

LEFT ARTILLERY BRIGADE.

Have Direct lines to two Battalions and two trunk lines to a forward exchange from which lines radiate to Batteries and O.P.s. Lines to Balloon and Heavy Group Exchanges, to left Infantry Brigade and Left Battalion of left Brigade.

VISUAL SYSTEM.

The Visual System is shewn on attached map, which also gives details of personnel, manning stations etc.,

Lucas Lamps only are in use. Owing to the number of lamps required to work this scheme they have had to be pooled and handed over when relief takes place.

Messages are sent both ways between the following stations :-

'A' to 'E'. 'F' to 'L'. 'F' to 'G'

Special tubes are being fitted at 'A' 'G' 'H' to enable messages to be sent both ways. Until this is done messages are being sent from front to rear only, being acknowledged by lamp during the daytime and by Fullerphone at night.

The following stations are manned permanently, signallers from the Signal School being relieved weekly.

'A'. 'E'. 'F'. 'L'. 'G'.

These stations are open for work as under:-

10am to 12 noon
2pm to 5 pm
9.30pm to 11.30pm.

There is always a lookout man on duty at the above stations.

All other stations are manned at least two hours by day and two hours by night.

Brigade Signal Officers are responsible for the supervision of the Permanent stations.

Practise messages are sent between 'F' and 'G' during the hours when the forward visual stations are not open.

WIRELESS: POWER BUZZER & AMPLIFIER.

Positions are shown on attached Map. Two Trench Wireless Sets are installed, one about N22c4.7 near Right Brigade Headquarters; the other about N29c5.3

Both these sets are in communication with Corps Directing Set at T7d2.8.,

A Power Buzzer is installed at each Battalion Headquarters, with the exception of that at the Headquarters of the extreme left Battalion the Power Buzzers are working satisfactorily to Amplifier installed near Forward Wireless Set N29c5.3.,

It is proposed to instal a second Amplifier in MAULINEN Caves to take messages from the Battalions of the Left Brigade.

PIGEONS.

Corps Mobile Pigeon Lofts are at M18b near NEUVILLE VITASSE. Pigeons are conveyed by Corps M.J.D.R., from lofts to Division Refilling Point (N21a2.2.) at 9.30 a.m. daily and left there.

The Infantry Brigades collect Pigeons from this point and send them up to the Battalions who send them forward to Companies.

Each Brigade has 8 pigeons supplied daily.

The pigeon loft is in communication with the Right Infantry Brigade and is also only a very short distance from the Reserve Brigade.

DESPATCH RIDER LETTER SERVICE.

The following are the times of the D.R.L.S.:-

A. To VII CORPS.

   Leave Division for Corps. 9.0 a.m., 3.0 p.m., 9.0 p.m.

B. To RIGHT BRIGADE

Leave Div	Arrive Bde	Leave Bde.	Arrive Div.
8.0 a.m.	8.30 a.m.,	8.45 a.m.	9.15 a.m.
1.0 p.m.	1.30 p.m.	1.45 p.m.	2.15 p.m.
8.0 p.m.	8.30 p.m.,	8.45 p.m.,	9.15 p.m.

C. To LEFT BRIGADE.

Leave Div.	Arrive Bde.	Leave Bde.	Arrive Div.
8.0 a.m.	8.30 a.m.	8.45 a.m.	9.15 a.m.
1.0 p.m.	1.30 p.m.	1.45 p.m.	2.15 a.m.
8.0 p.m.	8.30 p.m.	8.45 p.m.	9.15 p.m.

D To RESERVE BRIGADE, PIONEER BATTALION, and LOCALS.

   Leave Div.

   8.0 a.m.
   1.0 p.m.
   8.0 p.m.   Local Calls.

   (235th Army Troops Coy.
   (Charing Cross Dump.
   (Div. Bomb Store.
   (13th and 14th Mobile
   (Workshops.
   (Divisional Burial Officer.
   (183rd Labour Coy.

E. To Artillery Brigades.

   Leave Div.R.A. 8.0 a.m. 2.0. p.m. 8.30 p.m.

F. All letters for despatch by D.R.L.S. will be handed in to Signal Office 15 minutes before the times of departure stated above.

G. One M.C.D.R. is attached to each Infantry Bde and two to the Div.R.A.,

RUNNER SYSTEM.

The Runner System between Brigade and Battalion Headquarters is shewn on attached map. Details of minimum number of runners required during offensive operations is shewn on diagram below.

Under present conditions the system is worked with fewer men.

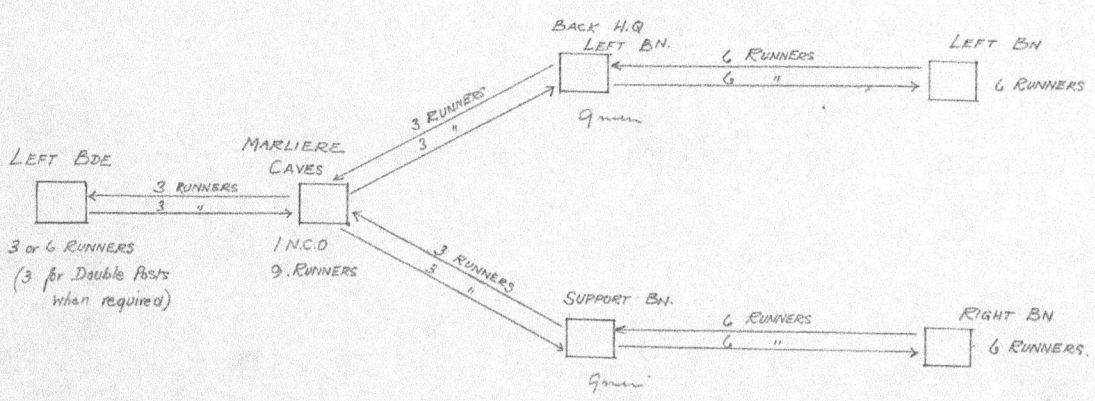

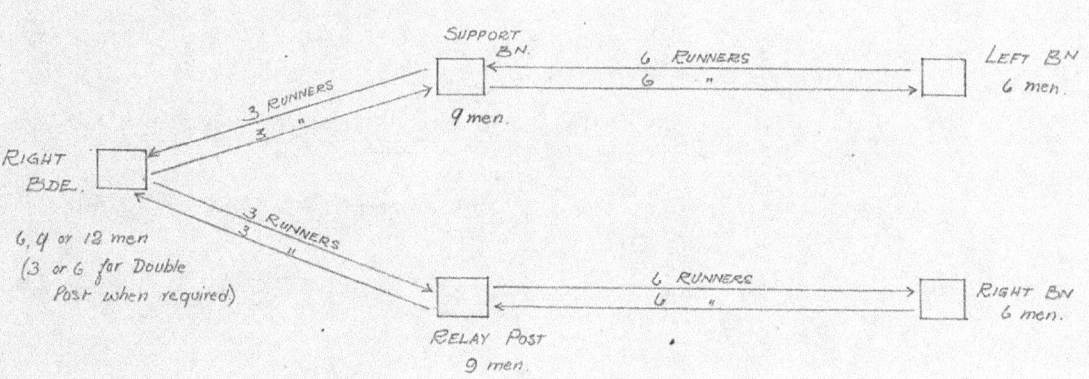

SYSTEM OF LABELLING.

A system of coloured labels is used. Labels of the correct shape are issued from Signal Company painted/as per table below on one side and with the letters GC stencilled thereon.

Numbers are allotted to formations as shewn and these numbers are painted or pencilled on opposite side of lable to GC.

Permanent or Semi-permanent Routes have distinguishing route letters in addition to numbers thus:- MM.10   AN.4

LINES	NUMBERS ALLOTTED	COLOUR of LABEL	REMARKS.
Division	1- 199	Red	
R. Inf. Bde.	200- 399	Blue	
L. Inf. Bde.	400- 599	Brown.	
Res. Inf. Bde.	600- 699	White.	Includes numbers
Divisional R.A.	700- 799	Red.	to be allotted
R.Bde R.F.A.	800- 899	Green	to battalions by
L.Bde R.F.A.	900- 999	Yellow.	Brigade Signalling
C. Bde R.F.A.	1000-1099	White	Officer.
Battalions R.Bde		Green	
Battalions L.Bde		Yellow.	

The following instructions have been issued:-

Line will be labelled at:-

(1) Intervals of not less than, for trench lines 100 yards, for open lines 200 yards.

(2) All junctions of lines and outside every dugout or Signal Office into which they are led.

(3) All points where they cross a road, track or trench, andwwhere they enter or leave a trench.

(4) All notice boards inscribed "All cables to be labelled here.

REPORT on GERMAN BURIES in DIVISIONAL AREA.

The following German buried cable routes exist.
(1) Crow Trench. (2) Starling Trench
(3) Curtain Trench.

(1) CROW TRENCH.
There are four armoured twins not more than one foot below the bottom of trench, or about 4 feet below ground level.

This Trench has been deepened and traversed for a considerable distance and is now used as a communication trench.
Cables have been tested with the following results:-

From last point where cables are visible to Test point marked T.P.1., all 'dis'.

Beyond T.P.1 is a break where only the southern ends of the cables can be found.

Cables all through from this point to another break 100 yards further south.

All through from this break to T.P.2.

Beyond T.P.2 all cables dis, back ends projecting through traverse; No cables through to T.P.2 and no southern ends to be found.

About 200 yard further along southern ends on side of trench. Of these only one pair through to T.P.3.,

From T.P.3 to break near T.P.4 no cables through. T.P.4 is not numbered.

From T.P.4 to T.P.5 all cables through.

At fork in trench cables turn to the left. From T.P.5 to T.P.6 nothing through.

(2) STARLING TRENCH.

There are four armoured twins similar to those in Crow Trench.

Testing was begun at a box (which has been marked 'A' about N30d0.9.

From TP'A' to TP'B' nothing through. Between TP'B' and TP'C' all cables dug up and out.

Between this cut and TP'C' all cables through and marked 1, 2, 3, & 4 by rings of wire round the lead sheathing.

Between cut and 'D' 1,2 & 3 through, 4 apparently shorted.

Test Point 'D' is about N30d9.6. Here cables were looped but no further Test Points found.

A cross trench was dug at O31b7.9 and nine lead covered pairs discovered. These were cut and forward ends well insulated.

Four small trenches were dug between this point and T.P.'D' four lead covered pairs being found at each point.

(3) CURTAIN TRENCH. Buried route apparently consists of 7 armoured pairs. Many test boxes have been buried and cables are exposed and broken at many points. No tests have been carried out.

VISUAL SIGNALLING
as applied to
TRENCH AND SEMI - MOBILE WARFARE.

TRENCH WARFARE.

Troops engaged in Trench Warfare on a Sector of the Front that has remained stationary for some time are merely performing garrison duties on a large scale and in close contact with the enemy.

Owing to the short interval between the launching of an attack and the time when it reaches our trenches it is necessary to provide for instantaneous communication between the infantry in the front line and the Artillery, so that effective artillery fire can be brought to bear at once.

The intensity of shell fire which develops in an attack makes the maintenance of communication an extremely difficult problem

In Trench Warfare Visual Signalling is regarded - and usually rightly so - as a subsidiary means of communication to the telegraph and telephone, but frequently it may be the only means possible.

Visual Signalling has great possibilities, even in Trench Warfare and its development should be encouraged in every way possible.

SEMI-MOBILE WARFARE.

Semi-Mobile Warfare may be defined as the stage reached after a successful attack in which several lines of Enemy Trenches have been taken.

It is most important that immediately an objective has been taken, communication should be established. Artillery Observation, Information regarding movement of enemy, impending Counter-attacks, replenishments of Bombs Ammunition, &c, sending up of re-inforcements are of vital importance and in several instances the full fruits of a successful attack have been lost owing to communication having broken down.

Visual thus becomes the most important method of communication, at any rate until such time as the captured position has been consolidated, and enemy counter-attacks repulsed. Lines are laid forward, duplicated, and the position becomes once more that of Trench Warfare.

MOBILE WARFARE.

In open fighting, without a Trench System, Visual ~~sib~~ Signalling becomes and remains the chief means of communication for fighting troops. Telegraph and Telephone becoming a subsidiary method.

A complete telephone system cannot be laid and maintained for the following reasons:-

Units constantly on the move, and scattered over large area.

A large amount of cable would be required and great difficulty would be experienced in reeling up disused cable.

Great difficulty in sending transport forward with cable etc owing to congestion of traffic.

~~SIGNALMENT~~ CONCEALMENT.

TRENCH WARFARE.

In Trench Warfare the concealment of visual stations is most important.

Great precautions must be taken to prevent messages being read by the enemy or the position of the station disclosed by the beam of a lamp or movement of signallers.

Visual Signalling from vicinity of front line trenches to Battalion, or from Battalion to Brigade Headquarters, can frequently be arranged without much difficulty. With care and with the aid of special apparatus Lamps may be used in some areas for signalling forward from Brigade and Battalion Headquarters.

The Lucas O.L. Daylight Signalling Lamp has proved very efficient for signalling in forward areas, especially where concealment is necessary.

The dispersion of rays can be reduced to a minimum by the use of diaphragm stop; and with the aid of long tube fitted with stops of various sizes used according to weather conditions, rays can be cut down to within a few yards of either side of receiving station.

Visual, if at all likely to be observed by the enemy, should not be established actually at the headquarters of a unit but rather a few hundred yards away, a short buried cable being used to connect with Headquarters.

Where possible Visual Stations should be fixed close to a communication trench. If this is done the dugout could also be used as a Runner relay post.

CONCEALMENT (cont)

SEMI-MOBILE WARFARE.

In Semi-mobile Warfare concealment is not of such vital importance as in Trench Warfare, and Visual can be worked from rear to front without special apparatus being used.

Should the enemy pick up a message, by the time it was sent back and translated it would probably be too late to be of use. It must not be forgotten that in the heat of battle the enemy is probably too much occupied to read visual messages.

SAFETY of SIGNALLER and APPARATUS.

In Trench Warfare it is essential that Signallers should be well protected and be provided with good accomodation. The efficient working and maintenance of communication depends largely on the accomodation provided for the personnel.
Owing to the amount of work to be done in improving and maintaining the defensive system this is often lost sight of with the result that unnecessary casualties are caused.

Good protection means good work, as a signaller exposed to shell and rifle fire becomes nervous and his sending un-readable.

Whereever possible a Signalling Lamp should be used; it can be concealed more readily than other appliances, and can usually be protected either by a concrete emplacement or an improvised sandbag shelter.
The operator can also signal from under cover.

Copper leads 15 to 20 yards long can be made to enable lamp to be operated from bottom of deep dugout.

The signalling shutter can also be worked from under headcover.

APPARATUS.

For Mobile or Semi-Mobile Warfare the following factors must be taken into consideration.

(a) Apparatus must be light and compact.

(b) Apparatus must not be conspicuous, men carrying lamps, flags etc make a special mark for enemy snipers.

With regard to (a) it has been found that heavy or clumsy apparatus will almost certainly be thrown away by signallers during an advance.

With regard to (b) flags should never be carried by attacking troops under Trench or Semi-Mobile conditions. They should only be carried and used in real open warfare.

APPARATUS. (cont)

For Mobile and Semi-Mobile Warfare the following apparatus is recommended.

O.L. Lucas Daylight Signalling Lamp.
Folding one handled pattern Signalling Fan.
Folding pattern Signalling Shutter.

The Lucas Lamp has already proved of very great value both in Trench and Semi-Mobile Warfare.

SIGNALLING LAMPS.

ADVANTAGES	DISADVANTAGES
Easily concealed.	Careful alignment required when used in conjunction with special apparatus.
Quickly aligned.	
Operator can work under cover.	
Can often be read through a barrage.	
BY DAYLIGHT.	
Difficult for enemy to pick up signals owing to <u>apparant</u> small lateral dispersion of rays.	Signals may be read by enemy when signalling forward without special apparatus.
	Range at which can be read is limited.
	Background must be carefully selected.
BY NIGHT.	
The only satisfactory method of Visual Signalling.	Signals more easily picked up by enemy. Lateral Rays much more pronounced.

In Trench Warfare each Company in the line should be provided with Signalling Lamps.

SIGNALLING DISCS.

Signalling Discs have not proved of much use in Trench Warfare and those issued have, sooner or later been 'lost'.

Signalling with this instrument must of necessity be very slow. In addition Discs are clumsy from a carrying point of view, and compared to Fans or Folding Shutters, heavy.

Discs may be of some value in Mobile Warfare but it is considered that the folding pattern Signalling Shutter is quicker in action and although slightly larger when in use possesses all the advantages without any of the disadvantages of the Disc.

SIGNALLING FANS.

Folding pattern, khaki on one side, white on the other should be carried. These fans are very ~~cons-~~ inconspicuous when folded.

Signalling Fans can be used in the same manner as the small flag, but can also be used by a man when lying down. Their range is not so great as that of the flag, but it is much more difficult for the enemy to pick up messages.

These Fans have also proved very useful as a means of disclosing to Contact Planes or Forward Observing Officers the position of advanced troops by day. This is done by exposing white side of a pre-arranged number of fans per Company at certain times, or when flares are called for by the Contact Patrol Aeroplane.

In Trench Warfare Fans should not be used unless well concealed.

SIGNALLING SHUTTERS.

Folding pattern only should be carried. This type possesses the same great advantage as the Signalling Fan in that it can be carried without being observed by the enemy.

It is impossible for enemy to read messages sent from front to rear; it is however more difficult to read and slower than the Fan. Great care must be taken to see that the sending shutter is always kept at right angles to the receiving station. Range at which Signals can be read is limited.

In Trench Warfare where Shutters can be used, fixed shutters of various sizes to suit distances between stations should be obtained. These should be supplied solely as Trench stores and issues made to suit the requirements of the Sector.

Fixed Shutters are not easily carried and invariably get broken.

TRAINING.

All Signallers should be taught the use of cover.

Considerable practise is required to become proficient with the Signalling Shutter and Fan. Practise with the Fan lying, kneeling, from behind cover, and with back to a parapet taking care that Fan is not visible above parapet.

Signallers should also be able to work Shutter from lying and kneeling positions and from under cover.

Full advantage should be taken of Brigade and Battalion attack practices, manoeuvres etc. The selection of good positions offers great opportunities for the exercise of initiative.

Young Officers of Artillery and Infantry should all know the various methods of communication. This should form part of their training.

A marked increase of efficiency results in battalions in which the Commanding Officers realize their responsibilities with regard to communications, and take an interest in their Signallers.

Signallers should be struck off all fatigues and with the exception of necessary Musketry and Square drill, devote their whole time to Signalling Training.

The common message "Position in front obscure" may often be traced to lack of training and initiative on the part of Visual Signallers.

PERISCOPES.

In Trench Warfare Periscopes have proved of value under certain conditions. They are useful for reading Visual Signals from an exposed position, and by their use lamps can be used under cover. Signals can only be read for a short distance by this method.

IMPORTANCE OF VISUAL SIGNALLING.

The importance of Visual Signalling cannot be over estimated.

During the long period of Trench Warfare visual has been allowed to fall into disuse, and in some cases Battalion Commanders have not realized the importance of this means of communication.

Again, before July 1916, Divisions got very little rest with the result that Signallers had very little time for training, the main training – owing to the universal use of the Diii telephone – being with that instrument.

In Trench Warfare Visual schemes should always be thought out and put into operation.

Visual in Semi-mobile Warfare is often the only means of communication. Again, after a successful attack, visual must be relied upon until such time as the enemy barrage has slackened and forward lines can be laid and maintained.

By continuous training only, can Battalion and Battery Signallers reach and maintain the high standard so necessary for successful intercommunication.

EMPLOYMENT OF SIGNALLING.

Visual Signalling should be employed in all stages of Warfare.

In Trench Warfare it can be employed as a subsidiary means of communication to relieve heavy traffic over the wires, and to bridge over periods when all lines are broken by shell fire.

During an attack and in Semi-mobile warfare Visual becomes of vital importance, and must be looked upon as the primary, if not the only means of communication.

Pigeons get killed, or lost through Pigeoneers becoming casualties, while Power buzzers get out of range of the Amplifier as the troops advance and difficulty is experienced ij moving the Amplifier forward.

Successful intercommunication by Visual Signalling depends in a great measure upon the closest co-operation existing between Brigade and Battalion Signal Officers.

Before an attack takes place, positions of Visual Stations to be taken up as troops advance must be carefully selected; probable future disposition s considered, detailed plans made, and necessary instructions issued. All concerned must be acquainted with the arrangements made.

EMPLOYMENT OF SIGNALLING (cont.)

A Central Visual Station should be established on each Brigade front, if possible at the end of the buried cable route. This station should be near a prominent object so that signallers can get into communication quickly as they advance.

Selecting signal stations near prominent objects is open to the objection that such positions are liable to be shelled, but it must not be forgotten that during active operation the enemy is too busy to concentrate his attention to picking up our visual signals.

Considerations of protection and concealment are of secondary importance in Semi-mobile and Mobile Warfare.

Shutters and fans only should be sent out with the troops actually attacking. Lamps, Telephones etc can be sent forward behind the last wave of the attacking Infantry.

DISADVANTAGES OF VISUAL SIGNALLING.

~~During the long period of Trench Warfare preceding the~~

Successful Visual Signalling is entirely dependant upon standard of Signalling within the unit.

With a low standard poor results are inevitable; with a high standard all things are possible.

Visual Stations are liable to give away Headquarters of Units.

Messages may be read by the Enemy; in Trench Warfare however this can usually be obviated by the use of special apparatus.

Visual communication may be delayed by barrages, smoke of guns firing, heavy bombardments etc. In recent fighting this has not been found to be a serious obstacle, Lucas Lamps fitted with a coloured screen having been read through enemy barrage.

Weather conditions, fog, mist snow etc. render visual impracticable and cause serious delays.

To overcome these disadvantages a D.R. and Runner system should be organised. Except in the case of important messages Runners should only be employed when Visual has broken down, and not as a duplicate system.

In Trench Warfare Stations that are in view of the ~~one~~ enemy should only be used for emergency purposes.

TRANSITION STAGE
from
TRENCH TO SEMI-MOBILE WARFARE.

Visual Signalling plays a very important part in the Transition stage.

No rules regarding procedure can be laid down. Thorough preliminary arrangements must be made (see page 7)

Position of all visual station and units with whom communication is established must be made known to all Commanders.

It is in the transition stage, no less than in actual mobile warfare that the value of thorough and continuous training will be felt. Indeed in the transition stage owing to heavy shell fire etc even higher training and discipline is needed than in Mobile Warfare.

THE SOMME ADVANCE.

During the long period preceding of Trench Warfare preceding the Battle of the Somme, Visual Signalling was allowed to fall into disuse. Signallers had little training and less practical experience, owing to every available man being employed to man and maintain the ever increasing number of telephone circuits.

In several of the big operations too many signallers were sent over with the attacking waves, in some cases signallers actually being sent over to fight with their platoons. This naturally resulted in very heavy casualties to highly trained specialists.

During the actual attacks it was generally found impossible to continue the existing lines forward and visual was resorted to. Telephone lines were laid forward and maintained without great difficulty after the enemy counter attacks had broken down.

Between September 15th and 25rd forward Visual proved invaluable. Combined visual and telephone stations near jumping off trenches were employed, and forward central stations established as attacks progressed. As soon as circumstances permitted telephone lines were extended to the forward central station which then became the advanced combined station.

In one case visual was maintained between Battalion headquarters and a forward sap for several days. Shutters and electric lamps were used.

Folding Signalling Fans proved of great value, 500 being distributed among the battalions of the Division.

Signalling shutters were also useful, These were unfortunately of the fixed type and soon got broken.

THE BATTLE OF ARRAS.

Lucas Lamps were used for the first time and proved invaluable. One lamp was read in daylight at a distance of 3,000 yards. Communication was also maintained through enemy barrage by use of lamps with coloured screens.

Fans and Shutters were also used to send messages back to jumping off trenches.

Lamp Signalling proved particularly valuable during German counter-attacks on night of April 16/17th.
Reinforcements and ammunition were sent up in response to messages sent on lamp before any other means of communication was established.

Communication by shutter was maintained by day and was comparatively successful. At times difficulty was experienced in reading shutter owing to smoke, and communication absolutely broke down when enemy barrage was put down.

Major.
Cmdg. 50th Divisional Signalling Co. R.E.,

SECRET.

WAR DIARY

of

50th. (NORTHUMBRIAN) DIVISIONAL SIGNAL COMPANY R. E.

Volume XXIX.

August 1917.

Vol 29

Army Form C. 2118.

WAR DIARY
or
INTELLIGENCE SUMMARY

(Erase heading not required.)

Instructions regarding War Diaries and Intelligence Summaries are contained in F. S. Regs., Part II. and the Staff Manual respectively. Title Pages will be prepared in manuscript.

114.

Place	Date	Hour	Summary of Events and Information	Remarks and references to Appendices
Boisleux St. Marc.	1917. August 5th	6 a.m.	The 150th Infantry Brigade completed relief of 149th Infantry Brigade in the VIS and GUEMAPPE Sectors.	O.O.115 dated 1 Aug.
do	6th		The 150th Infantry Brigade extended its right so as to include OTTO ALLEY	Ref 1/20000 Trench Map
do	7th	6 a.m.	The 151st Infantry Brigade took over from the 62nd Infantry Brigade, 21st Division, a portion of their front up to PUG LANE inclusive.	O.O.116 dated 3rd Aug/17
do	13th	midday	The 50th Division was transferred from the VIIth to the VIth Corps.	O.O.117 dated 10th Aug/17
do		6 a.m.	The 149th Infantry Brigade relieved the 151st Infantry Brigade in the CHERISY sector.	
do	21st	6 a.m.	The 151st Infantry Brigade relieved the 150th Infantry Brigade in the VIS and GUEMAPPE sectors.	O.O.118 dated 14th Aug/17
do	29th	6 a.m.	The 150th Infantry Brigade relieved the 149th Infantry Brigade in the FONTAINE and CHERISY sectors.	O.O.119 dated 26th Aug/17.
do	30th		The 149th Infantry Brigade moved to Winter quarters, Brigade Head-Quarters at M3609.2 Sheet 51b S.W.	

1st Sept.1917.

[signed] Major,
Comdg 50th (Nbn) Divl Sig Coy R.E.

WAR DIARY
of
50TH. (NORTHUMBRIAN) DIVISIONAL SIGNAL COMPANY R. E.

VOLUME XXX.

SEPTEMBER 1917.

Army Form C. 2118.

WAR DIARY
or
INTELLIGENCE SUMMARY.
(Erase heading not required.)

Instructions regarding War Diaries and Intelligence Summaries are contained in F. S. Regs., Part II. and the Staff Manual respectively. Title pages will be prepared in manuscript.

Place	Date 1917.	Hour	Summary of Events and Information	Remarks and references to Appendices
BOISLEUX ST. MARC.	Sept. 6th.	6 am.	The 149th. Brigade relieved the 151st. Inf. Bde. in the Left Sector.	O.O.120 of 2nd. Sept. 1917.
"	12th.		No. 475928 Pioneer BRUNTLETT J.E., wounded.	
"	14th.	6 am.	The 151st. Inf. Bde. relieved the 150th. Inf. Bde. in the Right Sector.	
"	15th.		The 151st. Inf. Bde. carried out a successful raid to the W. of CHERISY. For this operation the Visual system was extended to Div. Hd-Qrs. The first message was received by visual at 4.18 pm,— 18 minutes after Zero.	
			No. 463039 Sapper Bullock S.C.W. wounded.	
			" " " " recommended for M.M.	
"	19th.		No. 463197 Sapper TURNBULL T. accidently wounded.	
"	22nd.	6 am.	The 150th. Inf. Bde. relieved the 149th. Inf. Bde. in the Left Sector.	
"	21st.		No. 463187 Sapper HENDERSON T. wounded (at duty).	
"	27th.		No. 463039 BULLOCK S.C.W. awarded the Military Medal for gallantry in action.	
"	30th.	6 am.	The 149th. Inf. Bde. relieved the 151st. Inf. Bde. in the Right Sector.	
"			During the month Semi-Permanent routes were built connecting Reserve Brigade Winter Hd-Qrs. with its 4 Battalions and M.G. Coy, and also with the 3 Brigade Transport Lines. The Winter Horse Standings and Camp for Signal Company was built and occupied. Signal Office at New Divl. Hd-Qrs wired and local routes buried and led into all offices. Plans will be included in next month's War Diary.	

Major,
Cmdg. 50th (Nbn) Divl. Signal Co. R.E.

On His Majesty's Service.

50th Signal Coy
Oct 1917

WAR DIARY

of

50TH. DIVISIONAL SIGNAL COMPANY R. E.

VOLUME XXXI.

OCTOBER 1917.

Army Form C. 2118.

WAR DIARY
or
INTELLIGENCE SUMMARY.
(Erase heading not required.)

Instructions regarding War Diaries and Intelligence Summaries are contained in F. S. Regs., Part II. and the Staff Manual respectively. Title pages will be prepared in manuscript.

Place	Date	Hour	Summary of Events and Information	Remarks and references to Appendices
Near BOISLEUX-AU-MARC (Ref Map 1/100000 Sheet 11 LENS)	Oct. 4th.		50th Division (less Artillery) relieved by the 51st Division (less Artillery) between 4th and 6th October. Command of Sector passed to G.O.C. 51st Division at 10 a.m. 6th October. C.R.A. 51st Division assumed command of 50th Divisional Artillery at the same hour. Details of communications and diagrams of lines attached hereto.	O.O. No 127 dated 1st Oct.
do	Oct 4th		149th Infantry Brigade relieved by 153rd Infantry Brigade and moved to Reserve Brigade Area. 151st Infantry Brigade relieved by 149th Infantry Brigade and moved to GOMIECOURT by march route.	do
do	Oct 5th		149th Infantry Brigade relieved by 150th Infantry Brigade and moved to COURCELLES. 150th Infantry Brigade relieved by 154th Infantry Brigade and moved to Reserve Brigade Area.	do
do	Oct 6th	10 a.m.	50th Division Headquarters opened at ACHIET-LE-PETIT.	do
do			150th Infantry Brigade relieved by 152nd Infantry Brigade and moved to ACHIET-LE-PETIT. 7th D.L.I. relieved by 8th Royal Scots and moved to COURCELLES.	do
ACHIET-LE-PETIT. Ref. Map 1/100000 Sheet 11 LENS	Oct. 16th p.m.	8.15 p.m.	150th Infantry Brigade Hdqrs. entrained at MIRAUMONT.	O.O. 128. dated 12th Oct.
do	do	9.45 p.m.	151st Infantry Brigade Hdqrs. entrained at BAPAUME.	
do	Oct 17th p.m.	5.45 p.m.	Divisional Headquarters and Signal Company entrained at BAPAUME.	do
do	Oct 18th	4.5 a.m.	149th Infantry Brigade Headquarters entrained at MIRAUMONT.	do

Army Form C. 2118.

WAR DIARY
or
INTELLIGENCE SUMMARY.
(Erase heading not required.)

Instructions regarding War Diaries and Intelligence Summaries are contained in F. S. Regs., Part II. and the Staff Manual respectively. Title pages will be prepared in manuscript.

Place	Date	Hour	Summary of Events and Information	Remarks and references to Appendices
LEDERZEELE Ref Map 1/100000 Sheet 5a	Oct 18th	2.45 a.m.	50th Division Signal Company R.E. detrained at ARNEKE and proceeded to LEDERZEELE by March Route.	O.O. No129 dated 18th Oct
HAZEBROUCK		Noon.	Divisional Headquarters opened at LEDERZEELE coming under the orders of IInd Corps. Signal office opened.	
do			149th Infantry Brigade Group billetted in ARNEKE Area. 150th Infantry Brigade Group billetted in RUBROUCK Area. 151st Infantry Brigade Group billetted in ERINGHEM Area. Communications to 149th Infantry Brigade through ARNEKE Exchange. Communications to 150th and 151st Infantry Brigades through ZEGGERS-CAPPEL Exchange.	do
do	Oct 20th		149th Infantry Brigade Group moved from ARNEKE to PROVEN, P5 Area. 151st Infantry Brigade Group moved from ERINGHEM to ARNEKE.	O.O. No131 dated 19th Oct
do	Oct 20th	Noon	Divisional Headquarters closed at LEDERZEELE and opened at PROVEN CENTRAL at same hour, coming under the orders of 14th Corps.	do
PROVEN Ref Map 1/100000 Sheet 5a	Oct 21st		150th Infantry Brigade Group moved from RUBROUCK to ARNEKE Area. 50th Divisional Artillery moved direct to XIV Corps Area by rail. 151st Infantry Brigade Group moved from ARNEKE to PROVEN No 1 Area.	O.O. No141 dated 19th Oct
HAZEBROUCK	Oct 22nd		151st Infantry Brigade Group moved from PROVEN No 1 Area to XIV Corps Staging Area No 1 150th Infantry Brigade Group moved from ARNEKE to PROVEN No 1 Area. (B14d)	do
	Oct 23rd		149th Infantry Brigade moved from P5 Area to WHITE MILL (Ref Maps 1/40000 Sheets 20 & 28)	O.O. No132 dated
	Oct 24th		149th Infantry Brigade relieved 101st Infantry Brigade in Front Line 150th Infantry Brigade moved from K1 Area to WHITE MILL (B14d) or Canal Bank. By rail to ELVERDINGHE.	22nd Oct do

Army Form C. 2118.

WAR DIARY
or
INTELLIGENCE SUMMARY.

(Erase heading not required.)

Instructions regarding War Diaries and Intelligence Summaries are contained in F. S. Regs., Part II. and the Staff Manual respectively. Title pages will be prepared in manuscript.

Place	Date Oct	Hour	Summary of Events and Information	Remarks and references to Appendices
ELVERDINGHE CHATEAU	24th	10 a.m.	Divisional Headquarters closed at PROVEN CENTRAL and opened at ELVERDINGHE CHATEAU same hour.	O.O. No.132 dated 22nd Oct.
(Refs Maps 1/40000 Sheets 20 and 28)	Oct 25th		No 463289 Sapper BREWER.T. wounded by hostile shell fire.	
	Oct 26th		Communication maintained throughout the operation to Battalions and in case of Left Battalion to Companies.	
			The 150th Infantry Brigade relieved the 149th Infantry Brigade in the line on the night of 26th/27th.	O.O. No.135 dated 26th Oct
			The 149th Infantry Brigade moved to WHITE MILL on the night of 26th/27th.	
	Oct 27th		The 149th Infantry Brigade moved from WHITE MILL to SANTE SIXTE Staging Area (X2865.3) with Headquarters at CARIBOO CAMP.	
			The 151st Infantry Brigade moved from X2865.3 to WHITE MILL.	do
	Oct 29th		The XIV Corps Headquarters relieved by the XIX Corps Headquarters.	
			No 458939 L/Cpl.JOHNSON B.M. wounded hostile shell fire and remains at duty.	
			No 532156 Sapper WINCOTE C.H. wounded hostile shell fire and remains at duty.	
	Oct 31st		Lieut. R.W. CRANAGE Gassed and admitted to Hospital.	
			No 254820 Pioneer CONNON A. Gassed and admitted to Hospital.	
			No 463118 Sergeant JENKINS W.E. do do do	
			No 463121 2nd Cpl DAY W. do do do	
			Full particulars of communications with diagrams will be included in next month's WAR DIARY.	

COMMUNICATIONS.

INFANTRY.

From Divisional Headquarters there are two telephone pairs to each Infantry Brigade, one pair having Sounder superimposed.

Between the Infantry Brigades in the line and Division there are three main routes.

I   Corps Route along COJEUL VALLEY to point near HENINEL.
II Armoured Quads.
III "A" Route.

IV A lateral route runs from "I" at N.33.b.3.6. – Test Station N.33.b.1.9. cuts "II" about N.27.Central, cuts "III" about N.21.a.2.2. to Advanced Divisional Exchange, N.21.a.4.4.

All lines from Division, including Artillery lines run along one or more of the above routes, and radiate therefrom.

V   A supplementary line (Corps "O" Route) provides communication between Advanced exchange and Right and Left Brigades forward, and backwards to Corps Mobile Pigeon Lofts.

Linesmen are stationed as follows :-

DIV. ADV. EXCHANGE. N.21.a.4.4. Four linesmen, 5 Telephones.

   Maintenance. Forward of Adv. Exchange to Left Brigade.
   "   "   "   "   along "O" Route.

An N.C.O. and forward working party are also stationed at this point.

'A' TEST POINT. N.33.b.1.9. N.C.O.? 3 linesmen, 2 Telephones.

   Maintenance 'I' forward of NEUVILLE VITASSE – HENIN – ST. LEGER Road.
            "II"   Ditto.   ditto.
            "IV"   to N.27. Central
   Line from right Brigade to A.D.S. N.27.d.9.1.
   One Artillery linesman is also stationed at this point.

RIGHT BRIGADE N.22.d.4.4.   Two linesmen 1 Telephone.

   To assist "A" with forward portion.

RESERVE BRIGADE TEST POINT.

   1 N.C.O. and 3 linesmen. Corps route N. & S. along main road, 18 pair route to NEUVILLE VITASSE and locals.

   "I" up to Maintenance A.

INFANTRY BRIGADES.

RIGHT BRIGADE.

   There are two pairs to both front line Battalions and to Support Battalion.

   All lines forward of Brigade are led into a Test Point at N.29.b.8.3.

   Brigade has communication to Flanking Brigades and to covering Artillery. Battalions are also in communication with Flanking Battalion.

COMMUNICATIONS. (Contd.)

INFANTRY BRIGADES.

In addition there are lines to M.G. Company, forward Wireless Station, Visual Transmitting station, Brigade O.P. Pigeon Lofts and A.D.S., near HENINEL.

All work to battalions is sent over the Fullerphone.

There is a buried route containing 20 pairs from point near Quarry along STARLING TRENCH to CURTAIN TRENCH.

LEFT BRIGADE.

From Brigade Headquarters to Test Point there are 4 pairs. The Test Point is in MARLIERE CAVES N.17.d.3.0. and is manned by 5 Linesmen operators, assisted by the signallers of Company of support Battalion living in the caves.

From Marliere there are two pairs to each front line Battalion. Both pairs to right Battalion are tapped into Support Battalion.

In addition there are lines to Reserve Battalion, to M.G. Coy, covering Artillery, and Flanking Brigades. Battalions are in communication laterally and to flanking Battalions. There is also a line to Brigade Visual Station.

All work to Forward Battalions is sent over the Fullerphone.

RESERVE BRIGADE.

Semi-Permanent Lines connect all Battalions of the Brigade, Div. Bomb Store, Mobile Workshops & 446th Field Coy. R.E.

In addition there are lines to Transport of all Brigades and to M.G. Company.

ARTILLERY.

There are lines to each Artillery Brigade for Ringing telephones. Fullerphones are superimposed on ringing lines to 250th and 251st Brigades.

In addition each Brigade has a line for message work by an alternative route.

The following subscribers are also on the Divisional Artillery Exchange :-

VI Corps.	VI Corps Heavy Artillery.
50th. Division.	Arty. of Div. on Right.
39th. H.A.G.	" " " " Left.
Div. Amn. Column.	A. R. P.
D. T. M. O.	No. 45 Kite Balloon Section.

RIGHT ARTILLERY BRIGADE.

There are lines to each Battery, Infantry Brigade, Arty. Brigades on each flank, Heavy Artillery Group exchange, Kite Balloon Exchange. Two pairs of Batteries are in communication laterally and each battery has a line to at least one O.P. In addition one battery has a line to the left and another battery a line to the right battalion.

Visual Signalling has been arranged between Bde. Hdqrs. and one pair of batteries, and the latter have visual with another pair of batteries.

COMMUNICATIONS. (Contd.)

ARTILLERY.

CENTRE ARTILLERY BRIGADE.

There are lines to each Battery, to left Infantry Bde., Right Battalion of Left Inf. Bde, Artillery Brigades on either flank and to Kite Balloon Exchange. There are lines from each Battery to the Brigade O.P. and visual communications between Brigade Hd. Qrs. and the Brigade O.P. 'A' & 'D' Batteries and 'A' & 'B' Batteries are in communication laterally.

LEFT ARTILLERY BRIGADE.

Have direct lines to two Battalions and two trunk lines to a forward exchange from which lines radiate to Batteries and O.P.s. Lines to Balloon and Heavy Group Exchanges to left Infantry Brigade and Left Battalion of left Brigade.

LIST OF SUBSCRIBERS.

50th. DIV. EXCHANGE.

- VI Corps, 2 lines.
- Division on Right.
- Division on Left.
- 149th. Infantry Brigade. 2 lines.
- 150th. Infantry Brigade. 2 "
- 151st. Infantry Brigade. 2 "
- Adv. Div. Exchange.
- Divisional R.A.
- G.S.O.1.
- 'O' Office.
- 'Q' Office.
- A.D.M.S.
- A.D.S. near HENINEL.
- A.D.S. MARLIERE Caves.
- C.R.E.
-   R.E. Dump, BENIN,
-   181. Tunnelling Company.
-   7th. Durham L.I. (Pioneers).
- SIGNALS, Orderly Room.
-   Mess.
-   Horse Lines.
-   Linemen.
-   Corps Wireless Station.
-   Div. Signal School.
-   Linemen 'A' Point.
-     "   Res. Bde. Test Point.
-     "   Adv. Exchange.
- Divisional Train.
- Public Call Office.
- Ordnance Stores.

Through DIV. ARTILLERY EXCHANGE.

- VI Corps.
- VI Corps Heavy Artillery.
- Artillery of Div. on Right.
- "   "   "   "   Left.
- 250. Brigade R.F.A.
- 251.   "   "
- 50.   "   "
- Flanking Brigades R.F.A.
- 30th. H. A. G.
- 50th. D. A. C.
- 50th. A. R. P.
- D. T. M. O.
- A.A. Guns MERCATEL Church.

Through RIGHT INF. BRIGADE.

- Units of Brigade.
- Flanking Brigades.
- Pigeon Loft.
- Amb. Loading Station near HENINEL.

Through LEFT INF. BRIGADE.

- Units of Brigade.
- Flanking Brigades.
- A.D.S. MARLIERE Caves.

Through RESERVE INF. BRIGADE.

- Units of Brigade.
- Adv. Div. Exchange.
- Div. Bomb Store.
- Nos. 13 & 14 Mobile Workshops.
- 446th. Field Company R.E.

SYSTEM OF LABELLING.

A system of coloured labels is used. Labels of the correct shape are issued from Signal Company painted on one side as per table below and with letters GC stencilled thereon.

SYSTEM OF LABELLING. (Contd.)

Numbers are allotted to formations as shown and these numbers are painted or pencilled on opposite side of label to GG.

Permant or Semi-permanent Routes have distinguishing route letters in addition to numbers thus :-   MM,10   AN,4

LINES.	NUMBERS ALLOTTED.	COLOUR OF LABEL.	REMARKS.
Division	1 - 199	Red.	
R. Inf. Bde.	200 - 399	Blue.	
L. Inf. Bde.	400 - 599	Brown.	
Res. Inf. Bde.	600 - 699	White.	Includes numbers to be allotted to battalions by Brigade Signalling Officer.
Divisional R.A.	700 - 799	Red.	
R. Bde. R.F.A.	800 - 899	Green.	
L. Bde. R.F.A.	900 - 999	Yellow.	
C. Bde. R.F.A.	1000 -1099	White.	
Battalions R. Bde.		Green.	
Battalions L. Bde.		Yellow.	

The following instructions have been issued :-

Line will be labelled at :-

(1) Intervals of not less than, for trench lines 100 yards, for open lines 200 yards.

(2) All junctions of lines and outside every dugout or Signal Office into which they are led.

(3) All points where they cross a road, track or trench, and where they enter or leave a trench.

(4) All notice boards inscribed " All cables to be labelled here ".

VISUAL SYSTEM.

The Visual System is shown on attached map, which also gives details of personnel manning stations etc.

Lucas Lamps only are in use. Owing to the number of lamps required to work this scheme they have had to be pooled and handed over when relief takes place.

Messages are sent both ways between the following stations :-   'A' to 'E'.   'F' to 'L'.   'F' to 'G'.

Special tubes are being fitted at 'A', 'G', 'H', to enable messages to be sent both ways. Until this is done messages are being sent from front to rear only, being acknowledged by lamp during the daytime and by Fullerphone at night.

The following stations are manned permanently, signallers from the Signal School being relieved weekly.

'A'.   'E'.   'F'.   'L'.   'G'.

VISUAL SYSTEM. (Contd.)

These stations are open for work as under :-

10 a.m. to 12 noon.
2 p.m. to 5 p.m.
9.30 p.m. to 11.30 p.m.

There is always a lookout man on duty at the above stations.

All other stations are manned at least two hours by day and two hours by night.

Brigade Signal Officers are responsible for the supervision of the Permanent stations.

Practise messages are sent between 'F' and 'G' during the hours when the forward visual stations are not open.

WIRELESS, POWER BUZZER, & AMPLIFIER.

Positions are shown on attached Map. Two Trench Wireless Sets are installed, one about N.22.c.4.7. near Right Brigade Headquarters; the other about N.29.c.5.3.

Both these sets are in communication with Corps Directing Set at T.7.d.2.8.

A Power Buzzer is installed at each Battalion Headquarters, with the exception of that at the Headquarters of the extreme left Battalion the Power Buzzers are working satisfactorily to Amplifier installed near Forward Wireless Set N.29.c.5.3.

It is proposed to instal a second Amplifier in MARLIERE Caves to take messages from the Battalions of the Left Brigade.

PIGEONS.

Corps Mobile Pigeon Lofts are at M.18.b. near NEUVILLE-VITASSE. Pigeons are conveyed by Corps M.C.D.R., from lofts to Division Refilling Point (N.21.a.2.2.) at 9.30 a.m. daily and left there.

The Infantry Brigades collect Pigeons from this point and send them up to the Battalions who send them forward to Companies.

Each Brigade has 8 pigeons supplied daily.

The pigeon loft is in communication with the Right Infantry Brigade and is also only a very short distance from the Reserve Brigade.

RUNNER SYSTEM.

The Runner System between Brigade and Battalion Headquarters is shewn on attached Map. Details of minimum number of runners required during offensive operations is shown on diagram below. Under present conditions the system is worked with fewer men.

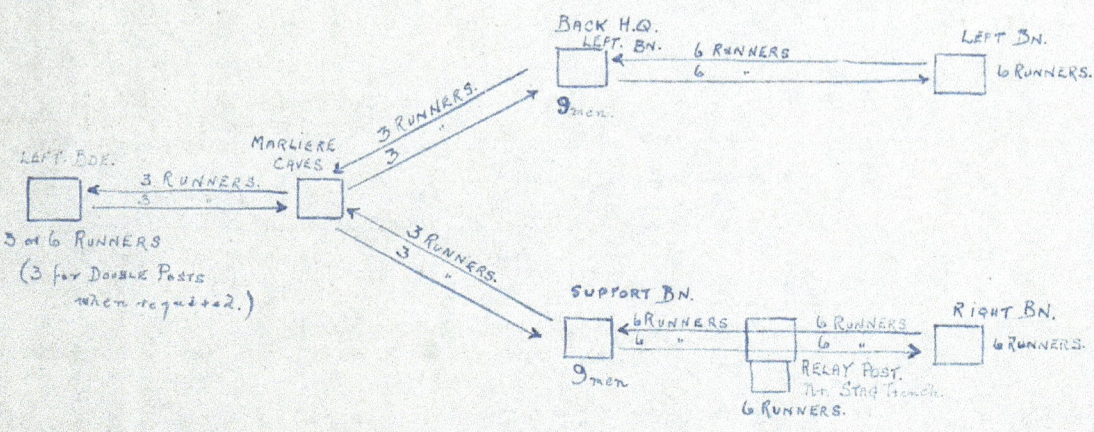

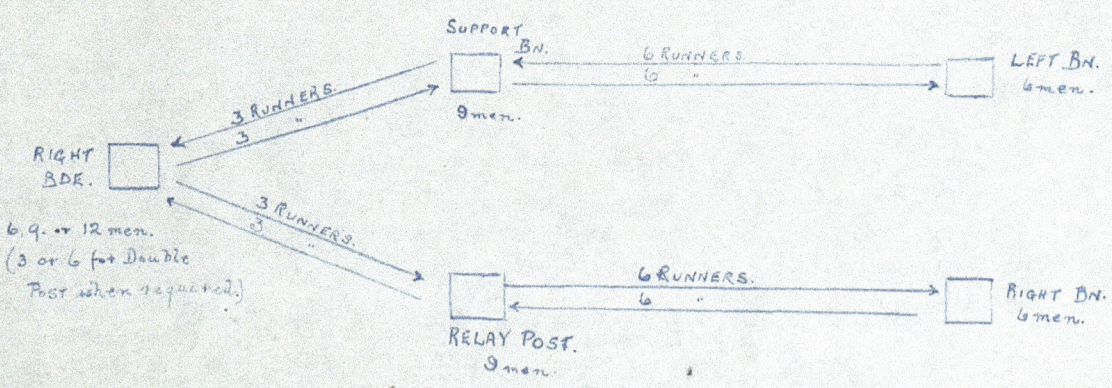

DESPATCH RIDER LETTER SERVICE.

The following are the times of the D.R.L.S :-

A. To VI Corps.

   Leave Division for Corps 7.45 a.m., 1.15 p.m. 4.5 p.m.
   8.30 p.m.

B. To RIGHT BRIGADE.

Leave Div.	Arrive Bde.	Leave Bde.	Arrive Div.
8.0 a.m.	8.30 a.m.	8.45 a.m.	9.15 a.m.
1.0 p.m.	1.30 p.m.	1.45 p.m.	2.15 p.m.
8.0 p.m.	8.30 p.m.	8.45 p.m.	9.15 p.m.

C. To LEFT BRIGADE.

Leave Div.	Arrive Bde.	Leave Bde.	Arrive Div.
8.0 a.m.	8.30 a.m.	8.45 a.m.	9.15 a.m.
1.0 p.m.	1.30 p.m.	1.45 p.m.	2.15 a.m.
8.0 p.m.	8.30 p.m.	8.45 p.m.	9.15 p.m.

D. To RESERVE BRIGADE, PIONEER BATTALION, and LOCALS.

Leave Div.		Local Calls.	(235th Army Troops Coy. (Charing Cross Dump. (Div. Bomb Store. (13th and 14th Mobile Workshops. (Divisional Burial Officer. (183rd Labour Coy.
8.0 a.m.			
1.0 p.m.			
8.0 p.m.			

E. To Artillery Brigades.

   Leave Div. R.A.   8.0 a.m., 2.0 p.m., 8.30 p.m.

F. All letters for despatch by D.R.L.S. will be handed in to Signal Office 15 minutes before the times of departure stated above.

G. One M.C.D.R. is attached to each Infantry Bde and two to the Div. R.A.

REPORT on GERMAN BURIES in DIVISIONAL AREA.

The following German buried cable routes exist :-
(1) Crow Trench.   (2) Starling Trench.
(3) Curtain Trench.

(1) **CROW TRENCH.**

There are four armoured twins not more than one foot below the bottom of trench, or about 4 feet below ground level.

This Trench has been deepened and traversed for a considerable distance and is now used as a communication trench.

Cables have been tested with the following results :-

From last point where cables are visible to Test Point marked T.P.1., all 'dis'.

Beyond T.P.1. is a break where only the Southern ends of the cables can be found.

Cables all through from this point to another break 100 yards further South.

All through from this break to T.P.2.

Beyond T.P.2 all cables dis, back ends projecting through traverse; No cables through to T.P.3 and no Southern ends to be found.

About 200 yards further along Southern ends on side of trench. Of these only one pair through to T.P.3.

From T.P.3. to break near T.P.4 no cables through. T.P.4. is not numbered.

From T.P.4. to T.P.5. all cables through.

At fork in trench cables turn to the Left. From T.P.5. to T.P.6 nothing through.

(2) **STARLING TRENCH.**

There are four armoured twins similar to those in CROW Trench.

Testing was begun at a box (which has been marked 'A' about N.30.d.0.9.)

From TP'A' to T.P'B' nothing through. Between TP'B' and TP'C' all cables dug up and cut.

Between this cut and TP'C' all cables through and marked 1,2,3,& 4 by rings of wire round the lead sheathings

Between cut and 'D' 1,2 & 3 through, 4 apparently shorted.

Test Point 'D' is about N.30.d.9.6. Here cables were looped but no further Test Points found.

A cross trench was dug at O.31.b.7.9. and nine lead covered pairs discovered. These were cut and forward ends well insulated.

Four small trenches were dug between this point and T.P.'D' four lead covered pairs being found at each point.

(3) **CURTAIN TRENCH.** Buried route apparently consists of 7 armoured pairs. Many test boxes have been buried and cables are exposed and broken at many points. No tests have been carried out.

COMMUNICATIONS.

INFANTRY.

From Divisional Headquarters there are two telephone pairs to each Infantry Brigade, one pair having Sounder superimposed.

Between the Infantry Brigades in the line and Division there are three main routes.

I   Corps Route along COJEUL VALLEY to point near HENINEL.
II   Armoured Quads.
III   "AN" Route.

IV   A lateral route runs from "I" at N.33.b.3.6. - Test Station N.33.b.1.9. cuts "II" about N.27.Central, cuts "III" about N.21.a.2.2. to Advanced Divisional Exchange, N.21.a.4.4.

All lines from Division, including Artillery lines run along one or more of the above routes, and radiate therefrom.

V   A supplementary line (Corps "O" Route) provides communication between Advanced exchange and Right and Left Brigades forward, and backwards to Corps Mobile Pigeon Lofts.

Linesmen are stationed as follows :-

DIV. ADV. EXCHANGE. N.21.a.4.4. Four linesmen, 5 Telephones.

Maintenance. Forward of Adv. Exchange to Left Brigade.
      "   "   "   "   along "O" Route.

An N.C.O. and forward working party are also stationed at this point.

'A' TEST POINT. N.33.b.1.9. N.C.O. & 3 linesmen, 2 Telephones.

Maintenance 'I' forward of NEUVILLE VITASSE - HENIN - ST. LEGER Road.
           "II"   Ditto.   ditto.
           "IV"   to N.27. Central
           Line from right Brigade to A.D.S. N.27.d.9.1.
One Artillery linesman is also stationed at this point.

RIGHT BRIGADE N.22.d.4.4.   Two linesmen 1 Telephone.

To assist "A" with forward portion.

RESERVE BRIGADE TEST POINT.

1 N.C.O. and 3 linesmen. Corps route N. & S. along main road, 16 pair route to NEUVILLE VITASSE and locals.

"I" up to Maintenance A.

INFANTRY BRIGADES.

RIGHT BRIGADE.

There are two pairs to both front line Battalions and to Support Battalion.

All lines forward of Brigade are led into a Test Point at N.29.b.8.3.

Brigade has communication to Flanking Brigades and to covering Artillery. Battalions are also in communication with Flanking Battalion.

COMMUNICATIONS. (Contd.)

INFANTRY BRIGADES.

In addition there are lines to M.G. Company, forward Wireless Station, Visual Transmitting station, Brigade O.P. Pigeon Lofts and A.D.S., near HENINEL.

All work to battalions is sent over the Fullerphone.

There is a buried route containing 20 pairs from point near Quarry along STARLING TRENCH to CURTAIN TRENCH.

LEFT BRIGADE.

From Brigade Headquarters to Test Point there are 4 pairs. The Test Point is in MARLIERE CAVES N.17.d.2.0. and is manned by 5 Linesmen operators, assisted by the signallers of Company of support Battalion living in the caves.

From Marliere there are two pairs to each front line Battalion. Both pairs to right Battalion are tapped into Support Battalion.

In addition there are lines to Reserve Battalion, to M.G. Coy, covering Artillery, and Flanking Brigades. Battalions are in communication laterally and to flanking Battalions. There is also a line to Brigade Visual Station.

All work to Forward Battalions is sent over the Fullerphone.

RESERVE BRIGADE.

Semi-Permanent Lines connect all Battalions of the Brigade, Div. Bomb Store, Mobile Workshops & 446th Field Coy. R.E.

In addition there are lines to Transport of all Brigades and to M.G. Company.

ARTILLERY.

There are lines to each Artillery Brigade for Ringing telephones. Fullerphones are superimposed on ringing lines to 250th and 251st Brigades.

In addition each Brigade has a line for message work by an alternative route.

The following subscribers are also on the Divisional Artillery Exchange :-

VI Corps.	VI Corps Heavy Artillery.
50th. Division.	Arty. of Div. on Right.
39th. H.A.G.	" " " " Left.
Div. Amn. Column.	A. R. P.
D. T. M. O.	No. 45 Kite Balloon Section.

RIGHT ARTILLERY BRIGADE.

There are lines to each Battery, Infantry Brigade, Arty. Brigades on each flank, Heavy Artillery Group exchange, Kite Balloon Exchange. Two pairs of Batteries are in communication laterally and each battery has a line to at least one O.P. In addition one battery has a line to the left and another battery a line to the right battalion.

Visual Signalling has been arranged between Bde. Hdqrs. and one pair of batteries, and the latter have visual with another pair of batteries.

COMMUNICATIONS. (Contd.)

ARTILLERY.

CENTRE ARTILLERY BRIGADE.

There are lines to each Battery, to left Infantry Bde., Right Battalion of Left Inf. Bde, Artillery Brigades on either flank and to Kite Balloon Exchange. There are lines from each Battery to the Brigade O.P. and visual communications between Brigade Hd. Qrs. and the Brigade O.P. 'A' & 'D' Batteries and 'A' & 'B' Batteries are in communication laterally.

LEFT ARTILLERY BRIGADE.

Have direct lines to two Battalions and two trunk lines to a forward exchange from which lines radiate to Batteries and O.P.s. Lines to Balloon and Heavy Group Exchanges to left Infantry Brigade and Left Battalion of left Brigade.

LIST OF SUBSCRIBERS.

50th. DIV. EXCHANGE.

- VI Corps, 2 lines.
- Division on Right.
- Division on Left.
- 149th. Infantry Brigade. 2 lines.
- 150th. Infantry Brigade. 2 "
- 151st. Infantry Brigade. 2 "
- Adv. Div. Exchange.
- Divisional R.A.
- G.S.O.1.
- 'G' Office.
- 'Q' Office.
- A.D.M.S.
- A.D.S. near HENINEL.
- A.D.S. MARLIERE Caves.
- C.R.E.
  - R.E. Dump, HENIN,
  - 181. Tunnelling Company.
  - 7th. Durham L.I. (Pioneers).
- SIGNALS, Orderly Room.
  - Mess.
  - Horse Lines.
  - Linemen.
  - Corps Wireless Station.
  - Div. Signal School.
  - Linemen 'A' Point.
  - " Res.Bde.Test Point.
  - " Adv. Exchange.
- Divisional Train.
- Public Call Office.
- Ordnance Stores.

Through DIV. ARTILLERY EXCHANGE.

- VI Corps.
- VI Corps Heavy Artillery.
- Artillery of Div. on Right.
- "   "   "   "   Left.
- 250. Brigade R.F.A.
- 251.   "   "
- 50.   "   "
- Flanking Brigades R.F.A.
- 39th. H. A. G.
- 50th. D. A. C.
- 50th. A. R. P.
- D. T. M. O.
- A.A. Guns MERCATEL Church.

Through RIGHT INF. BRIGADE.

- Units of Brigade.
- Flanking Brigades.
- Pigeon Loft.
- Amb. Loading Station near HENINEL.

Through LEFT INF. BRIGADE.

- Units of Brigade.
- Flanking Brigades.
- A.D.S. MARLIERE Caves.

Through RESERVE INF. BRIGADE.

- Units of Brigade.
- Adv. Div. Exchange.
- Div. Bomb Store.
- No. 13 & 14 Mobile Workshops.
- 446th. Field Company R.E.

SYSTEM OF LABELLING.

A system of coloured labels is used. Labels of the correct shape are issued from Signal Company painted on one side as per table below and with letters GC stencilled thereon.

SYSTEM OF LABELLING. (Contd.)

Numbers are allotted to formations as shown and these numbers are painted or pencilled on opposite side of label to GO.

Permant or Semi-permanent Routes have distinguishing route letters in addition to numbers thus :-   MM,10   AN,4

LINES.	NUMBERS ALLOTTED.	COLOUR OF LABEL.	REMARKS.
Division	1 - 199	Red.	
R. Inf. Bde.	200 - 399	Blue.	
L. Inf. Bde.	400 - 599	Brown.	
Res. Inf. Bde.	600 - 699	White.	Includes numbers to be allotted to battalions by Brigade Signalling Officer.
Divisional R.A.	700 - 799	Red.	
R. Bde. R.F.A.	800 - 899	Green.	
L. Bde. R.F.A.	900 - 999	Yellow.	
C. Bde. R.F.A.	1000 - 1099	White.	
Battalions R. Bde.		Green.	
Battalions L. Bde.		Yellow.	

The following instructions have been issued :-

Line will be labelled at :-

(1) Intervals of not less than, for trench lines 100 yards, for open lines 200 yards.

(2) All junctions of lines and outside every dugout or Signal Office into which they are led.

(3) All points where they cross a road, track or trench, and where they enter or leave a trench.

(4) All notice boards inscribed " All cables to be labelled here ".

VISUAL SYSTEM.

The Visual System is shown on attached map, which also gives details of personnel manning stations etc.

Lucas Lamps only are in use. Owing to the number of lamps required to work this scheme they have had to be pooled and handed over when relief takes place.

Messages are sent both ways between the following stations :-

'A' to 'E'.   'F' to 'L'.   'F' to 'G'.

Special tubes are being fitted at 'A', 'G', 'H', to enable messages to be sent both ways. Until this is done messages are being sent fromx front to rear only, being acknowledged by lamp during the daytime and by Fullerphone at night.

The following stations are manned permanently, signallers from the Signal School being relieved weekly.

'A'.   'E'.   'F'.   'L'.   'G'.

VISUAL SYSTEM. (Contd.)

These stations are open for work as under :-

    10 a.m. to 12 noon.
    2 p.m. to 5 p.m.
    9.30 p.m. to 11.30 p.m.

There is always a lookout man on duty at the above stations.

All other stations are manned at least two hours by day and two hours by night.

Brigade Signal Officers are responsible for the supervision of the Permanent stations.

Practise messages are sent between 'F' and 'G' during the hours when the forward visual stations are not open.

WIRELESS, POWER BUZZER, & AMPLIFIER.

Positions are shown on attached Map. Two Trench Wireless Sets are installed, one about N.22.c.4.7. near Right Brigade Headquarters; the other about N.29.c.5.3.

Both these sets are in communication with Corps Directing Set at T.7.d.2.8.

A Power Buzzer is installed at each Battalion Headquarters, with the exception of that at the Headquarters of the extreme left Battalion the Power Buzzers are working satisfactorily to Amplifier installed near Forward Wireless Set N.29.c.5.3.

It is proposed to instal a second Amplifier in MARLIERE Caves to take messages from the Battalions of the Left Brigade.

PIGEONS.

Corps Mobile Pigeon Lofts are at M.18.b. near NEUVILLE-VITASSE. Pigeons are conveyed by Corps M.C.D.R., from lofts to Division Refilling Point (N.21.a.2.2.) at 9.30 a.m. daily and left there.

The Infantry Brigades collect Pigeons from this point and send them up to the Battalions who send them forward to Companies.

Each Brigade has 8 pigeons supplied daily.

The pigeon loft is in communication with the Right Infantry Brigade and is also only a very short distance from the Reserve Brigade.

RUNNER SYSTEM.

The Runner System between Brigade and Battalion Headquarters is shewn on attached Map. Details of minimum number of runners required during offensive operations is shewn on diagram below. Under present conditions the system is worked with fewer men.

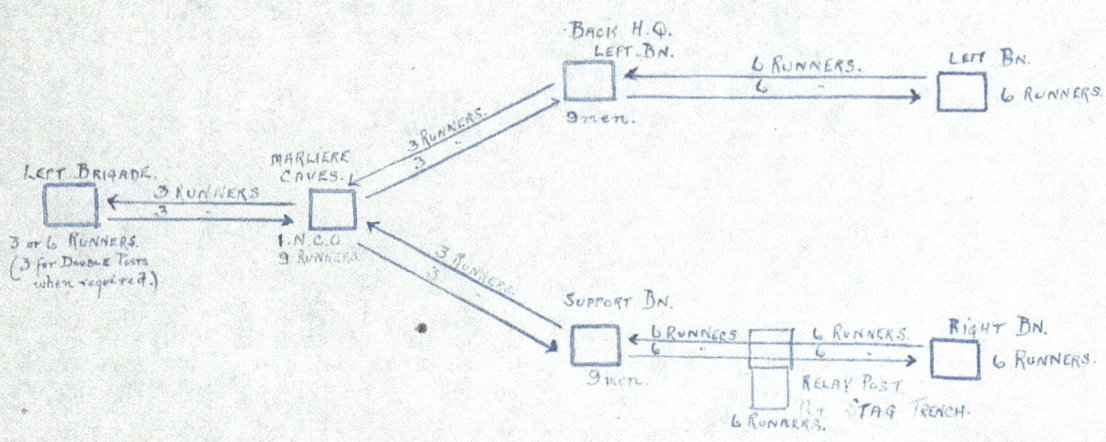

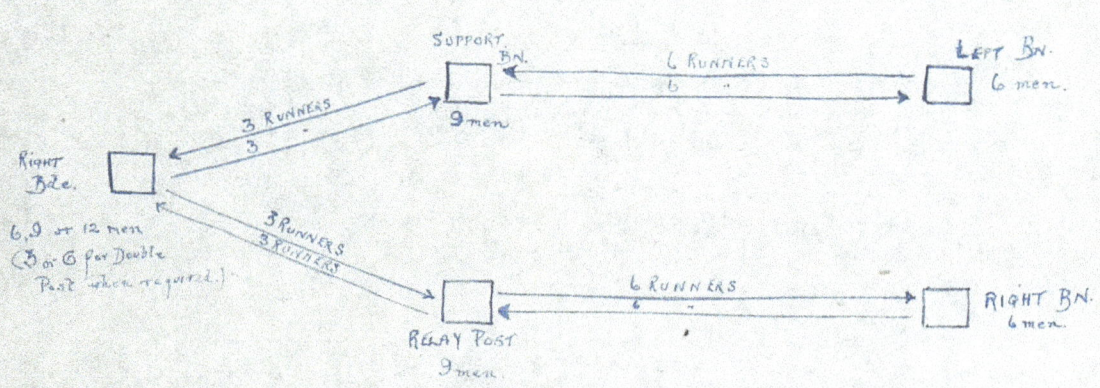

DESPATCH RIDER LETTER SERVICE.

The following are the times of the D.R.L.S :-

A. To VI Corps.

    Leave Division for Corps 7.45 a.m., 1.15 p.m. 4.5 p.m.
                                    8.30 p.m.

B. To RIGHT BRIGADE.

Leave Div.	Arrive Bde.	Leave Bde.	Arrive Div.
8.0 a.m.	8.30 a.m.	8.45 a.m.	9.15 a.m.
1.0 p.m.	1.30 p.m.	1.45 p.m.	2.15 p.m.
8.0 p.m.	8.30 p.m.	8.45 p.m.	9.15 p.m.

C. To LEFT BRIGADE.

Leave Div.	Arrive Bde.	Leave Bde.	Arrive Div.
8.0 a.m.	8.30 a.m.	8.45 a.m.	9.15 a.m.
1.0 p.m.	1.30 p.m.	1.45 p.m.	2.15 a.m.
8.0 p.m.	8.30 p.m.	8.45 p.m.	9.15 p.m.

D. To RESERVE BRIGADE, PIONEER BATTALION, and LOCALS.

Leave Div.		
8.0 a.m.		(235th Army Troops Coy.
1.0 p.m.		(Charing Cross Dump.
8.0 p.m.	Local Calls.	(Div. Bomb Store.
		(13th and 14th Mobile Workshops.
		(Divisional Burial Officer.
		(183rd Labour Coy.

E. To Artillery Brigades.

    Leave Div. R.A.   8.0 a.m., 2.0 p.m., 8.30 p.m.

F. All letters for despatch by D.R.L.S. will be handed in to Signal Office 15 minutes before the times of departure stated above.

G. One M.C.D.R. is attached to each Infantry Bde and two to the Div. R.A.

REPORT on GERMAN BURIES in DIVISIONAL AREA.

The following German buried cable routes exist :-
(1) Crow Trench.   (2) Starling Trench.
(3) Curtain Trench.

(1) **CROW TRENCH.**

There are four armoured twins not more than one foot below the bottom of trench, or about 4 feet below ground level.

This Trench has been deepened and traversed for a considerable distance and is now used as a communication trench.

Cables have been tested with the following results :-

From last point where cables are visible to Test Point marked T.P.1., all 'dis'.

Beyond T.P.1. is a break where only the Southern ends of the cables can be found.

Cables all through from this point to another break 100 yards further South.

All through from this break to T.P.2.

Beyond T.P.2 all cables dis, back ends projecting through traverse; No cables through to T.P.2 and no Southern ends to be found.

About 200 yards further along Southern ends on side of trench. Of these only one pair through to T.P.3.

From T.P.3. to break near T.P.4 no cables through. T.P.4. is not numbered.

From T.P.4. to T.P.5. all cables through.

At fork in trench cables turn to the Left. From T.P.5. to T.P.6 nothing through.

(2) **STARLING TRENCH.**

There are four armoured twins similar to those in CROW Trench.

Testing was begun at a box (which has been marked 'A' about N.30.d.0.9.)

From TP'A' to T.P'B' nothing through. Between TP'B' and TP'C' all cables dug up and cut.

Between this cut and TP'C' all cables through and marked 1,2,3,& 4 by rings of wire round the lead sheathing.

Between cut and 'D' 1,2 & 3 through, 4 apparently shorted.

Test Point 'D' is about N.30.d.9.6. Here cables were looped but no further Test Points found.

A cross trench was dug at O.31.b.7.9. and nine lead covered pairs discovered. These were cut and forward ends well insulated.

Four small trenches were dug between this point and T.P.'D' four lead covered pairs being found at each point.

(3) **CURTAIN TRENCH.** Buried route apparently consists of 7 armoured pairs. Many test boxes have been buried and cables are exposed and broken at many points. No tests have been carried out.

Report on Communications During Operations

of October 25th and 26th 1917.

Telegraph and Telephone:-

1. Division to Brigades -

(a). Preliminary Work.
On October 24th it was finally decided that the Forward Brigade would occupy MARTIN'S MILL.

Two pairs were obtained through the 14th Corps bury to WOOD HOUSE and two pairs through Corps bury to AU BON GITE.

Two existing pairs of ground cable from WOOD HOUSE to MARTIN'S MILL were taken over and two pairs were laid from AU BON GITE to MARTIN'S MILL.

To assist the Brigade Section two additional pairs were laid from MARTIN'S MILL to JAPAN HOUSE which was used as a forward test station.

Later a laddered line was built between these two points.

Personnel of No 1 Section were lent to Brigade Section for maintenance of all lines from MARTIN'S MILL to JAPAN HOUSE.

Unfortunately, although the two pairs between AU BON GITE and MARTIN'S MILL were kept through for two days despite very heavy shell fire, no communication could be kept over the bury.

This was apparently due to lack of co-ordination between Corps and Right Division personnel, who were dividing the maintenance.

The maintenance of bury between CANAL BANK and WOOD HOUSE was divided, O.C. Signals of Division on left taking the responsibility.

An advanced Divisional Exchange and Test Point was established near BOESINGHE STATION and was in communication with Brigade Rear Headquarters at HUDDERSFIELD HUTS and with Support Battalion at MARSOUIN FARM.

There was telegraphic and telephonic communication to the 150th Infantry Brigade in support at WHITE MILL near ELVERDINGHE CHATEAU and with the 151st Infantry Brigade in Reserve at XIV Corps Staging Area No 1 (X28d5.4 Sheet 19) through XIV Corps.

Lines were laid to the Corps Walking Wounded Dressing Station at CHEAPSIDE and communication was obtained through Left Division to the Divisional Bomb Store at GOUVY FARM.

There were also direct lines to the Corps Wireless Directing Station at B.11.a.9.8. and to No 20 H.D. Mobile Pigeon Loft near STEENJE MILL on ELVERDINGHE - POPERINGHE Road.

2. Brigade to Battalions -

When the 149th Infantry Brigade took over the Sector West of POELCAPELLE Brigade Headquarters was at MARTIN'S MILL, a Brigade Test Point at JAPAN HOUSE and Battalion Headquarters at PASCAL FARM and EGYPT HOUSE respectively.

According to orders issued on October 24th PASCAL FARM was to be Advanced Brigade Headquarters with Left Battalion Headquarters at EGYPT HOUSE, Centre and Right Battalions at TAUBE FARM and Support Battalion at PASCAL FARM.

From MARTIN'S MILL to JAPAN HOUSE there existed two pairs and from PASCAL FARM to EGYPT HOUSE one pair of ground cable.

For the operations of October 26th the following work was done:-

A three legged laddered cable laid between JAPAN HOUSE
/and

and PASCAL FARM with rungs about 200 yards apart. This was afterwards strengthened by additional legs and rungs near JAPAN HOUSE and PASCAL FARM where shelling was more concentrated.

Laddered cables were laid from PASCAL FARM to EGYPT HOUSE and to TAUBE FARM.

These ladders were very badly cut up by shell fire on the night of the 24/25th but by selection of better routes, as the worst shelled areas became known, and with the co-operation of Battalion Signallers the lines were rebuilt.

On October 25th it was decided that one Battalion H.Q. would remain near the RIFLE PITS and the forward ladder was extended to this Headquarters.

During operations constant telegraphic and telephonic communication was maintained as far as JAPAN HOUSE notwithstanding heavy and continuous shell fire.

Forward of JAPAN HOUSE communication by wire was intermittent but communication by lamp never failed.

VISUAL.

A visual squad comprising one Officer and 18 O.R. was selected from the Divisional Signal School to maintain Visual communication from the end of the bury at WOOD HOUSE to JAPAN HOUSE.

The Brigade had Visual communication from JAPAN HOUSE to PASCAL FARM and from PASCAL FARM to all Battalions, transmitting stations being necessary between PASCAL FARM and EGYPT HOUSE and PASCAL FARM and TAUBE FARM.

Visual communication proved of great value and during the operation of 26th communication was maintained with the Battalions throughout the day, one Battalion also maintaining constant communication with its three forward companies.

Later due to the heavy casualties to linemen and increasing intensity of shelling Visual was more and more used, linemen <u>not</u> being sent out during heavy shelling.

The casualties in the Company whilst the Division was in the line were three Officers and sixty-five Other Ranks, without considering attached personnel.

The only difficulty with Visual was when the Visual Signallers occupied the same pill-box as the Staff or F.O.O.

POWER BUZZER AND WIRELESS:-

A wireless set was established at MARTIN'S MILL and remained in constant communication with the Corps Directing Station at BOESINGHE except for a few very short intervals when the aerial was shot down and had to be put up again.

During actual operations there was a good deal of interruption caused by the trench aeroplane wireless sets.

Power Buzzers and Amplifiers were distributed as follows:-

Power Buzzer at EGYPT HOUSE (Left Battalion H.Q.)
" " at TAUBE FARM (Centre & Right Battn H.Q.)
" " at PASCAL FARM (Support Battn H.Q.)
" " at JAPAN HOUSE (Advanced Bde H.Q.)
" " at MARTIN'S MILL (Brigade Headquarters)
Amplifier at PASCAL FARM
" at MARTIN'S MILL.

Communication by these means was maintained although very few messages were sent between EGYPT HOUSE and PASCAL FARM and both ways between MARTIN'S MILL and PASCAL FARM.

It would have been better if another Amplifier had been available at JAPAN HOUSE as MARTIN'S MILL to PASCAL FARM was too far (3000 yards) owing to having to cross two streams besides the interruptions from other instruments owing to the very bad state of the lines caused by shell fire.

If another Amplifier had been available to have been placed at JAPAN HOUSE in spite of all interruption continual communication could have been kept between MARTIN'S MILL and
/JAPAN

JAPAN HOUSE and PASCAL FARM.

PIGEONS:-

Division was allotted No 20 H.D. Mobile Loft (near STEENJE MILL on ELVERDINGHE - POPERINGHE Road) and about 70 birds were available.

The loft was in communication with the Divisional Headquarters via Park Exchange XIV Corps.

Division collected Pigeons by D.R.

From BOESINGHE STATION 10 Runners (Pigeoneers) from Reserve Brigade carried them to Battalion Headquarters and a proportion were sent forward before Zero in assault baskets to Companies.

A good many messages were sent in this way but the casualties amongst the birds were fairly heavy.

40 pigeons were sent to Battalion Headquarters for this operation.

RUNNERS:-

As it was found almost impossible for D.R.s to go beyond the CANAL BANK a Runner Post was established at BOESINGHE STATION. 20 trained runners were supplied by the Reserve Brigade who took the messages to Brigade Headquarters (MARTIN'S MILL).

Two runners were sent each time, an interval of about fifty yards being kept between them.

Report on Communications During Operations

of October 25th and 26th 1917.

Telegraph and Telephone:-

1. Division to Brigades -

   (a). Preliminary Work.

   On October 24th it was finally decided that the Forward Brigade would occupy MARTIN'S MILL.

   Two pairs were obtained through the 14th Corps bury to WOOD HOUSE and two pairs through Corps bury to AU BON GITE.

   Two existing pairs of ground cable from WOOD HOUSE to MARTIN'S MILL were taken over and two pairs were laid from AU BON GITE to MARTIN'S MILL.

   To assist the Brigade Section two additional pairs were laid from MARTIN'S MILL to JAPAN HOUSE which was used as a forward test station.

   Later a laddered line was built between these two points.

   Personnel of No 1 Section were lent to Brigade Section for maintenance of all lines from MARTIN'S MILL to JAPAN HOUSE.

   Unfortunately, although the two pairs between AU BON GITE and MARTIN'S MILL were kept through for two days despite very heavy shell fire, no communication could be kept over the bury.

   This was apparently due to lack of co-ordination between Corps and Right Division personnel, who were dividing the maintenance.

   The maintenance of bury between CANAL BANK and WOOD HOUSE was divided, O.C. Signals of Division on left taking the responsibility.

   An advanced Divisional Exchange and Test Point was established near BOESINGHE STATION and was in communication with Brigade Rear Headquarters at HUDDERSFIELD HUTS and with Support Battalion at MARSOUIN FARM.

   There was telegraphic and telephonic communication to the 150th Infantry Brigade in support at WHITE MILL near ELVERDINGHE CHATEAU and with the 151st Infantry Brigade in Reserve at XIV Corps Staging Area No 1 (X28d5.4 Sheet 19) through XIV Corps.

   Lines were laid to the Corps Walking Wounded Dressing Station at CHEAPSIDE and communication was obtained through Left Division to the Divisional Bomb Store at GOUVY FARM.

   There were also direct lines to the Corps Wireless Directing Station at B.11.a.9.8. and to No 20 H.D. Mobile Pigeon Loft near STEENJE MILL on ELVERDINGHE - POPERINGHE Road.

2. Brigade to Battalions -

   When the 149th Infantry Brigade took over the Sector West of POELCAPELLE Brigade Headquarters was at MARTIN'S MILL, a Brigade Test Point at JAPAN HOUSE and Battalion Headquarters at PASCAL FARM and EGYPT HOUSE respectively.

   According to orders issued on October 24th PASCAL FARM was to be Advanced Brigade Headquarters with Left Battalion Headquarters at EGYPT HOUSE, Centre and Right Battalions at TABBE FARM and Support Battalion at PASCAL FARM.

   From MARTIN'S MILL to JAPAN HOUSE there existed two pairs and from PASCAL FARM to EGYPT HOUSE one pair of ground cable.

   For the operations of October 26th the following work was done:-

   A three legged laddered cable laid between JAPAN HOUSE
   /and

and PASCAL FARM with rungs about 200 yards apart. This was afterwards strengthened by additional legs and rungs near JAPAN HOUSE and PASCAL FARM where shelling was more concentrated.

Laddered cables were laid from PASCAL FARM to EGYPT HOUSE and to TAUBE FARM.

These ladders were very badly cut up by shell fire on the night of the 24/25th but by selection of better routes, as the worst shelled areas became known, and with the co-operation of Battalion Signallers the lines were rebuilt.

On October 25th it was decided that one Battalion H.Q. would remain near the RIFLE PITS and the forward ladder was extended to this Headquarters.

During operations constant telegraphic and telephonic communication was maintained as far as JAPAN HOUSE notwithstanding heavy and continuous shell fire.

Forward of JAPAN HOUSE communication by wire was intermittent but communication by lamp never failed.

VISUAL.

A visual squad comprising one Officer and 18 O.R. was selected from the Divisional Signal School to maintain Visual communication from the end of the bury at WOOD HOUSE to JAPAN HOUSE.

The Brigade had Visual communication from JAPAN HOUSE to PASCAL FARM and from PASCAL FARM to all Battalions, transmitting stations being necessary between PASCAL FARM and EGYPT HOUSE and PASCAL FARM and TAUBE FARM.

Visual communication proved of great value and during the operation of 26th communication was maintained with the Battalions throughout the day, one Battalion also maintaining constant communication with its three forward companies.

Later due to the heavy casualties to linemen and increasing intensity of shelling Visual was more and more used, linemen not being sent out during heavy shelling.

The casualties in the Company whilst the Division was in the line were three Officers and sixty-five Other Ranks, without considering attached personnel.

The only difficulty with Visual was when the Visual Signallers occupied the same pill-box as the Staff or F.O.O.

POWER BUZZER AND WIRELESS:-

A wireless set was established at MARTIN'S MILL /// /// and remained in constant communication with the Corps Directing Station at BOESINGHE except for a few very short intervals when the aerial was shot down and had to be put up again.

During actual operations there was a good deal of interruption caused by the French aeroplane wireless sets.

Power Buzzers and Amplifiers were distributed as follows:-

Power Buzzer at EGYPT HOUSE (Left Battalion H.Q.)
    "   " at TAUBE FARM (Centre & Right Battn H.Q.)
    "   " at PASCAL FARM (Support Battn H.Q.)
    "   " at JAPAN HOUSE (Advanced Bde H.Q.)
    "   " at MARTIN'S MILL (Brigade Headquarters)
Amplifier at PASCAL FARM
    " at MARTIN'S MILL.

Communication by these means was maintained although very few messages were sent between EGYPT HOUSE and PASCAL FARM and both ways between MARTIN'S MILL and PASCAL FARM.

It would have been better if another Amplifier had been available at JAPAN HOUSE as MARTIN'S MILL to PASCAL FARM was too far (3000 yards) owing to having to cross two streams besides the interruptions from other instruments owing to the very bad state of the lines caused by shell fire.

If another Amplifier had been available to have been placed at JAPAN HOUSE in spite of all interruption continual communication could have been kept between MARTIN'S MILL and

/JAPAN

JAPAN HOUSE and PASCAL FARM.

PIGEONS:-

Division was allotted No 20 H.D. Mobile Loft (near STEENJE MILL on ELVERDINGHE - POPERINGHE Road) and about 70 birds were available.

The loft was in communication with the Divisional Headquarters via Park Exchange XIV Corps.

Division collected Pigeons by D.R.

From BOESINGHE STATION 10 Runners (Pigeoneers) from Reserve Brigade carried them to Battalion Headquarters and a proportion were sent forward before Zero in assault baskets to Companies.

A good many messages were sent in this way but the casualties amongst the birds were fairly heavy.

40 pigeons were sent to Battalion Headquarters for this operation.

RUNNERS:-

As it was found almost impossible for D.R.s to go beyond the CANAL BANK a Runner Post was established at BOESINGHE STATION. 20 trained runners were supplied by the Reserve Brigade who took the messages to Brigade Headquarters (MARTIN'S MILL).

Two runners were sent each time, an interval of about fifty yards being kept between them.

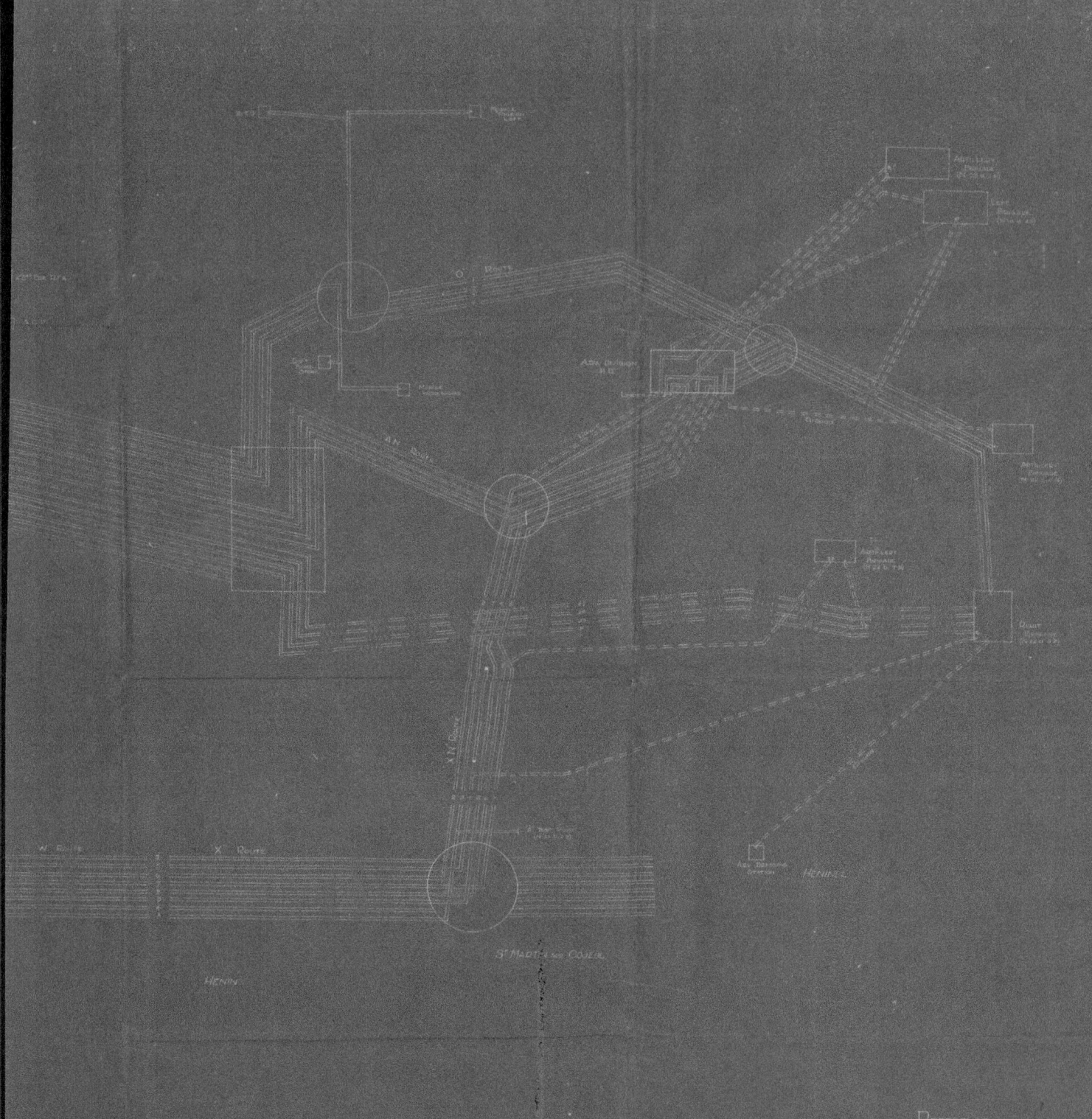

CIRCUIT DIAGRAM OF COMMUNICATIONS

50th (Northumbrian) Divisional Signal Coy. R.E.

Sept. 1917

2 COPIES

CROP - DIAGRAM (NEW)

2 to Meg Lacy

War Diary

50 D Signal
Vol 31

War Diary

of

50th (Northumbrian) Divisional Signal Company.

Royal Engineers

Volume XXXII

Nov. 1917.

WAR DIARY.

of

50TH DIVISIONAL SIGNAL COMPANY

ROYAL ENGINEERS.

VOLUME XXXII.

NOVEMBER 1917.

Army Form C. 2118.

124

WAR DIARY
or
INTELLIGENCE SUMMARY.
(Erase heading not required.)

Instructions regarding War Diaries and Intelligence Summaries are contained in F. S. Regs., Part II. and the Staff Manual respectively. Title pages will be prepared in manuscript.

Place	Date	Hour	Summary of Events and Information	Remarks and references to Appendices
ELVERDINGHE	Nov 2nd.		Casualties:-	
			463125 Spr Wilby A Gassed Enemy Shell.	
			463123 " Williams P do	
			237819 Pnr Langshawe A do	
			463126 Spr Peacock C do	
			86726 " Ditton R do	
			473909 Pnr Morgan T do	
			463103 Sgt MacDonald A T do	
			463251 Spr Waterman T do	
			127811 Pnr McLaughlin G B do	
			463162 Spr Stewart H do	
			Lieut W R Stewart do	
do	Nov 3rd.		Casualties:-	
			268097 Pnr Luker H C Gassed Enemy Shell.	
			463071 2/Cpl Richardson A do	
			463029 L/Cpl Larner R do	
			461563 Spr Gardiner C H do	
			500559 " Gunter T J do	
			237341 " Murdock A do	
			463206 L/C Rothera R do	
			463116 Sgt Main D O do	
do	Nov 4th		Casualties:-	
			548860 Spr Bateman A W Gassed Enemy Shell.	
			463138 Cpl Tissiman J do	
			463076 Spr Mole E do	
			316526 Pnr Shaw P W Killed in action Enemy Shell Fire.	
do	Nov 7/8th		The 149th Infantry Brigade relieved 151st Infantry Brigade in front line. Brigade Headquarters at MARTIN'S MILL. 151st Infantry Brigade Headquarters moved to WHITE MILL relieving 150th Infantry Brigade Headquarters who moved to CARIBOU.	OO No 142 dated 4-1-17

Army Form C. 2118.

WAR DIARY
or
INTELLIGENCE SUMMARY.
(Erase heading not required.)

125

Place	Date	Hour	Summary of Events and Information	Remarks and references to Appendices
ELVERDINGHE	Nov 9th		50th Divisional Signal Company R.E. moved by road to WULVERDINGHE.	O.O. No 143 dated 8-1-17
			Casualties:-	
			458939 Cpl Johnson R M Killed in Action Enemy Shell Fire	
			480532 Spr Verity J Gassed Enemy Shell	
			253358 Pnr Alexander W H do	
			253233 " Borkett C do	
			253236 " Davidson A T do	
			553913 " Morrison J R do	
			253234 " Page G do	
			481962 " Dungworth A E do	
			463110 Spr Finch D J do	
			463239 " Hannan J do	
			253235 Pnr Sneap P W do	
			497933 " Mapes O do	
			253232 Cpl Thomas W do	
			Lieut R.M. Graham R F A do	
do	Novr 9/10th		The 50th Division (less Artillery) were relieved by the 17th Division in the front line. Command of the area passed to G.O.C. 17th Division on completion of relief. 149th Infantry Brigade were relieved by the 52nd Infantry Brigade in the line, Brigade Headquarters moving to CARIBOU.	O.O. No 143 & 144 dated 8-11-17
do	Novr 10th		50th Division Headquarters closed at ELVERDINGHE CHATEAU and opened at EPERLECQUES at 10 a.m. 151st Infantry Brigade Group moved from WHITE MILL to HOULLE area by train. Brigade Headquarters opened at HOULLE (Q.5.c.5.6 Sheet 27a S.E. 1/20000) 150th Infantry Brigade Group moved from ELVERDINGHE area to TOURNEHEM area by train. Brigade Headquarters opened at TOURNEHEM (J.31.a.9.1 Sheet 27a N.E. 1/20000) 50th Divisional Signal Company R.E. Transport moved by road from WULVERDINGHE to EPERLECQUES. Telegraphic and Telephonic communication to XVIII Corps and all Brigades.	O.O. No 143 & 144 dated 8-11-17

Army Form C. 2118.

WAR DIARY
or
INTELLIGENCE SUMMARY.
(Erase heading not required.)

126

Instructions regarding War Diaries and Intelligence Summaries are contained in F. S. Regs., Part II. and the Staff Manual respectively. Title pages will be prepared in manuscript.

Place	Date	Hour	Summary of Events and Information	Remarks and references to Appendices
EPERLECQUES	Nov 12th		Casualties:- 475950 Cpl Mennel J Wounded Hostile Shell Fire.	
do	Nov 13th		The 149th Infantry Brigade Group moved from CARIBOU area to SERQUES area, by train. Brigade Headquarters opened at SERQUES (R.7.a.2.3 Sheet 27a S.E. 1/20000).	O.O. No 143 & 144 dated 8-11-17.
			Note:- The following units remained in the forward area on the relief of the Division:— Artillery, 7th D.L.I. (Pioneers), 1/4th East Yorks Regt, 7th Field Company R.E., 1/3rd Northumbrian Field Ambulance, No 4 Cable Detachment of the 50th Divisional Signal Company R.E., 250th and 251st Artillery Brigade Signal Subsections of the 50th Divisional Signal Company R.E.	
			Awards:- 463138 Cpl Tissiman J Awarded D.C.M.	
do	Nov 18th		Awards:- 463198 Cpl White R.R. Awarded Bar to M.M.
500559 Spr Gunter T J   Awarded M.M.
463097 " Laws R H   "   "
532214 " Roberts G W   "   "
236938 " McHugh R   "   "
463189 " Henderson T   "   "
463185 Sgt Readhead G " "	

Army Form C. 2118.

WAR DIARY
or
INTELLIGENCE SUMMARY.

(Erase heading not required.)

Place	Date	Hour	Summary of Events and Information	Remarks and references to Appendices
EPERLECQUES	Nov 24th		Awards:- 86726 Spr Ditton R. Awarded M.M. 96639 " Inns F H " " 458940 Pnr Thorgilson F C " " 253233 " Borkett C " "	
do	Nov 28th		Awards:- Lieut A E Odell M.C. Awarded Bar to M.C. 463076 Spr Mole E Awarded D.C.M.	
			Report on communications during operations of October 25th/26th with diagrams attached.	

Lieut.
a/Comdg 50th (Nbn) Divisional Signal Company R.E.

1-12-17.

SECRET.

WAR DIARY

of

~~A.R.E.~~ 50th (Northumbrian) Divisional SIGNAL Co, R.E.

VOLUME No XXXIII.

DECEMBER 1917.

Army Form C. 2118.

Vol XXXI

WAR DIARY
or
INTELLIGENCE SUMMARY.
(Erase heading not required.)

Instructions regarding War Diaries and Intelligence Summaries are contained in F. S. Regs., Part II. and the Staff Manual respectively. Title pages will be prepared in manuscript.

Place	Date	Hour	Summary of Events and Information	Remarks and references to Appendices
EPERLEQUES	Dec. 2nd.		AWARDS. No. 25626 A/L.Cpl. Rowe B.J. Awarded M.M. " 235079 Pte. Padgett J.R. " 463128 C.S.M. King F. Awarded D.C.M. Lieut. W. Pyemont M.C. Awarded Bar to M.C.	G.O. No 1-48 dated 7-12-17
do.	Dec. 10th.		The 150th. Infantry Brigade moved from WATTEN to BRANDHOEK by train. Relieved the 100th. Infantry Brigade.	Do.
do.	Dec. 11th.		The 150th. Infantry Brigade moved from BRANDHOEK to POTIJZE by train. Relieved the 19th. Infantry Brigade.	do.
			The 149th. Infantry Brigade moved from WATTEN to BRANDHOEK by train. Relieved the 110th. Infantry Brigade.	do.
do.	Dec. 12th.		The 149th. Infantry Brigade marched from BRANDHOEK to POTIJZE. Relieved the 98th. Infantry Brigade.	do.
			The 151st. Infantry Brigade moved from WATTEN to BRANDHOEK by train. Relieved the 149th. Infantry Brigade.	do.
Ref. Map. Sheet 28. 1/40,000.			The 150th. Infantry Brigade relieved the 98th. Infantry Brigade in the line on the night 12/13th.	do.
	Dec. 13th.		Divisional H.Q. closed at EPERLEQUES at 12 noon. Adv. H.Q. re-established at the RAMPARTS, YPRES same hour in relief of the 33rd. Division. Rear H.Q. opened at BRANDHOEK. A fire broke out in the early hours of the 15th. at the Ramparts, destroying 33rd. Division H.Q. A large amount of Technical equipment belonging to the 33rd. & 50th. Signal Companies was lost. A temporary Signal Office was opened at "H" Test Point and later moved to small dug-outs in RAMPARTS N. of MENIN GATE.	do.

Army Form C. 2118.

WAR DIARY
or
INTELLIGENCE SUMMARY.
(Erase heading not required.)

Instructions regarding War Diaries and Intelligence Summaries are contained in F. S. Regs., Part II. and the Staff Manual respectively. Title pages will be prepared in manuscript.

Place	Date	Hour	Summary of Events and Information	Remarks and references to Appendices
YPRES.	Dec.16th.		The 149th. Infantry Brigade relieved the 150th. Infantry Brigade in the line on the night of 16/17th. The 150th. Infantry Brigade moved to Div. Reserve at BRANDHOEK. Relieved 151st. Infantry Brigade. The 151st. Infantry Brigade moved from Reserve at BRANDHOEK to Support at POTIJZE. Relieved the 149th. Infantry Brigade.	C.O. No. 149 dated 14-12-17. do.
Ref. Map Sheet 28 1/40,000.				
Do.	Dec. 17th.		Advanced Division H.Q. established at the RAMPARTS YPRES at 10 a.m.	G.X. 4981 dated 16-12-17
Do.	Dec. 20th.		The 151st. Infantry Brigade relieved the 149th. Infantry Brigade in the line on the night of 20/21st. The 150th. Infantry Brigade moved into Support in the POTIJZE Area in relief of the 151st. Infantry Brigade. The 149th. Infantry Brigade moved from the Front line to Div. Reserve at BRANDHOEK. Relieved the 150th. Infantry Brigade.	C.O. No. 152 dated 18-12-17. do.
Do.	Dec. 23rd.		AWARDS. No. 463025 Sapper Barrass J.W. Awarded Bar to M.M. " 254820 " Connon A. Awarded M.M.	
Do.	Dec. 24th.		CASUALTIES. No. 463209 Sapper Stearman J. Gassed Enemy Shell. " 463248 " Seyburn R.F. do.	
Do.	Dec. 25th.		CASUALTIES. No. 463118 Sergeant Jenkins W.E. Gassed Enemy Shell. " 463239 Sapper Lowes N. do.	

Army Form C. 2118.

WAR DIARY
or
INTELLIGENCE SUMMARY.
(Erase heading not required.)

Instructions regarding War Diaries and Intelligence Summaries are contained in F. S. Regs. Part II. and the Staff Manual respectively. Title pages will be prepared in manuscript.

Place	Date	Hour	Summary of Events and Information	Remarks and references to Appendices
YPRES.	Dec. 25th.		The 149th. Infantry Brigade relieved the 150th. Infantry Brigade in Support.	O.O. No.152. dated 21-12-17.
Ref. Map. Sheet 28 of 1/40,000.			The 150th. Infantry Brigade relieved the 151st. Infantry Brigade in the line on the night 24/25th. The 151st. Infantry Brigade moved from the Front line to Div. Reserve at BRANDHOEK. Relieved the 149th. Infantry Brigade.	do.
YPRES.	Dec. 29th.		The 151st. Infantry Brigade moved from Div. Reserve at BRANDHOEK to YPRES in relief of the 149th. Infantry Brigade. The 150th. Infantry Brigade moved from the Front line to Div. Reserve at BRANDHOEK. Relieved the 151st. Infantry Brigade. The 149th. Infantry Brigade moved from Support to the Front line in relief of the 150th. Infantry Brigade.	O.O. No.154 dated 26-12-17. do.
			Diagrams and details of communications will be included in January War Diary.	
	1-1-18.			

Major.
Cmdg. 50th. (Nbn) Div. Signal Co. R.E.

On His Majesty's Service.

Signal Coy
30 Div
Jan 11/8

-SECRET-

WAR DIARY

of

50TH (NORTHUMBRIAN) DIVISIONAL SIGNAL COMPANY, ROYAL ENGINEERS.
---oOo---

VOLUME XXXIV.

JANUARY, 1918.

Army Form C. 2118.

WAR DIARY
or
INTELLIGENCE SUMMARY
(Erase heading not required.)

Vol XXIV

Instructions regarding War Diaries and Intelligence Summaries are contained in F. S. Regs., Part II. and the Staff Manual respectively. Title pages will be prepared in manuscript.

Place	Date	Hour	Summary of Events and Information	Remarks and references to Appendices
YPRES.	Jan. 2nd.		CASUALTIES. No. 463066 L/Cpl. Scott R.E. Gassed Enemy Shell.	
" Ref. Map. Sheets 27 & 28 1/40,000.	Jan. 3rd.		The 149th. Inf. Bde. moved by train from BRANDHOEK to WATOU.	O.O. 159 dated 1-1-18.
"	Jan. 4th.		The 150th. Inf. Bde. moved by train from POTIJZE to WINNEZEELE.	O.O. 158 dated 1-1-18.
"	Jan. 5th.		The 151st. Inf. Bde. were relieved in the line by 19th. Inf. Bde. on the night of the 5/6th. and moved to POTIJZE.	—do—
"	6th.		The 151st. Inf. Bde. moved by train from POTIJZE to EECKE.	—do—
"	"		Divl. H.Q. closed at YPRES & BRANDHOEK at 10 a.m. and re-opened at same hour at STEENEVOORDE Relieved by 33rd. Division.	—do—.
STEENEVOORDE. Ref. Map. Sheet HAZEBROUCK 5a. 1/100,000.				
	Jan. 16th.		The 150th. Inf. Bde. moved by train from WINNEZEELE to ESQUERDES area.	O.O. 159 d.9-1-18.
	17th.		The 151st. Inf. Bde. moved by train from EECKE to BOISDINGHEM area	—do—
	18th.		149th. Inf. Bde. moved by train from WATOU to TATINGHEM	—do—
	19th.		Divl. H.Q. closed at STEENEVOORDE at 10 a.m. and re-opened at WIZERNES same hour. Relieved by 8th. Division.	—do—

Army Form C. 2118.

WAR DIARY
or
INTELLIGENCE SUMMARY.
(Erase heading not required)

Place	Date	Hour	Summary of Events and Information	Remarks and references to Appendices
WIZERNES. Ref. Map. Sheets 27 & 28 1/40,000.	Jan. 27th.		The 149th. Inf. Bde. moved by train from TATINGHEM to YPRES	O.O. 161 d.24-1-18.
	Jan. 28th.		The 150th. Inf. Bde. moved from from ESQUERDES to BRANDHOEK by train	--do--.
	" 29th.		The 150th. Inf. Bde. moved from BRANDHOEK to YPRES	--do--.
	Night 29/30th.		The 149th. Inf. Bde. moved from YPRES to Front Line	--do--.
	Jan. 30th.		The 151st. Inf. Bde. moved from BOISDINGHEM to BRANDHOEK by train	--do--.
	"		Divl. H.Q. moved from closed at WIZERNES at 12 noon and re-opened at RAMPARTS	--do--.
YPRES			same hour in relief of the 33rd. Division.	
			Notes on Communications for December 1917, and diagrams relating thereto are appended.	
	31-1-18.			

Major,
Cmdg. 50th.(Nbn) Divl. Signal Co. R.E.

Telegraphic and Telephonic Communications.

From Adv. Division to the Forward Infantry Brigade there are two pairs running in the Corps Bury, one being a telephone pair and the other a Buzzer Pair.

A third telephone pair runs to the Rear H.Q. of the Forward Brigade and thence to Forward Brigade H.Q.

From Z.E. Test Point (D.20.d.2.6) to Forward Brigade there are three overland lines, for the purpose of bridging any faults or breaks that may occur on the bury.

There is also a line from Z.E. to W.H.(DD20d.2.6) for bridging any fault between these points.

The Forward Brigade has buried laterals to its right and left Flanking Brigades.

The Advanced Division is connected to its Flanking Divisions by lines in buries and on Corps routes.

The following stations are also connected to the Advanced Division Exchange (Ramparts) by local lines, in buries and open routes:-

        Support Brigade (Convent YPRES)
        Corps Main Dressing Station.(Prison YPRES).
        Field Companies.
        Pioneers (7th. D.L.I. & 18th. Middlesex).
        Rear Visual Station and Divisional Runner Post.
        Divisional Bomb Store.

The Divisional Advanced Exchange is connected to Divisional Rear Exchange by three pairs. There are also four pairs from Advanced Division direct to Corps.(3 in use and one spare for emergencies) and one pair direct to Corps from Divisional Rear H.Q.

VISUAL SYSTEM :-

There is a Brigade Visual Station at Brigade H.Q. in the line D.21.a.85.30 (L.C.).

This Station communicates with a transmitting Divisional Station at Hill 35 D.19.b.2.7. (G.G.).

The Transmitting Station communicates with a Rear Divisional Station near BAVARIA HOUSE C.29.d.3.6. (B.H.).

The Rear Visual Station is in communication by telephone with Advanced Divisional H.Q. through Division Post I.5.a.1.7 (D.R.P.).

Map references are taken from Sheet 28 N.W. 1/20,000.

Strength of Divisional Stations is as under :-

G.G. 6 men.
B.H. 3 men.

Lucas Lamps only are in use.

Messages are sent both ways between the Stations L.C. to G.G. and G.G. to B.H.

The Stations are manned permanently and are relieved every 6 days.

The Brigade in the line has Visual communication to its Battalions and Battalions have Visual communication to some of their Companies.

WIRELESS, POWER BUZZERS, & AMPLIFIERS.

Position is as under :-
1 Wireless Trench Set at L.C.(H.Q. of Bde in line D.21.a.85.30). This wireless set is in communication with Corps Directing Set at I.1.b.8.8.

A Power Buzzer is installed at Company H.Q. D.12.c.5.9 (P.R.). and is working to Company H.Q. D.17.b.15.80. (H.F.).

H.F. is in communication by telephone with Battalion H.Q. at HAMBURG HOUSE D.16.b.6.8. (H.H.).

Further Power Buzzers and Amplifiers are being installed.

Map references are taken from Sheet 28 N.W. 1/20,000.

PIGEONS.

Corps Pigeon Lofts are at 16 Rue de Cassell POPERINGHE in telephonic communication with Advanced Division H.Q.

Pigeons are conveyed by M.C.D.R. from the lofts to Division refilling points, MILL COTTAGE. D.R.P. I.5.a.1.7. at 11 a.m. daily.

The Pigeons are taken up to H.Q. of brigade in line daily by Runners from whence they are sent forward in assault baskets to Battalions for distribution to Companies.

The Brigade has 8 Pigeons supplied daily i.e. 4 per Battalion in the line.

CONTACT PLANES.

Dropping Station is maintained in Square YPRES opposite Cloth Hall. Visual Signallers are constantly on duty during daylight.

D.R.L.S. & RUNNERS.

1 Despatch Clerk and 12 Runners at "O" Dug-out MILL COTTAGE I.5.a.1.7.

Motor Cyclists deliver despatches to this point and Runners deliver them to Brigade in the line.

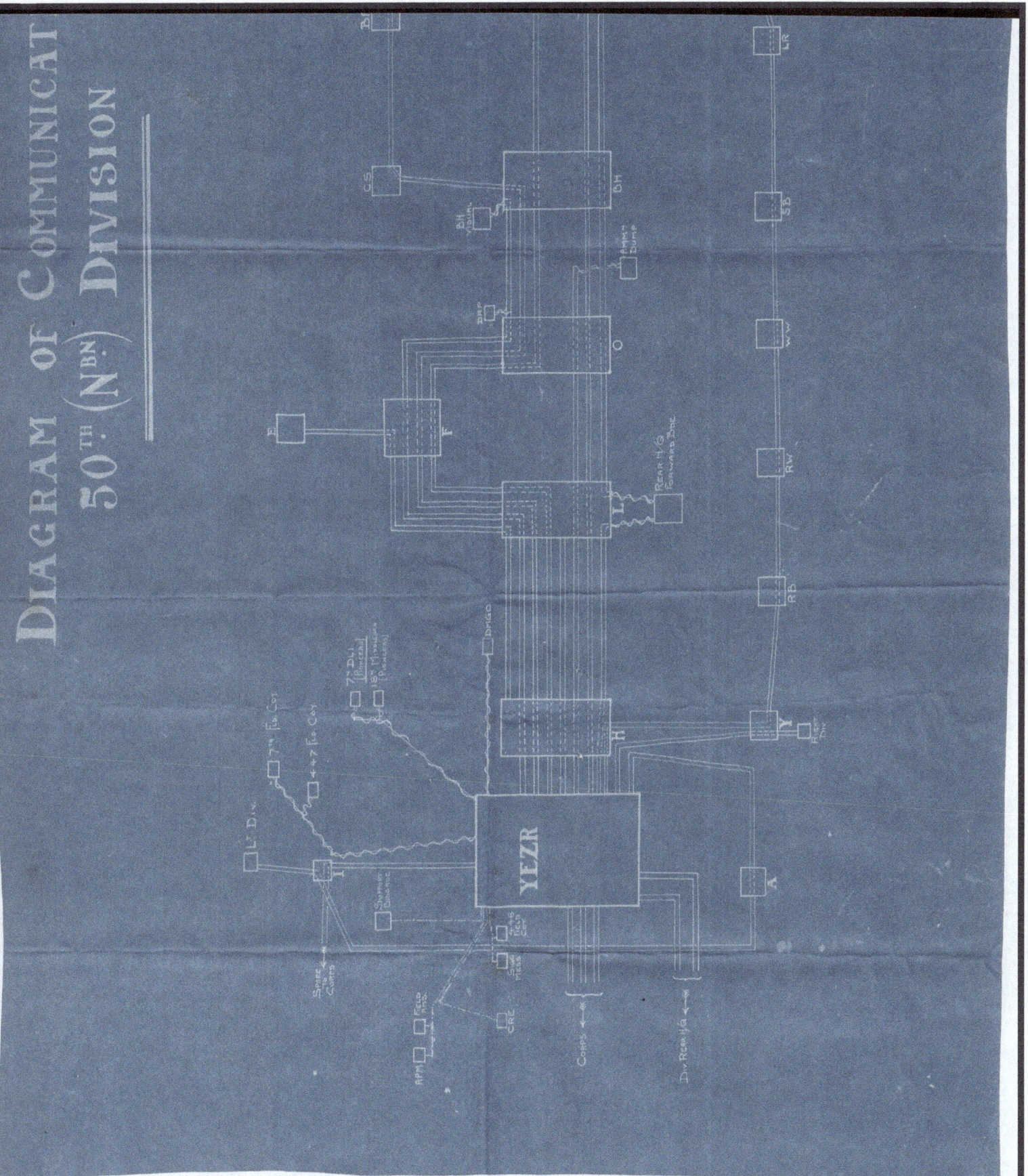

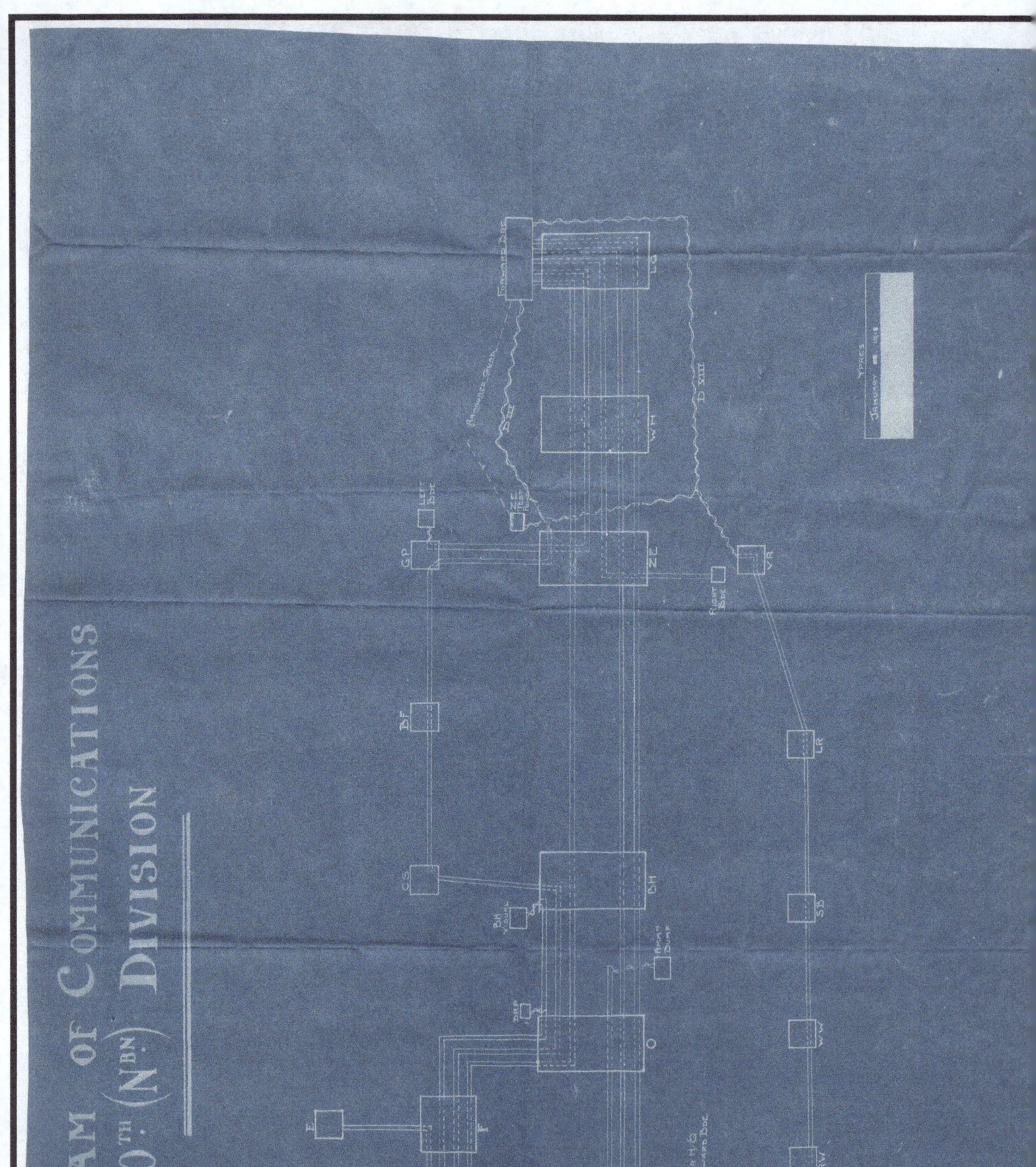

On His Majesty's Service.

-SECRET-

WAR DIARY

of

50TH (NORTHUMBRIAN) DIVISIONAL SIGNAL COMPANY, ROYAL ENGINEERS.

VOLUME XXXV.

FEBRUARY, 1918.

Army Form C. 2118.

50th (North) [handwritten]

WAR DIARY
or
INTELLIGENCE SUMMARY.
(Erase heading not required.)

Instructions regarding War Diaries and Intelligence Summaries are contained in F. S. Regs., Part II. and the Staff Manual respectively. Title pages will be prepared in manuscript.

Place	Date	Hour	Summary of Events and Information	Remarks and references to Appendices
YPRES. Ref. Map. Sheet 28 1/40,000.	Feb. 2nd.		149th. Inf. Bde. relieved in the line by 150th. Inf. Bde. and moved to Divl. Reserve at BRANDHOEK, relieving 151st. Inf. Bde.	O.O. No. 165 dd 31-1-18.
			150th. Inf. Bde. moved from YPRES to Front Line, Relieved 149th. Inf. Bde.	-do-.
			151st. Inf. Bde. moved from Divl. Reserve at BRANDHOEK to Support at YPRES.	-do-.
	Feb. 7th.		149th. Inf. Bde. moved from BRANDHOEK to Support at YPRES. Relieved 151st. Inf. Bde.	O.O. No. 168 d.3-2-18.
			151st. Inf. Bde. moved from YPRES to Front Line. Relieved 150th. Inf. Bde.	-do-.
			150th. Inf. Bde. relieved in the line by 151st. Inf. Bde. and moved to Divl. Reserve at BRANDHOEK, relieved 149th. Inf. Bde.	-do-.
YPRES. Ref. 1/10,000 French Map. Sheet 28 N.E.1 ZONNEBEKE.	Night 9/10th.		(a) 50th. Division handed over to 29th. Division the Front line from present inter-Divisional Boundary to D.6.d.90.85. (b).50th. Division took over from 66th. Division Front Line from TIBER to D.23.d.1.7. Transfers carried out as follows :— 151st. Inf. Bde. handed over the/as in (a) to 86th. Inf. Bde. and took over the line to the South as far as D.18.a.65.15 from 199th. Inf. Bde. 149th. Inf. Bde. took over the line from D.18.a.65.15 to D.23.d.1.7 from 199th. Inf. Bde. 150th. Inf. Bde. moved from BRANDHOEK to YPRES.	O.O. No. 167 dated 1-2-18.
-do-	Night 10/11th.		The 150th. Inf. Bde. moved from YPRES. to the Left Brigade Front. Relieved 151st. Inf. Bde.	O.O. No. 167 dated 1-2-18.
			151st. Inf. Bde. moved from Left Brigade Front to YPRES. Relieved by 150th. Inf. Bde. Became Reserve Brigade.	
YPRES.	Night 14/15th.		The 151st. Inf. Bde. relieved the 150th. Inf. Bde. in the line .	O.O. No. 174 dated 12-2-18.
			The 150th. Inf. Bde. moved from the Front line to YPRES and became Reserve Brigade.	-do-.

Army Form C. 2118.

WAR DIARY
or
INTELLIGENCE SUMMARY.
(Erase heading not required.)

Instructions regarding War Diaries and Intelligence Summaries are contained in F.S. Regs., Part II. and the Staff Manual respectively. Title pages will be prepared in manuscript.

Place	Date	Hour	Summary of Events and Information	Remarks and references to Appendices
YPRES.	Night 18/19th.		The 150th. Inf. Bde. relieved the 151st. Inf. Bde. in the line.	O.O. No. 177 dated 17-2-18.
			The 151st. Inf. Bde. moved from the Front Line to YPRES and became Reserve Brigade.	-do-.
-do-.	Feb. 20th.		The 151st. Bde. Group moved by train from YPRES to TATINGHEM.	O.O. No. 175 dated 15-2-18.
	Night 21/22nd.		The 150th. Inf. Bde. was relieved in the Line (Left Bde. Sector) by the 19th. Inf. Bde. and moved to YPRES.	O.O. No. 175 dated 15-2-18.
	Feb. 22nd.		The 150th. Bde. Group moved by train from YPRES to ESJUERDES.	-do-.
	Night 22/23rd.		The 149th. Inf. Bde. was relieved in the Line (Right Bde. Sector) by the 100th. Inf. Bde. and moved to YPRES.	-do-.
	Feb. 23rd.		The 149th. Inf. Bde. Group moved from YPRES to BOISDINGHE" by train.	-do-.
YPRES.	Feb.23rd.		The 50th. Divl. Headquarters closed at the RAMPARTS YPRES at 12 noon and re-opened at WIZERNES same hour. Relieved by the 33rd. Division, and became G.H.Q. Reserve.	O.O. No. 175 dated 15-2-18.

WORK ON LINES — FEBRUARY 1918.

The lines taken over from the 33rd. Division were substantially the same as those handed over in the early part of JANUARY with two exceptions. Owing to the breakage of the centre buried cable route in advance of G.R., three pairs had been put out overland from G.R. to Z.E.; and on account of trouble in the southern bury (via V.R.) a line had been laid overland from W.W. to G.R. so that the fourth pair to the Bde. began in the southern bury and finished in the centre bury.

The southern bury having been proved good, we reverted to the original scheme. The line from G.R. to W.W. was taken up and laid out to '08 test box. It was there joined to No.1 pair on the poled cable route from 'H', this and the permanent route between 'H' and 'O' having been put in the Divl. maintenance. At G.R. this line was joined to one of the pairs to Z.E., so as to form a complete overland line from Divn. to Z.E. As this line proved very good it was brought into use as one pair to Bde., and the buried pair thus thrown spare was utilized as a service line to the linemen at Z.E.

A buried route from V.R. to Z.E. commenced by the 33rd. Division was completed by two parties of 80 pioneers. The route was tested and jointed, put on boards at Z.E. & V.R., and 4 pairs brought into use.

Army Form C. 2118.

WAR DIARY
or
INTELLIGENCE SUMMARY.
(Erase heading not required.)

Place	Date	Hour	Summary of Events and Information	Remarks and references to Appendices
			3.	
			WORK ON LINES (Contd.)	
			A low trestle route was built beside JUDAH TRACK and the three pairs from Z.E. to G.R. above-mentioned were brought on to it, together with a pair from Z.E. to B.Y. in use by Divl. Arty. Owing to insufficiency of trestles this route was continued on stakes to G.R. When a Brigade Front was taken over from the 66th. Division on the 10th, that Division handed over two lines to the Bde. H.q. at V.R. A third line in a route further south (I.D. - L.R. route) was arranged for through the XXIInd. Corps. An additional pair was put out on existing poles to the Barracks, where the Right Bde. had its Rear H.q.	
			The poled route carrying local lines in YPRES was improved and extended. Some salved poles were used to pole the overland pair forward of 'O'. This work had reached as far as B.H. test-box when the Division was relieved. A pair was laid from V.R. to FROST HOUSE for the use of the medical service.	
			DURING THE PERIOD THE DIVISION WAS IN THE LINE CABLE WAS SALVED AS PER DETAILS ATTACHED.	
			FULL DETAILS OF COMMUNICATIONS TOGETHER WITH 6 SHEETS OF DIAGRAMS ARE ATTACHED.	
	1-3-18.		*[signature]* Major, Cmdg. 50th.(Nbn) Divl. Signal Co. R.E.	

50th (NORTHUMBRIAN) DIVISIONAL SIGNAL COMPANY, R.E. No. 10951

50th. Division "Q".
A.D. Signals, VIIIth. Corps. (For information).

Return of Cable Salved by 50th. Divl. Signal Co. R.E.

Description of Cable.	Sent to VIIIth. Corps - Miles.	Re-issued. Miles.	Salved by 149 Bde & re-issued or handed over - miles.	TOTAL MILES.	Salvage Value per mile.	T O T A L.
						£. s. d.
D.ii Twisted.	5¾		1½	7¼	£10.	72 - 10 - 0.
D.iii Twisted.	8¼	5	3	16¼	£16.	260 - 0 - 0.
D.V. Twisted or Single.	24¼ Twisted.	8¼	½	33	£24.	792 - 0 - 0.
D.8 Twisted.	9½	3½	2	15	£22.	330 - 0 - 0.
D. Twin.	8	4		12	£15.	180 - 0 - 0.
3 Strand Copper.	2			2	£25.	50 - 0 - 0.
Various Types of above, in coils & on stakes.	5			5	£15.	75 - 0 - 0.
Various Types of 1 Pr. 2 Pr. & 7 Pr. Brass Sheathed & Armoured Cable.	6½		¼	6¾	£25.	168 - 15 - 0.
						£1928 - 5 - 0.

Approximate Vocabulary Value over £4,000. Bulk of Cable in very good condition. (Drums and coils of new Cable not included).

Major,

20-2-18.

Cmdg. 50th.(Nbn) Divl. Signal Co. R.E.

War Diary 2

DETAILS of COMMUNICATION

50TH DIVISION.

TELEGRAPHIC and TELEPHONE COMMUNICATION.
---oOo---

1. **DIVISION to VIIIth CORPS.**

    There are 3 pairs (1/2, 13/14, 21/22.) on "Y" route to Corps, also 1 pair (7/8) on the Z.E. - Z.I. route to Corps Report Centre GOLDFISH CHATEAU and 1 emergency pair on "X" route to Corps Report Centre. Communication can also be obtained through BRANDHOEK EXCHANGE and flanking Divisions.

11. **DIVISION TO FLANKING DIVISIONS.**

    Lines in buried routes through H.A. and I Test boxes to Division on left and through "H" and "Y" test boxes to Division on right.

    To Division on left 7."H" 8/43.A 32.I.
    To Division on right 6. H.2.Y.

111. **DIVISION TO BRIGADES.**

    To each of the Brigades in Line there are buried Lines in three different routes.
    In case of damage to the buried cables overland pairs are maintained from each Brigade to the Linemen's dug-out in D.20.d; from there three overland pairs run each on a low trestle route to GODLEY ROAD, and one pair is continued through the lesser shelled area back to YPRES.

    LINES TO LEFT BRIGADE.

    H 21. L 23. F 30. O 3. B.H.3. G B 13. B F 3. G F 14.

    Z B local // H 29. L 9. O 40. B H 35. G R 35. Z B 47.

    W H local // H 45. L 6. F 15. O 39. B H 16. G R 16.

    Z B 7. W H local // H 10. Y 50/42. R B 17. W W 12. S B 12. *RW 10*

    L R 12. V R 1. Z B local.

    LINES TO RIGHT BRIGADE.

    H 4. Y 8. Z B 8. R B 7. R W 7. W W 6. S B 7. L R 7.

    V R local // H 56/57. Y 4. L 11. O 47. B H 27. D V 30.

    S B 29. L R 29. V R local // H 16. Y 12. R B 17. B X 9.

    I D 52. J T 64. A Z 28. L R 28. V R local.

    In addition there is communication from Division to Back Headquarters of the Brigades in Line and to the BRIGADE in SUPPORT at the CONVENT, YPRES.

IV. A list of Subscribers is given in Appendix "A". This also includes Divisional Units obtained through BRANDHOEK EXCHANGE.

V. BRIGADES TO FLANKING BRIGADES.

RIGHT Brigade has buried Lines to Brigades on either flank.

(a) To Brigades on Right (1) V R 1.   L R.
                         (2) V R 4.   L R.

(b) To Brigades on Left. (1) V R 3.   Z E 23.
                         (2) W H local.

LEFT Brigade also has buried Lines to Brigades on either flank.

(c) To Brigades on Right   as (b) above.

(d) To Brigade on Left   W H 43.   Z E 31. G.P

VI BRIGADES TO BATTALIONS.

The Brigade in Support has Lines partly on buried system and partly overland to all its Battalions.

The Right Brigade has two routes to its Battalion in Line, the Lines being buried as far as test boxes L C and K F respectively. It is also joined to the M.G.Group at DEVILS CROSSING, to Support Battalion and to No. 3 Group R.F.A.

Left Brigade Lines are overland from L C and include a pair to each Battalion and Machine Gun Co and a laddered Line serving <u>all</u> Units. Intermediate test points enable sound portions of broken Lines to be utilised in maintaining communication.

VII. BATTALIONS TO FLANKING BATTALIONS.

All Battalions have lateral communication and Right and Left Flank Battalions of Division are in communication with Battalions on Right and Left respectively.

VIII. BATTALIONS TO COMPANIES.

The Front Line Battalion, Right Brigade is connected by overland Lines to all its Companies.

Left Battalion, Left Brigade is joined to all its Companies by metallic pair.

Right Battalion, Left Brigade is joined to its Reserve Support and Right Companies by metallic pair, and to all Companies by a Ladder. This ladder extends also to Right Company, Left Battalion of the ~~Left~~ Right Brigade.

DIVISIONAL ARTILLERY COMMUNICATIONS

IX. DIVISIONAL ARTILLERY TO GROUPS.

All forward Lines are on the Corps buried system. They are allotted and maintained by Corps. Only the overland Lines from the test points to Unit Exchange are maintained by respective Units.

Nos. 1 and 2 Groups jointly man a Group Forward Exchange, and an O.P. Exchange.

List of Subscribers on Divisional Artillery Exchange is shewn in Appendix "A".

X. No. 1 GROUP.

No. 1 Group has direct Lines to "A", "B" and "D" Batteries, a Heavy Artillery Group, Kite Balloon and laterals to Nos. 2 and 3 Groups.

The forward Exchange has Lines to each Battery, O.P. Exchange, Left Infantry Brigade, and Right Battalion of Left Brigade, "A" and "B" Batteries are also in direct communication with O.P. Exchange.

Visual communication has been arranged from Group H.Q. to each Battery and to the O.P. Exchange. The latter is also in visual communication with the O.P.'s

XI. No. 2 GROUP.

No. 2 Group works through the forward Exchange to to which it has 3 trunks. It has lateral communication with Nos. 1 and 3 Groups.

The forward Exchange has Lines to each Battery and O.P. Exchange

Each Battery is on the O.P. Exchange.

Batteries have visual communication with the forward Exchange and the forward Exchange has visual to Group H.Q.

XII. No. 3 GROUP.

No. 3 Group has Lines to a Heavy Artillery Group, Groups Nos. 1 and 3, the Left Group of the D.A. on our Right and the Right Infantry Brigade. A Battery Exchange is used as a forward Exchange and has Lines to each other Battery and O.P. As the Batteries of this Group are occupying more or less Reserve positions no visual has been arranged.

Diagram of all communications attached.

WIRELESS POWER BUZZER and AMPLIFIER

---oOo---

Sheet 28. N.W. 1/20,000
" 28. N.E. "

Two Wireless, 50 Watt Trench Sets are installed, one at HAMBURG D.10.d.3.2. and the other at Brigade H.Q. D.20.d1.6. These are in direct communication with Corps directing Set at C.28.b.60.85.

There is a Power Buzzer in PASSCHENDAELE working back to CREST FARM D.12.a.2.8. where there is a P.B & A.

At HAMBURG D.10.d.3.2. a P.B.& A is also installed. HAMBURG is in communication with CREST FARM and also with P.B. & A Station of Brigade on Right [RIGHT] at DASH CROSSING D.17.c.3.9. and as before stated is in communication by Wireless to Corps Directing Set at C.28.b.60.85.

Each P. B. & A. station is manned by three men, and relieved every four days. Personnel is supplied from P.B. Squad attached to Divisional Signal Company. Fresh accumulators are taken up every other day.

Wireless P.B.& A. communications are shewn on attached diagram.

VISUAL SYSTEM

---oOo---

VISUAL STATIONS are situated at positions shewn below. Personnel are supplied from Visual Signallers of Visual Section of 50th Divisional Signal Co. R.E. assisted by men from Divisional Power Buzzer Squad.

Lucas Lamps are mainly used, Nos. are shewn below against Map Reference.

B.H.   Map Reference C.29.d.5.5.   (Equipment :-
                                         1 Lucas Lamp.
         (Personnel 3)   1 Telescope
                                         2 Flags
                                         1 Shutter
                                         1 Message case.

         communicating to :-

G.G.   D.19.b.3.8.   (Equipment :-
                                         3 Lamps
         (Personnel)   4 Flags, 2 Blue, 2 White.
              6   1 Telescope
                                         1 Message case.

         communicating to :-

Brigade Station at L C, D.21.a.7.4. and V R, D.26.a.1.4. (Left Brigade).

Brigades are responsible for Battalion Visual Stations communicating with V R and L C.

Equipment at L C and V R supplied by Brigade, also personnel.

The Stations are manned permanently and there is always a look-out man on duty.

O.K. is sent through every two hours at night.

B.H. Station is in communication with Divisional H.Q. by telephone

Visual communications are shewn on attached diagram.

D.R.L.S. & RUNNERS

Motor Cyclist D.R's. carry despatches direct to the Right Brigade, leaving those for the Left Brigade at the Runner Post near FROST HOUSE on their way forward. Runners carry from this post to the Left Brigade, and the despatches they bring back are collected by the M.C.D.R. on his return journey. Time table of D.R.L.S. is attached.

PIGEONS

Pigeons are forwarded daily by Corps to the Divl Runner Post at FROST HOUSE and distributed by Runners to Brigades in Line for forwarding to Battalions or Coys. At present each Brigade receives four Pigeons daily. Pigeon Loft is in POPERINGHE and is in direct communication with the Corps.

APPENDIX "A".

A. 50th DIVISION TELEPHONE EXCHANGE.		B. BRANDHOEK EXCHANGE (CORPS).	
No.	SUBSCRIBER.	No.	SUBSCRIBER.
1	G.O.C.	1	MERSEY Camp.
2	G.S.O.1	2	Corps P of W Cage.
3	G. Office.	3	Area Commandant BRANDHOEK.
4	G.S.O.3, Night.	4	"H" Corps H.A.
5	A & Q Offices.	5	No. 3 Traffic Control.
6	VlIIth Corps, 3 Lines.	6	BRANDHOEK A.A.
7	Right Division through E Y 2 Ex.	7	Area Commandant, VLAMERTINGHE.
8	Left Division.	8	48 Water Point.
9	Right Brigade. (2 Lines)	9	9th D.A. W.L.
10	Right Brigade, back H.Q.	10	6 Water Point.
11	Left Brigade (2 Lines)	11	VlIIth Corps (2 Lines).
12	Left Brigade, back H.Q.	12	66 Labour Group.
13	Support Brigade.	13	GOLDFISH CHATEAU.
14	BRANDHOEK Exchange.	14	HOP FACTORY.
15	50th Division Artillery.	15	23rd Supply Column.
16	C.R.E.	16	S.X. Exchange.
17	7th Field Co, R.E.	17	Main Dressing Station.
18	446th Field Co, R.E.	18	"R" Battery A.A.
19	447th Field Co, R.E.	19	Corps Advanced.
20	7th D.L.I (Pioneers).	20	23rd Brigade Transport, 2 rings.
21	TRANSIT Dump.	21	24th " " 3 "
22	O.C. SIGNALS.	22	25th " " 4 "
23	VlIIth Corps Wireless.	23	Camouflage Officer "H" Corps.
24	GOLDFISH CHATEAU.	24	50th Division.
25	Divl Runner Post, FROST HOUSE.	25	557 A.T. Coy.
26	BAVARIA HOUSE (B.H.) Visual Station.	26	D.A.D.O.S. 50th Division.
27	Superintendant Signal Office.	27	50th Divisional Train.
28	Signals Mess.	28	RED FARM Field Ambulance.
29	Horse Lines & C Q.M.S.		
30	Lineman BRANDHOEK.		
31	D.M.G.O.		C. DIVISIONAL ARTILLERY EXCHANGE.
32	A.D.M.S.		
33	1/3rd Nbn Field Ambulance.	1	C.R.A.
34	A.P.M.	2	Brigade Major.
35	Traffic Control, OXFORD ROAD.	3	Staff Captain.
36	Bomb Store, CAMBRIDGE Dump.	4	VlIIth Corps Heavy Artillery.
37	Divisional Gas Officer.	5	50th Division.
38	Camp Commandant, BRANDHOEK.	6	250 Brigade R.F.A. (2 Lines)
39	French & Belgian Mission, BRANDHOEK.	7	251 " " "
		8	38 " " "
		9	"O" Brigade H.A.G.
		10	Counter Battery Report Centre.
		11	Left Divisional Artillery.
		12	Right " "
		13	Liaison Line, Left Inf. Brigade.
		14	" " Right "
		15	D L Exchange.
		16	D.A.C.
		17	Trench Mortars
		18	No. 1 Group Wagon Lines.

APPENDIX "A".

Page. 2.

D. LEFT INFANTRY BRIGADE EXCHANGE.		E. RIGHT INFANTRY BRIGADE EXCHANGE.	
NO.	SUBSCRIBER.	NO.	SUBSCRIBER.
1	Brigade Commander.	1	Brigade Major.
2	Brigade Major.	2	Brigade Signal Officer.
3	Liaison Officer & Signal Officer.	3	Rear Brigade H.Q.
4	Rear Brigade H.Q.	4	Division (2 Lines)
5	Division (2 Lines).	5	Divisional Artillery.
6	Divisional Artillery.	6	Brigade on Right.
7	Brigade on Right.	7	" " Left.
8	Brigade on Left.	8	Forward Exchange (3 Lines).
9	Right Battalion, E J 1.	9	Support Battalion.
10	Left Battalion, E M 2.	10	Machine Gun Company.
11	Reserve Battalion, E J 19.	11	Medical Post TWICKER.
12	No 1 Group 250 Brigade R.F.A.	12	Medical Post FROST HOUSE.
13	No. 2 Group 251 " "		
14	No. 3 " 38 " "		
15	"O" Group Corps H.A.		
16	Machine Gun Company.		

———oOo———

50TH DIVISION.
POSITION CALLS.

50th Divisional H.Q. B Y 5.

LEFT BRIGADE	E C 37.	**RIGHT BRIGADE**	B G 2.

LEFT BATTALION B M 2. **RIGHT BATTALION** B J 8.

Left Coy.   B V 1.   Right Coy   B D 2.
Right " Coy.   B V 3.   Left Coy   B J 10.
Support " Coy.   B V 17.   Support Coy   B J 12.
                              Reserve Coy   B J 14.

RIGHT BATTALION. B J 1. **LEFT BATTALION.** E J 16.

Left Coy.   B V 21.   Right Coy)   E V 2.)
Right Coy.   B V 20.   Left Coy)   E V 2.)
Support Coy.   B J 13.   Support Coy   E J 18.
Reserve Coy.   B J 31.   Reserve Coy   B J 20

SUPPORT BATTALION. B J 19. **SUPPORT BATTALION.** F C 5.

                              Company H.Q.   F C 7.
                                 "   "   B J 22.
                                 "   "   F C 9.
                                 "   "   B J 24.

50TH DIVISIONAL ARTILLERY.
POSITION CALLS.

R.A. H.Q. B Y 3.

No. 1 GROUP.	B G 25.	**No. 3 GROUP.**	B K 27.
A/250	B D 35.	Forward Exchange	B C 27.
B/250	B N 11.	A/119	B C 39.
C/250	B G 7.	B/119	B G 45.
D/250	B G 13.	B/119 (Sect)	B G 5.
D/250 (Single How.)	B G 15.	C/119	B C 41
B/250 -do-	B G 17.	D/119	B C 43.

No. 2 GROUP. B G 13.

Forward Exchange B G 21.
A/251   E G 12
B/251   E M 3.
C/251   B D 34.
D/251   B D 6.

O.P.'s :-
D.12.c.05.70.   B V 27.
D.6.b.45.10.   B V 29.
D.9.d.23.   B K 15.
D.10.d.55.10.   B J 41.
D.17.c.7.4.   B J 45.
D.22.b.90.10.   B J 47.

O.P. EXCHANGE D.10.a.55.10 B J 43.

DESPATCH RIDER LETTER SERVICE
50th DIVISION.

---oOo---

The following will be the times of the D.R.L.S. from this date inclusive :-

A. <u>VIII Corps, Reserve Brigade, etc.</u>

VIII Corps.	Dep.	7.0 a.m.	ˣ11.30 a.m.	3.45 p.m.	8.30 p.m.
BRANDHOEK.		7.30 a.m.	NOON.	4.15 p.m.	9.0 p.m.
VIII Corps H.A.		7.45 a.m.	12.15 p.m.	4.30 p.m.	9.15 p.m.
~~VIII Corps~~					
GOLDFISH CHATEAU.		8.15 a.m.	12.45 p.m.	5.0 p.m.	9.45 p.m.
Left Division		8.45 a.m.	1.15 p.m.	5.30 p.m.	10.15 p.m.
Right Division		9.0 a.m.	1.30 p.m.	5.45 p.m.	10.30 p.m.
GOLDFISH CHATEAU		9.15 a.m.	1.45 p.m.	6.0 p.m.	10.45 p.m.
VIII Corps H.A.		9.45 a.m.	2.15 p.m.	6.30 p.m.	11.15 p.m.
BRANDHOEK		10.0 a.m.	2.30 p.m.	6.45 p.m.	11.30 p.m.
VIII Corps	Arr.	10.30 a.m.	3.0 p.m.	7.15 p.m.	Midnt.

ˣThis run is timed to carry back Intelligence Reports.

B. <u>To Right and Left Brigades.</u>

Leave Div.	Arrive Rear H.Q. Left Brigade.	Arrive Div Runner Post	Arrive Left Brigade (by Runner)	Arrive Right Brigade.
7.30 a.m.	7.45 a.m.	8.15 a.m.	8.45 a.m.	8.30 a.m.
11.0 a.m.	11.15 a.m.	11.45 a.m.	12.15 p.m.	12.0 Noon.
2.0 p.m.	2.15 p.m.	2.45 p.m.	3.15 p.m.	3.0 p.m.
5.0 p.m.	5.15 p.m.	5.45 p.m.	6.15 p.m.	6.0 p.m.
8.0 p.m.	8.15 p.m.	8.45 p.m.	9.15 p.m.	9.0 p.m.

Leave Right Brigade.	Leave Left Brigade.(by Runner).	Leave Div. Runner Post	Leave Rear H.Q. Left Brigade.	Arrive Division
8.45 a.m.	9.0 a.m.	9.45 a.m.	10.0 a.m.	10.15 am
12.15 p.m.	12.30 p.m.	1.15 p.m.	1.30 p.m.	1.45 pm
3.15 p.m.	3.30 p.m.	4.15 p.m.	4.30 p.m.	4.45 pm
6.15 p.m.	6.30 p.m.	7.15 p.m.	7.30 p.m.	7.45 pm
9.15 p.m.	9.30 p.m.	10.15 p.m.	10.30 p.m.	10.45 pm

C. <u>LOCAL SERVICE</u> (Telegrams and D.R.L.S.)

To Support Brigade, C.R.E., A.D.M.S., A.P.M., Town Major, Corps Main Dressing Station, A.P.M. YPRES, Field Coy, R.E., 244 Employment Coy, and other Units in YPRES.

<u>Leave Divn.</u> 7.0 a.m. 9.0 a.m. 11.0 a.m. 2.0 p.m.

4.0 p.m. 6.0 p.m. 8.6 p.m.

D. All letters for despatch by D.R.L.S. will be handed in to Signal Office 15 minutes before the time of departure stated above.

NOTE :- D.R's and Runners must on no account be delayed by Units.

50th Northumbrian Division.

50th DIVISIONAL SIGNAL COMPANY R. E.

MARCH 1918

SECRET.

WAR   DIARY

- of -

50th.(Northumbrian) Divisional Signal Company R.E.

Volume No. 36

March 1918.

Army Form C. 2118.

WAR DIARY
or
INTELLIGENCE SUMMARY.
(Erase heading not required.)

VOL XXXVI

Instructions regarding War Diaries and Intelligence Summaries are contained in F. S. Regs., Part II. and the Staff Manual respectively. Title pages will be prepared in manuscript.

Place	Date	Hour	Summary of Events and Information	Remarks and references to Appendices
WIZERNES.	1918. Mar. 1st. to Mar. 7th. Mar. 8th.		Division in G.H.Q. Reserve, held ready to move at 24 hours notice. O.O. 180 dated 26-2-18. Division entrained for MOREUIL. Company detrained at BO/ES and marched to MOREUIL.	
do.				
MOREUIL.	Mar. 9th.		Office closed at WIZERNES at 6 a.m. and re-opened at MOREUIL same hour.	
HARBONIERES.	Mar. 11th.		Division moved to TROYARD AREA; office closed MOREUIL at 10 a.m. and re-opened HARBONIERES same hour. O.O. 181 dated 10-3-18.	
do.	Mar. 12th. to Mar. 20th.		Lines to 149th. Inf. Bde. at MESIERES, 150th. Inf. Bde. at CAYEUX, and 151st. Inf. Bde. at MARCELAVE, and line to VILLERS BRETONNEUX.	
do. BEAUBETZ)	Mar. 21st.		Division, less Artillery, Field Companies R.E. and Pioneer Battalion allotted to XIXth. Corps. Divisional Headquarters established at BEAUBETZ; Lines to 151st. Inf. Bde. in BEAUBETZ, 150th. Inf. Bde. at HANCOURT, and 149th. Inf. Bde. at THERRY, and line to XIXth. Corps at JATELET.	
BEAUBETZ &) LE MESNIL.)	Mar. 22nd.		Divl. H.Q. moved to LE MESNIL at 2 p.m. Lines to XIXth. Corps at VILLERS CARBONNEL and 149th. Inf. Bde. at THERRY working on permanent routes.	
VILLERS CARBONNEL) FOUCAUCOURT.)	Mar. 23rd.		Moved to VILLERS CARBONNEL AT 8 a.m.; at 2 p.m. Divl. H.Q. ordered to CHAULNES, but position changed on arrival there to FOUCAUCOURT. Line obtained on permanent route to ESTREES for 151st. Inf. Bde. Adv. H.Q. and line laid across country to 149th. Inf. Bde. Adv. H.Q. at point on FAY-ASSEVILLERS road, half a mile northeast of FAY; these lines were joined by cable laid along the ESTREES-FAY road, which enabled communication to be maintained when the permanent route was damaged by shell fire. Line to Corps at "A" Camp. 1000 yards west of FOUCAUCOURT.	
FOUCAUCOURT) to)	Mar. 24th. to Mar. 26th.		Divl. H.Q. moved to "A" Camp at 8 p.m. on 24th. March. Corps having mov'd back to VILLERS BRETONNEUX. Lines to Bdes. and Corps were extended to "A" Camp and a cable line laid back through HERBEVILLE and VAUVILLERS, HARBONIERES, GUILLAUCOURT to MARCELAVE, that being the line on which the Division was to retire. At noon on 25th. March Divl. H.Q. were established at the crossroads one mile south of VAUVILLERS, and at 9 p.m. moved back to MARCELAVE.	

Army Form C. 2118.

WAR DIARY
or
INTELLIGENCE SUMMARY.
(Erase heading not required.)

Instructions regarding War Diaries and Intelligence Summaries are contained in F. S. Regs., Part II. and the Staff Manual respectively. Title pages will be prepared in manuscript.

Place	Date	Hour	Summary of Events and Information	Remarks and references to Appendices
MERICOURT. VILLERS BRETONNEUX.	Mar. 27th.		At 2.30 p.m. Divl. H.Q. were ordered back to VILLERS BRETONNEUX, and Adv. Divl. H.Q. were established at crossroads one mile southwest of CAIX, communication forward being obtained by visual and wireless.	
	do.		CASUALTIES. No. 301461 Cpl. Wood L. Killed in Action. " 198864 Spr. Barber A.G. Killed in Action. " 463187 Spr. Carr L.S. Wounded " 463057 " Curry J.A. do.	
VILLERS BRETONNEUX. HANGARD. SOURDON.	Mar. 28.		Divl. H.Q. moved at 11 a.m. to HAYLAND. Adv. H.Q. remaining at CAIX. Cable detachment were sent out to link up HANGARD with Adv. Divl. H.Q. and 149th. Inf. Bde., but before this could be completed, Divl. H.Q. were ordered to SOURDON and Adv. Divl. H.Q. and 149th. Inf. Bde. were retiring on MORUEIL, where their H.Q. were established beside the same night.	
SOURDON BOVES.	Mar. 29th.		Divl. H.Q. moved to BOVES at noon on the 29th. March. Adv. Divl. H.Q. being fixed at BERTRANCOURT, where communication was established with 20th. and 39th. Divisions and XIXth. Corps by wire, and with 149th. Inf. Bde. at crossroads one mile southwest of DEMUIN by wire and wireless, and by visual from H.Q. of 20th. Division at DOMMARTIN. Corps were also in touch by wireless. Divl. H.Q. at BOVES were in telephone communication with 61st. Division.	
BOVES. SAINS en AMIENOIS.	Mar. 30th.		Divl. H.Q. at 11 a.m. were transferred to SAINS EN AMIENOIS, where communication was obtained with XIXth. Corps and 3rd. Cav. Division.	
SAINS en AMIENOIS.	Mar. 31st.		31st. Division transferred to XIIIth. Corps and H.Q. moved to DOURIEZ. Company staged night 31st. March/1st. April at BOURDON.	O.O. 190 dated 31-3-18.

Graham Adams
Capt. & Adjt.
Major
Comdg. 50th (North'bn.) Divisional Signal Company R.E.

50th Divisional Engineers

50th (Northumbrian) DIVISIONAL SIGNAL COMPANY R.E.

APRIL 1918.

SECRET.

WAR DIARY.

OF

50TH (NBN) DIVISIONAL SIGNAL COMPANY, ROYAL ENGINEERS.

for month of

APRIL 1918.

VOLUME XXXVII.

****

Army Form C. 2118.

WAR DIARY
or
INTELLIGENCE SUMMARY.

Vol. XXXVII

(Erase heading not required.)

Instructions regarding War Diaries and Intelligence Summaries are contained in F. S. Regs., Part II. and the Staff Manual respectively. Title pages will be prepared in manuscript.

Place	Date	Hour	Summary of Events and Information	Remarks and references to Appendices
POUPIEZ	Apl. 1st. to 3rd.		Div. H.Q. at DOURIEZ; cable wagons sent out to establish communication with three Bdes at LIESCOURT, MACHIEL & VILLERS-sur-AUTHIE were withdrawn on receipt of orders for transfer to to First Army.	
BOBECQ	Apl. 4th to 7th.		Division transferred from Fourth to First Army. H.Q. closed at DOURIEZ at 10 a.m. & re-opened at BOBECQ at the same hour. Communication established with XIth Corps at HINGES. 149th. Inf. 191 Bde. at GONNEHEM, 150th. Inf. Bde. at LOCON. 151st. Inf. Bde. at VERDIN les BETHUNE. dated 3.4.18.	O.O.
BOBECQ Ref. map sht. 1/40,000. 36B 30 & 36B	Apl. 7th.		151st. Inf. Bde. transferred to XV Corps and Bde. H.Q. moved to ESTAIRES.	
"	Apl. 8th.		Remainder of Division (less Artillery) transferred to XV Corps. Div. H.Q. closed at BOBECQ at 10 a.m. and opened at WHITE CHATEAU on MERVILLE - LA MOTTE road, K.2.a.5.1 Sheet 36a. at the same hour. Communication established with XV Corps at LA MOTTE. 149th. Inf. Bde. dated 7.4.18 at LES LAURIERS. 150th. Inf. Bde. at DOULIEU, and 151st. Inf. Bde. at ESTAIRES.	O.O. 193
MERVILLE	Apl. 9th.		151st. Inf. Bde. was to relieve the 6th. Portuguese Bde. at LES HUITES MAISONS. 150th. Inf. Bde. moved to ESTAIRES and LA COROUE. 50th. Division was to relieve 2nd Portuguese Division at LESTREM at 10 a.m. on 10th. April, but enemy attack began in early morning of 10th. April and relief was never completed. CASUALTIES. 40032 Spr. Edwards J.E. Wounded. 46151 L/C. Houliston W.H. -do-. 46309 Spr. Hollamby J.P. -do-.	
MERVILLE	Apl. 10th.		151st. Inf. Bde. H.Q. remained at ESTAIRES and communication was established by line on permanent route, extended by poled cable and buried cable. 150th. Inf. Bde. moved to TROU BAYARD, north of ESTAIRES and a similar line was obtained. 149th. Inf. Bde. opened at CHAPELLE DUVELLE and two lines were used from the WHITE CHATEAU one being permanent as far as ROBERMETZ then cable over the ground. Each Bde. had a Wireless Set which obtained and kept communication with the Division throughout, Wireless being used on occasions to send operation orders in clear in emergency.	

Army Form C. 2118.

WAR DIARY
or
INTELLIGENCE SUMMARY.
(Erase heading not required.)

Instructions regarding War Diaries and Intelligence Summaries are contained in F. S. Regs., Part II. and the Staff Manual respectively. Title pages will be prepared in manuscript.

Place	Date	Hour	Summary of Events and Information	Remarks and references to Appendices
MERVILLE.	Apl. 11.		Early in the morning H.Q., 149th. & 150th. Inf. Bdes. moved to L.12.c. communication being obtained by extending the two lines between Division and BOULIEU, and 151st. Inf. Bde. moved to CHAPELLE DUVELLE, taking over 149th. Bde. line to Division. One cable line was laid from Division to BOULIEU and 149th. & 150th. Bdes. retired on this line, the first step being VIEUX MOULIN in NEUF BERQUIN. 151st. Inf. Bde. moved back to ROBERMETZ along the cable line.	
			In the afternoon all line was traced from LE HAUTE DUC Estaminet in K.1.d. (to which place Division H.Q. had moved after being heavily shelled in the WHITE CHATEAU) to NEUF BERQUIN via VIERHOUCK and were kept in communication continuously by telephone. Wireless communication was also maintained throughout the day from the Bdes. to Division.	
	CASUALTIES.		No. 463072 M/S. Cpl. Morow F. Wounded.	
LA MOTTE.	Apl. 12.		Early in the morning Advanced Div. H.Q. moved back to LA MOTTE Chateau, Rear H.Q. having meantime moved to THIENNES. Orders were issued for 149th. & 151st. Inf. Bdes. to co-operate in the LA MOTTE Chateau Grounds at night after relief by the 5th. Division. 149th. Inf. Bde. H.Q. were out of touch with Division and were working under the 29th. Division on our left.	
	CASUALTIES.		No. 463196 a/Cpl. Turnbull J. Killed in Action.	
			" 463191 a2/Cpl. Johnstone J.W. -do-	
			" 463296 W/O. Carr T. Wounded.	
			" 463204 " Henderson T. -do-	
			" 424078 Spr. Steven G. -do-	
			" 56617 a2/Cpl. Bleakley D. -do-	
			" 463091 Spr. Horner E.B. Shell Shock	
			" 267289 Pte. Coulson H.B. 6th. North'd. Fus. } Killed in Action.	Attached Div'l. Power Buzzer Squad.
			" 240442 " Hollingsworth R. 4th. Yorks. Regt. }	
			" 300704 " Graham R. 8th. D.L.I. Killed in Action.	
			" 300450 " Dobson F. 8th. D.L.I. Missing.	
			" 250921 " Blakey J. 6th. D.L.I. -do-	
			" 314425 " Metcalfe G. 6th. North'd. Fus. -do-	
			" 20147 " Dawson F. 4th. E. Yorks. Regt. -do-	

Army Form C. 2118.

WAR DIARY
or
INTELLIGENCE SUMMARY.
(Erase heading not required.)

Instructions regarding War Diaries and Intelligence Summaries are contained in F. S. Regs., Part II. and the Staff Manual respectively. Title pages will be prepared in manuscript.

Place	Date	Hour	Summary of Events and Information	Remarks and references to Appendices
J.3.d.9.7. West of LA MOTTE.	Apl. 13th.	to 1 p.m.	After concentration at LA MOTTE, Advanced Divl. H.Q. were established at J.3.d.9.7. where the Inf. Bdes. H.Q. were also fixed. The division was then under orders of 5th. Division. H.Q. at THIENNES. Rear H.Q. at THIENNES. Wireless communication was and two lines laid by alternative routes to J.3.d.9.7. Wireless communication was also established between Rear and Adv. H.Q. and between Rear H.Q. and Corps. A line was also laid to WITTES to which place near Div. H.Q. moved, a small office being opened there.	
ROQUETOIRE.	Apl. 16th.	to 19th.	Divl. H.Q. moved from WITTES and THIENNES to ROQUETOIRE, office closing at former at noon and re-opening at ROQUETOIRE at the same hour. A line was laid to pick up an open wire that ran nearly into WITTES, the latter being extended to 151st. Inf. Bde. 150th. Inf. Bde. were put into communication with Division through 151st. Inf. Bde. by diverting the WITTES-THIENNES line to LA LACQUE. 149th. Inf. Bde. H.Q. were established in MAMETZ and a line was laid from ROQUETOIRE via WARNE, where 75th. D.L.I. H.Q. were, to MAMETZ, both H.Q. being on the same line.	
CASUALTIES.	18th.		No. 311124 a/Sergt. Mennell J.H. Wounded. 480799 Spr. Paul C. -do-.	
AIRE.	Apl. 20th. to 26th.		Divl. H.Q. moved to AIRE, the ROQUETOIRE office closing at 11.30 a.m. and AIRE opening at the same hour. A line was laid to AIRE Exchange for temporary communication with Corps and the three Bdes. through ROQUETOIRE Exchange. A line to LA LACQUE was extended to 150th. Inf. Bde. and 151st. Bde. communication established that way in addition to the line through ROQUETOIRE. Another line was laid to WARNE to pick 149th. Bde. and the 7th. D.L.I. and later a direct line to Corps was obtained and a D.C. set installed. AIRE Exchange being intermediate on the line.	
AIRE. FERE-en-TARDENOIS SOISSONS Ref. map SOISSONS 30N. 1/100,000.	Apl. 26th 27th		Division commenced entraining for FERE-e-TARDENOIS Area. Divl. H.Q. closing at AIRE at 3.30 p.m on 27th. Apl. and opening at ARCIS-le-PONSART at 5 p.m. on Apl. 28th. Lines were first obtained through the French Civil Exchanges and then laid to 149th. Bde. at COULONGES, 150th. Bde. at COUPVILLE and 151st. Bde. in ARCIS-le-PONSART.	
AWARDS.			Capt. H.M.S. Porter R.G.A., O.I/C Signals 50th. Divn. Arty. awarded M.C. 15-4-18, while under the XIXth. Corps.	

Signed [illegible] Major
Comdg. 50th (North bn.) Divisional Signal Company R.E.

WAR DIARY

OF

50TH (NORTHUMBRIAN) DIVISIONAL SIGNAL COMPANY,

ROYAL ENGINEERS.

VOLUME XXXVIII.

****

May, 1918.

VOL XXXVIII

WAR DIARY of 50 DIVISIONAL SIGNAL COMPANY

INTELLIGENCE SUMMARY

(Erase heading not required.)

Instructions regarding War Diaries and Intelligence Summaries are contained in F.S. Regs., Part II. and the Staff Manual respectively. Title pages will be prepared in manuscript.

Place	Date	Hour	Summary of Events and Information	Remarks and references to Appendices
ARCIS-LE-PONSART	1918 May 1 to May 5		On arrival, lines to IX Corps at FERE-EN-TARDENOIS, 1HQ Inf Bde at COULONGES, and 150 Bde at COURVILLE were obtained through French Buried Exchange. 151 Bde was in ARCIS-LE-PONSART. Lines were laid by cable wagon to COURVILLE, COULONGES, and to CRUGNY, the latter being for CRA and MG Bn. The communications of 51st French Division (HQ VAILLY) were reconnoitred as it was thought the Division was relieving there, but orders were cancelled and lines of 21st French Divn (HQ BEAURIEUX) were gone over, and eventually, at 10 am on 5th, taken over. The French communications, including Wireless and Power Buzzer, Visual and Pigeons	SHEET No. 22 SOISSONS
BEAURIEUX	May 5		were taken over as they stood, but the Divl HQ of the French Divn had been	
ROMAIN	May 5 to 31		at ROUCY. Lines on the various buried systems were obtained, but were	
BREUIL-sur-VESLE			not very satisfactory as the lines were old, and cable lines were	
BRANSCOURT			laid to 150 and 1HQ Inf Bdes (PC CALVAIRE) (permanent line to BRABANT was extended)	
FAVEROLLE			by cable to 151 Bde at PC EVREUX and alternating lines in the buried were	
CUISLES			used for buzzer work. The Sector was very quiet until the morning of the	
IGNY LE JARD			27 May when the attack by the enemy on the CHEMIN DES DAMES began. The	
LE BRUIL			bombardment opened at 1 am and is reported to have been the heaviest on record.	
VERT LA GRAVELLES				

WAR DIARY or INTELLIGENCE SUMMARY

Army Form C. 2118.

(Erase heading not required.)

Place	Date	Hour	Summary of Events and Information	Remarks and references to Appendices
BEAUVIEUX	1918 May 5		All Headquarters received great attention, including gas shell, and respirators were worn for several hours even at Divl H.Q. Warning of the impending attack having been received on the evening of the 26 May, the Divl Signal Office was moved to a dugout under CHATEAU HANATEAU and all lines led into it. All overland lines were cut within an hour of the opening of the bombardment and communication maintained by the faulty buried lines. 151 Bde H.Q. was very heavily shelled and it was found impossible, after many attempts, to maintain the line from the Signal Office at the Bngde to the Bd Test Box on its buried route between BEAUVIEUX and CALVAIRE where the lines came off. Touch was lost with this Bde, was lost about 11am and was never restored, runners and despatch riders being used. Through BEAUVIEUX CENTRALE and CAMP OUEST telephone communication was maintained to 150 Bde at LA HUTTE and through them to 149 Bde at CALVAIRE until both H.Q. retired this circuit being wholly buried. 150 Bde moved to P.C. TERRASSE at 1.30am but apparently the enemy reached that point first, as nothing further was heard of this Bde H.Q. 151 Bde had orders to proceed to the same	
ROMAIN	May 31			
BREUIL s/VESLE				
BRANSCOURT				
FAVEROLLE				
CUISLES				
IGNY-LE-JARD				
LE BRUIL				
VERT-LA-GRAVELE				

Army Form C. 2118.

WAR DIARY
or
INTELLIGENCE SUMMARY.
(Erase heading not required.)

Instructions regarding War Diaries and Intelligence Summaries are contained in F. S. Regs., Part II. and the Staff Manual respectively. Title pages will be prepared in manuscript.

Place	Date	Hour	Summary of Events and Information	Remarks and references to Appendices
	1918			
BEAURIEUX	May 5		place, but to move on BEAURIEUX and on reaching the latter they were	
ROMAIN	May 31		informed that the enemy was already in possession of P.C. TERRASSE.	
BREUIL S/VESLE			HQ Bde HQ. moved to CHAUDARDES and the original cable line was	
BRANSCOURT			diverted there, but soon after the Bde retired across the AISNE and	
FAVEROLLE			communication to the Bdes ceased when the Bde HQ ceased to function	
CUISLES			as such, which happened about 10 am at which hour the line was withdrawn	
IGNY LE JARD			to the south side of the AISNE. The 7th Inf Bde 25th Divisione then came	
LE BRUIL			under the orders of 50th Div. and established HQ at BEAUREGARDE FARM	
VERT LA GRAVELLE			when the GOC 50 Div was also established. About 3pm HQ 50 Div moved	
			back to ROMAIN and 7th Bde to dugouts on the road between ROMAIN	
			and BEAUREGARDE FARM where a cable line was run out to them from	
			ROMAIN, to which place IX Corps had also laid a cable line. At 5 pm	
			Div HQ moved back to BREUIL sur VESLE and 7th Bde to ROMAIN. The line from	
			Corps was split at BREUIL giving communication to Corps and the 7th Bde, the	
			line forward of ROMAIN being used by the Bde to one of its Battalions.	
			At 3 am on the 28th Div HQ moved to BRANSCOURT where 8 Div HQ was	

BEAUREUX	1918
ROMAIN	May 5
BREVIL S/VESLE	to
BRANSCOURT	May 31
FAVEROLLE	
CUISLES	
IGNY LE JARD	
LE BRUIL	
VERT LA GRAVELLE	

already established and a line was put on 8th Div Exchange to obtain communication with Corps. At 9.30 am Div HQ moved to FAVEROLLE. 8th Div HQ were also there and IX Corps ran two lines to them. A line was put in to 8 Div, who had also communication with 74th Bde. At 8.30 pm. command of 74th Bde passed to 8 Div. and 50 Div H.Q. moved to LHERY but only for two hours, after which they moved to CUISLES CHATEAU. At 2 pm. 29th May. Div. Rear H.Q. was established at the FARM half a mile south of CHATILLON and a line laid from there to CUISLES CHATEAU which remained Advd Divl. HQ. A tap was also taken from a line laid to IX Corps which passed near the farm. At 10 am. on the 30th May Div. H.Q. moved to IGNY LE JARD where an office was established for despatch work only; and at 4.30 pm. H.Q. again moved to LE BRUIL when an office was also opened for despatch work. At 10 am on the 31st May Div. H.Q. was opened at VERT LA GRAVELLE. IX Corps had moved to VERTUS and communication with them was established by putting a line on the Civil Exchange at VERT, Corps being on to VERTUS Civil Exchange.

No Wireless messages were received on the 27th May during the attack. 151 Bde & the Bde with which communication was lost at 1 am, were subjected to such heavy shelling that

	1918	
BEAURIEUX	May 5	It is scarcely possible the aerials could have been maintained.
ROMAIN	"	No messages were received by Pigeon and it is not known
BREUIL S/VESLE	May 31	what became of the birds which had been issued to the
BRANSCOURT		Brigades. All the Wireless personnel and equipment are
FAVEROLLE		missing.
CUISLES		The retirement of Divl HQ. from BEAURIEUX was very
IGNY LE JARD		sudden and the Electric Light Lorry with all Orderly Room papers,
LE BRUIL		and the 3 ton Lorry, with officers kits and the contents of the
VERT LA GRAVELLE		C.Q.M.S. stores must have been destroyed or captured. Efforts
		were made to destroy the papers and instruments in the Signal
		Office, but the N.C.O. detailed for this work is Missing and
		it is not known how far the efforts were successful.

Casualties sustained were as follows:-

Officers Lt. D. V. L. Braddock 9th DLI   i/c Wireless   Missing
         Lt. Lt. W. J. Hunter   R.E.   Missing
         Lt.   S. G. Wood   " 11 B.   No 5 Section   Wounded
         Lt.   C. C. Kennedy   R.E.   No. 4 Section Missing
         Lt.   S. A. Brown   Queens   No. 3 Section Wounded
         Lt. Lt. E. B. Judliffe R.F.A.   No. 2 Section Missing
                                          251 Bde Subsection Missing

O.R. 85. Permanently attached O.R. 49   Total 6 Officers 134 O.R.

AHHBagnall
mjr

50 DIVISIONAL SIGNAL COMPANY R.E.

CIRCUITS IN USE AT BEAURIEUX AT 12.30 am, 27th May 1918.

CIRCUIT	NATURE of CIRCUIT	LIFE of CIRCUIT
IX CORPS LINE No 1	Permanent Route	Held throughout
do. do. No 2	Permanent Route	Held throughout
do. do. No 3	Permanent Route	Held throughout
149 INF BDE LINE No. 1	Cable	Held within ½ hour of bombardment opening
do. do. No. 2	Permanent to BRABANT, Buried to CALVAIRE	do.
150 INF BDE No. 1	Cable	Held throughout
do. No. 2	Buried	Cut after ½ an hour of bombardment opening
151 INF BDE No. 1	Permanent Route to BRABANT, Cable to Bde.	Held till H.Q. Trench
do. No. 2	Buried, 200 yds cable from Test Box to Bde.	Held till Divn moved
8 DIVN (RIGHT)	Buried	Held till Dn moved
22 (French) DIVN (LEFT)	Buried	Held throughout
BEAURIEUX Army Exchange	Buried	Held throughout
CAMP OUEST do.	Buried	Held within the hour of bombardment opening
MOULIN ROUGE do.	Permanent Route	do.
BRABANT	Permanent Route	
150 Bde Rear HQ, MAIZY	Buried	Held throughout
151 Bde do., MUSCOURT.	Buried to MAIZY, cable to Bde.	Cut before 5 am.
C.R.A.	Buried	Held throughout.

CASUALTIES
27-5-18

SIGNAL SCHOOL STAFF

No	Rank	Name	Unit	Remarks
	MISSING			
	Private	Brown Chas	6 NF	
	"	Baker E.J.	5 DLI	
	"	James T.F.	244 Bns N 6	
	"	Holland G.A.	-do-	
224186	"	Bassett J	-do-	
	WOUNDED (hung Gas)			
	Sergt	Wardlaw H.J.	"E" Corps Signal Co.	

CASUALTIES 27-5-18 POWER BUZZER SQUAD.

No	Rank	Name	Unit	Remarks
MISSING				
	Private	Jessup	5 NF	
	"	Burridge	8 D.L.I.	
	"	David	6 NF	
	"	Wilkinson	4/6 Yorks	
	"	Searle	5 Yorks	
	"	Gee	6 D.L.I.	
	"	Seed	5 Yorks	
200810	"	Parkin R.	5 D.L.I.	
	"	Redford	4 NF	
	"	Worcup	4/6 Yorks	
	"	Darby	5 NF	
	"	Allott	6 NF	
	"	Overment	4 Yorks	
	"	Bradford	4 NF	
	"	Lumley	5 York	
200443	"	Cattermole H.	5 D.L.I.	
	"	Wilkinson	D.L.I. ?6th	
	"	Baldwin	5 Yorks	
	"	Davies	5 "	
	"	Carter	4 "	
	"	Carmody	?6th D.L.I.	
202800	"	Barron J	6th D.L.I.	
	"	Ambler	4 NF	
	"	Gillingham	4 NF	
	"	Everett	5 NF	
	"	Hodgetts	5 Yorks	
	"	Gallagher	?6th D.L.I.	
KILLED				
241812	Private	Marche H.B.	5 NF	

CASUALTIES
27.5.18

251 Brigade
R.F.A.
Sub-Section

No	Rank	Name	Unit	Remarks
		Missing		
	2/Lieut	E.D. Judhope	R.F.A.	
475930	2/Corpl	Vare C	R.E.	
475925	Sapper	Anderson C	"	
475933	"	Dobson W	"	
475929	"	Beadnell R	"	
475931	"	Dale J	"	
471931	Corpl	Bainbridge J	"	
471932	Sapper	Young F	"	
471933	"	Dubb W	"	
221790	Pioneer	Webber C.J.	"	
142964	Sapper	Shatters K.J.	"	
237211	Pioneer	Morgan C	"	
127913	Sapper	Sagg H	"	
463092	"	Schooler A	"	
129919	"	Griffiths G.R.	"	
69130	"	Davenport R.J.	"	

CASUALTIES
27.5.18

260 Brigade
R.F.A.
Sub Section.

No	Rank	Name	Unit	Remarks
MISSING				
474095	Sapper	Kerr D.	RE	
406088	"	Scott J.A.	"	
497932	Pioneer	Mapes O.	"	
WOUNDED				
463236	Sapper	Harman J.J.	"	
ACCIDENTALLY INJURED				
45086	A/Sergt	Daniels C.C.	"	

CASUALTIES 27.5.18 — HEAD QUARTERS AND No 1 SECTION

No	Rank	Name	Unit	Remarks
		INFANTRY ATTACHED		
	Missing			
	Private	Clark J.O.	9th D.L.I.	(Batman)
	"	Whitehead Wb.	9th RScots	"
	L/C	Marsh	7 D.L.I.	"
	Private	Hudson J.	5 NF	"
	"	Powell E.	5 D.L.I.	"
	"	Best J.	6 D.L.I.	Orderly
		A.S.C., MT ATTACHED		
	Missing			
	Private	Mathews J.M.		
	"	Gush P.A.		

Head Quarters & No 1 Section CASUALTIES (Including Wireless)
27.5.18

No	Rank	Name	Unit	Remarks
	MISSING			
	Lieut	D.V.L. Craddock	9th D.W.	Off i/c Wireless
463058	C.Q.M.S.	Charlton L.	R.E.	
463054	L/C	Davison W.R.	"	
463065	Sapper	Worrall R.	"	? Wounded
78644	"	McCarthy W	"	
463158	"	Munro W	"	
482341	"	Vicker W	"	
463165	"	Williams J.H.	"	
127698	Pioneer	Boyd W	"	
463015	Sergt	Bartram C	"	
281754	Sapper	Sowton C.R.	"	Dvr attached No 3 Section
31712	Sergt	Harvey R.J.	"	
463083	L/C (W)	Ness W.R.	"	
198157	L/C	Rollason H	"	
126912	Sapper	Barham E.G.	"	
172565	"	Carter G.E.	"	
134209	"	Cole G.W.	"	
232009	"	Finlayson J.A.	"	
198865	L/C	Lewis F	"	
357545	"	Richardson J.A.	"	
126425	"	Stebbins G.H.	"	
254475	"	Warburton E.H.	"	
582399	"	Alwynne C	"	
316743	Pioneer	Dutton S.E.	"	
463146	Driver	Rushforth W.J.	"	
	L/C	West	"	
	2/Corpl	Blakeley D.	"	
	WOUNDED AND MISSING			
463097 (?)	Sapper	Laws R.H.	"	
	WOUNDED			
463038	Corpl	Sadler H.A.	"	Rejoined 2.6.18
502232	Sapper	Hammond J	"	
	SICK TO HOSPITAL			
255127	Pioneer	Cole C.C.	"	
42087	Sapper	Littlewood A.J.	"	1.6.18

CASUALTIES   N° 2 SECTION
27.5.18

N°	Rank	Name	Unit	Remarks
MISSING				
302114	Pioneer	Wilcock A.	RE	
WOUNDED				
	Lieut	D.A. Brown	1/W Surreys	
463207	Corpl	Lawton W.	RE	Rejoined 29.5.18
463192	Sapper	Pilson W	"	
463211	"	Kirby H	"	
GASSED				
463287	Sapper	Parker W	RE	

INFANTRY ATTACHED

MISSING				
242296	Private	Keighley W.B.	5 NF	
GASSED				
240402	Private	McDonald J	6 NF	
262557	"	Thompson J	6 NF	
265696	"	Robbie F.A.	6 NF	

N°	Rank	Name	Unit	Remarks
MISSING				

CASUALTIES No 3
27.5.18 SECTION

No	Rank	Name	Unit	Remarks
MISSING				
	2/Lieut	C.A. Kennedy	R.E.	
463118	Sergt	Jenkins W.E.	"	
463140	L/C	Kilsington C.H.	"	
463215	Pioneer	Edwards B.	"	
463237	Sapper	Halse C.	"	
463208	"	Lazenby C.	"	
463234	"	Munro H.	"	
463153	"	Laverick J.C.	"	
496890	"	Schuttrbruck J.H.G.	"	
475959	Pioneer	Waters	"	
473936	"	Robson C.P.	"	
WOUNDED AND MISSING				
463016	2/Cpl	Scott R.G.	"	
		INFANTRY ATTACHED		
MISSING				
300342	Private	Harrison W.	4th East Yorks
29463	"	Thompson J.W.	-do-	
200567	"	Jackson R.	"	
200528	"	Cherry J.	4th Yorks	
23968	"	Ferguson J.	"	
203034	"	King C.	"	
240213	"	Knaggs J.	5 Yorks	
240370	"	Catlin H.	"	
19347	"	Johnson U.	"	
240859	"	Jackson J.W.	"	
WOUNDED AND MISSING				
200919	Private	Pearson G.H.	4th E Yorks	
WOUNDED				
205198	Private	Longhton C.	5 Yorks	

CASUALTIES
27-5-18

Nº 4 SECTION

Nº	Rank	Name	Unit	Remarks
WOUNDED				
463109	Sergt	Pringle L	T.E.	
463176	Corpl	Blenkinsopp W	"	
GASSED (Enemy Shell)				
	Lieut	A.G. Wood M.C.	7th N.F.	
INFANTRY ATTACHED				
MISSING				
200135	Private	Hobday H	5 D.L.I.	
WOUNDED, believed Prisoner of War				
200327	Private	Hancock L	5 D.L.I.	
WOUNDED				
300327	Private	Barrett J	8 D.L.I.	
SICK TO HOSPITAL				
300707	Private	Gibbons J.W.	8 D.L.I.	

CASUALTIES
27.5.18

No 5 SECTION

No	Rank	Name	Unit	Remarks
MISSING				
	Lieut	W.J. Hunter	R.E.	
275630	Private	Musgrave M.O.	7 D.W.	x
267305		Thompson G.	6 N.F.	x
WOUNDED, believed Prisoner of WAR				
20319	Private	Clarke A.	A&Yorks	x

x. All three men in process of being transferred to the R.E. Signal Service.

No	Rank	Name	Unit	Remarks

SECRET.

WAR DIARY

OF

50TH (NORTHUMBRIAN) DIVISIONAL SIGNAL COMPANY,

ROYAL ENGINEERS.

VOLUME. XXXIX.

June, 1918.

JUNE 1918   VOL XXIX

WAR DIARY 50 DIVISIONAL SIGNAL Coy Army Form C. 2118.

INTELLIGENCE SUMMARY.

Place	Date	Hour	Summary of Events and Information	Remarks and references to Appendices
VERT-LA-GRAVELLE (MARNE)	1918 June 1 to June 8		Fine to IX Corps through VERTUS exchange. Visual training and riding drill carried out daily	
MONTGIVROUX CHATEAU (MONDEMENT)	June 9 to June 17		at FERE CHAMPENOISE. Fine to IX Corps through 25 Div at ALLEMANT. Fine to BROYES through 149 Inf Bde in that village. Lines laid from 149 Inf Bde to 150 and 151 Inf Bdes who were also in BROYES. Special DR at 100am daily to Benfroit Bde which was in the line near BLIGNY under orders of 19 DIV. Visual training continued. Combined Bde Section made up of elements of 150 and 151 Bde Sections sent up on 4 inst. together with cable detachment under Lt. Odell to 19th DIV. Visual training continued.	
LA NOUE	June 14 to June 30		Moved to LA NOUE. Fine to IX Corps at FERE CHAMPENOISE. Lines laid to ESTERNAY Bird Exchange (for Corps), to LACHY for CRA and from RA Exchange to BROYES for 149 and 151 Inf Bde and to CHAPTON CHATEAU for	

WAR DIARY
or
INTELLIGENCE SUMMARY.
(Erase heading not required.)

Place	Date	Hour	Summary of Events and Information	Remarks and references to Appendices
LA NOUE	1915 June 19th to June 30		Machine gun Battalion, to MOEURS for 150 Inf Bde. Bonfoeuits Bde rejoined on 19th June and Lt Odell with cable detachment on same day. On 21st June new Bonfoeuite Bde section was formed chiefly of 149 Bd Section and joined Bonfoeuite Bde at BROYES under Lt Barnard. Elements of 150 and 151 Bdes sent to Artillery to complete 251 Bde sub section and R.A. H.Qrs detachment. No 5 Section sent out to Machine Gun Battalion. Wireless Section and cable detachment joined from 25 Div. and Brigade section came with Bonfoeuits Bde from 25 DIV. No. 3 Detachment sent to O/C Div Arty Signals. On the 25th June, Lt Odell with 2 Cable Detachments proceeded to IGNY-LE-JARD with a view to taking over from 8th (Cavalry) Div. On the 26th inst, orders for take over were cancelled and Lt Odell ordered to return with cable detachments. Lines to ESTERNAY and MOEURS had been tested in and lines to MOEURS was re laid on the 2nd inst. Warning Order for return to British zone was	

WAR DIARY
or
INTELLIGENCE SUMMARY.
(Erase heading not required.)

Army Form

Instructions regarding War Diaries and Intelligence Summaries are contained in F. S. Regs., Part II. and the Staff Manual respectively. Title pages will be prepared in manuscript.

Place	Date	Hour	Summary of Events and Information	Remarks and references to Appendices
	1918			
LA NOUE	June 1 to June 30		received entrainment to begin on 2nd July.	
			Honours and Awards	
			1918	
			June 5 Bar to MM	
			463129 Cpl Wilson, R. 28th June MM	
			163066 T/Bpl Scott, RE. MM 218754 - Brown, G.R. 463193 Cpl Piloon, W.	
			163118 Sgt Jenkins, W.E. MM 463269 - Hales, G. 463129 Sgt Bingley, I.	
			MM 20 June 3rd June 1918	
			M.M. M.C.	
			463017 W/C BM Morley, B. 463293 Boon Sgt Pattinson, F.H.	
			31712 Bpl Gorery, R.I. 463016 Sgt Mitcheson, G.A.G. Capt L.G. Adam	
			161606 MCBpl Halley, W. 463055 Pnr Crowley, W.M. Lieut W.R. Stewart	
			32228 Sgt Birmingham, J. 22nd June MM MSM	
			463113 - Bright, H.M. 532214 Sgt Roberts, G.W. 463058 CQMS	
			463046 Cpl Watt, J.B. 221786 W/Cpl Pearce, S.E. Sharlton, I.	
			463244 W/Cpl Smith, P.Q. 182080 L. Bowen, A.I.	
			126913 Sgt. Barham, E.G.	
			56617 T/Bpl Bleakly, D.	

Sgd W.H. Brigmon Major
Cmdg 52nd Div Signal Co A.I.F.

A6915 Wt. W1442/M1160 350,000 12/16 D.D.&I. Forms/C./2118/14.

50th DIVL. COMMUNICATIONS
Artillery Lines to Brigades
Feb 1917

Reference
- Buried Cable
- Overhead
- Poled
- Airline
- Exchange Phone
- Junction
- Buzzer

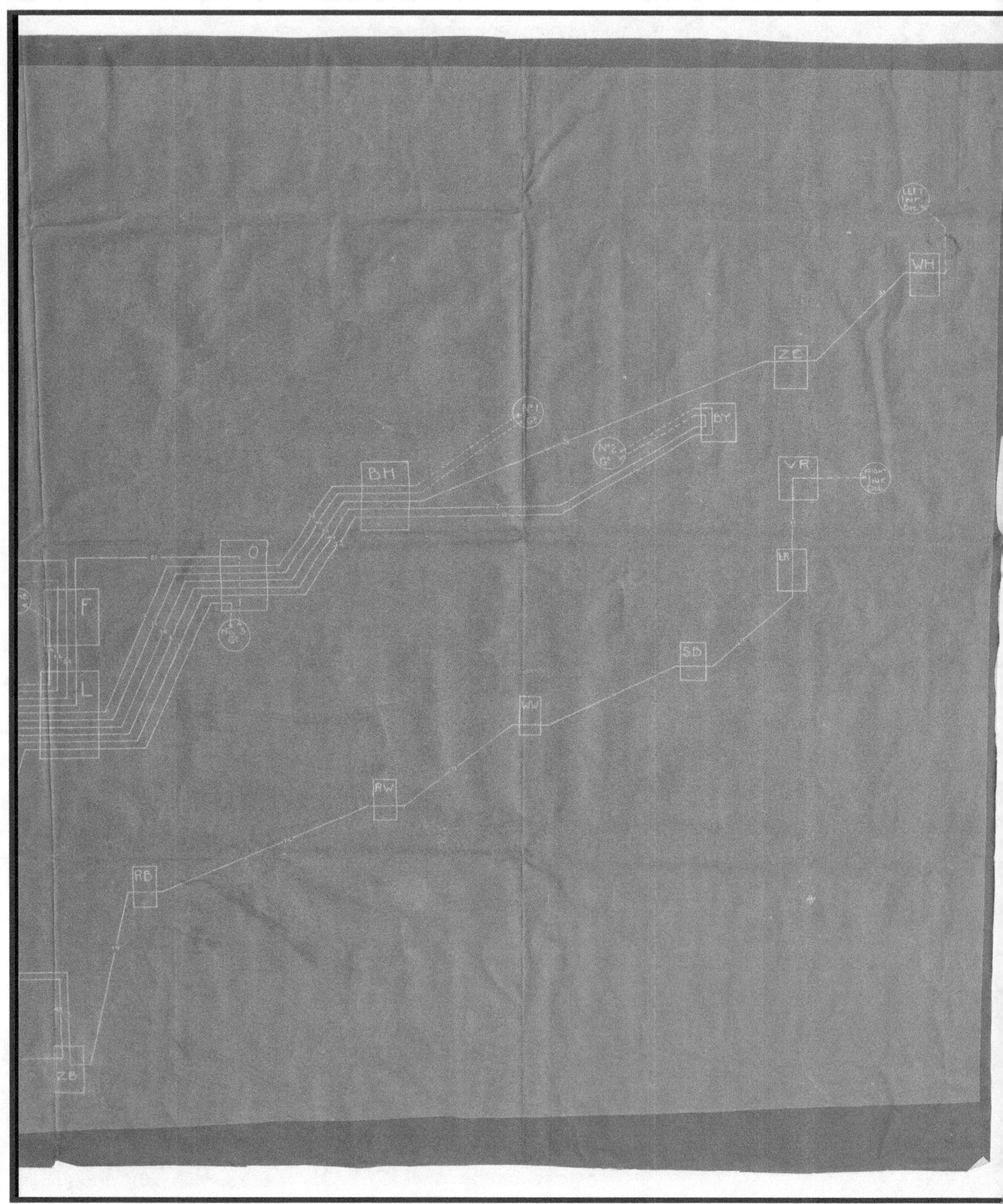

50th Divl. Communications
Left Infantry Bde.
Feb. 2/16

Reference
Metallic Route shewn
Ladder "
Buried "

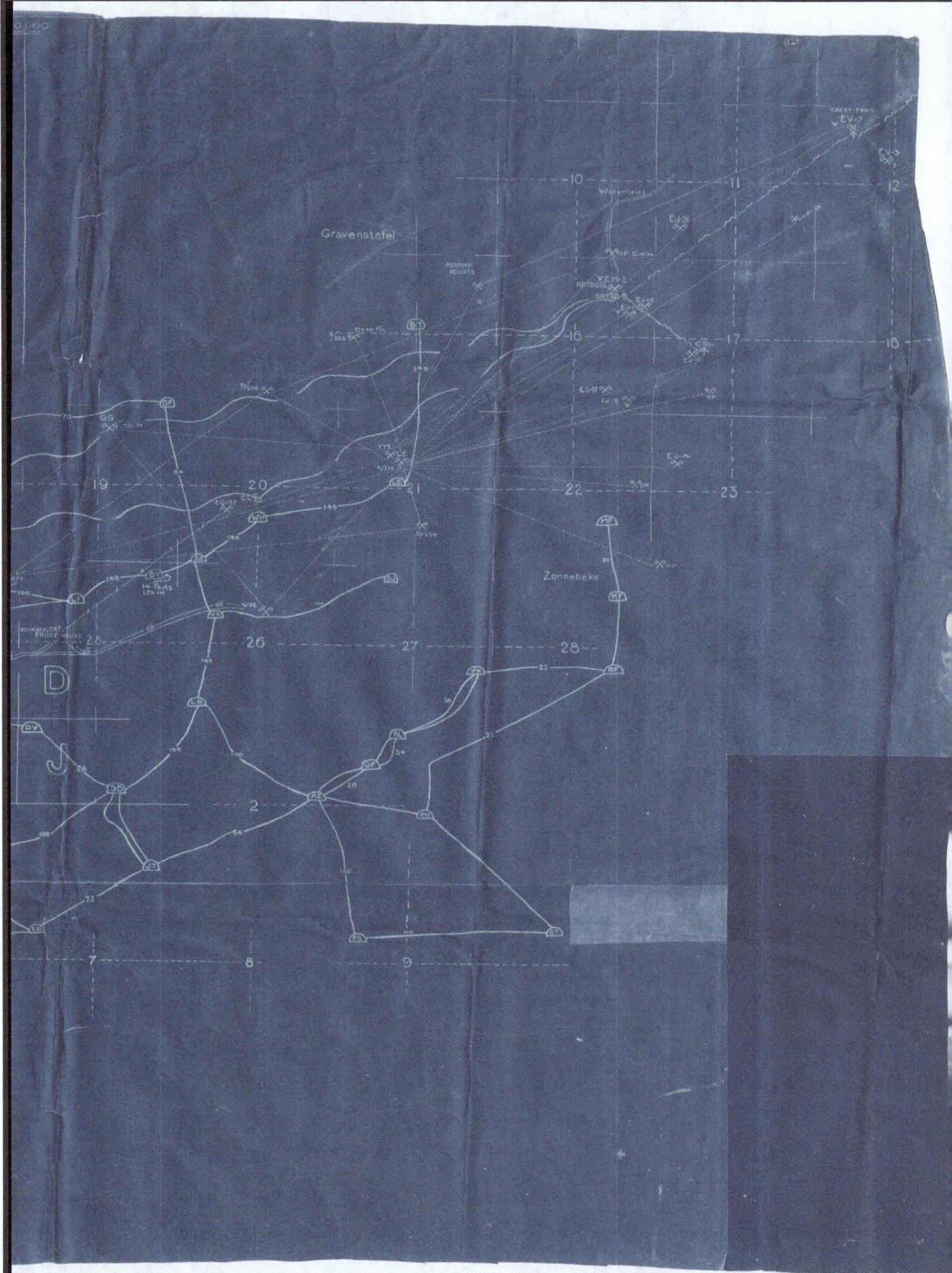

50 D Signal

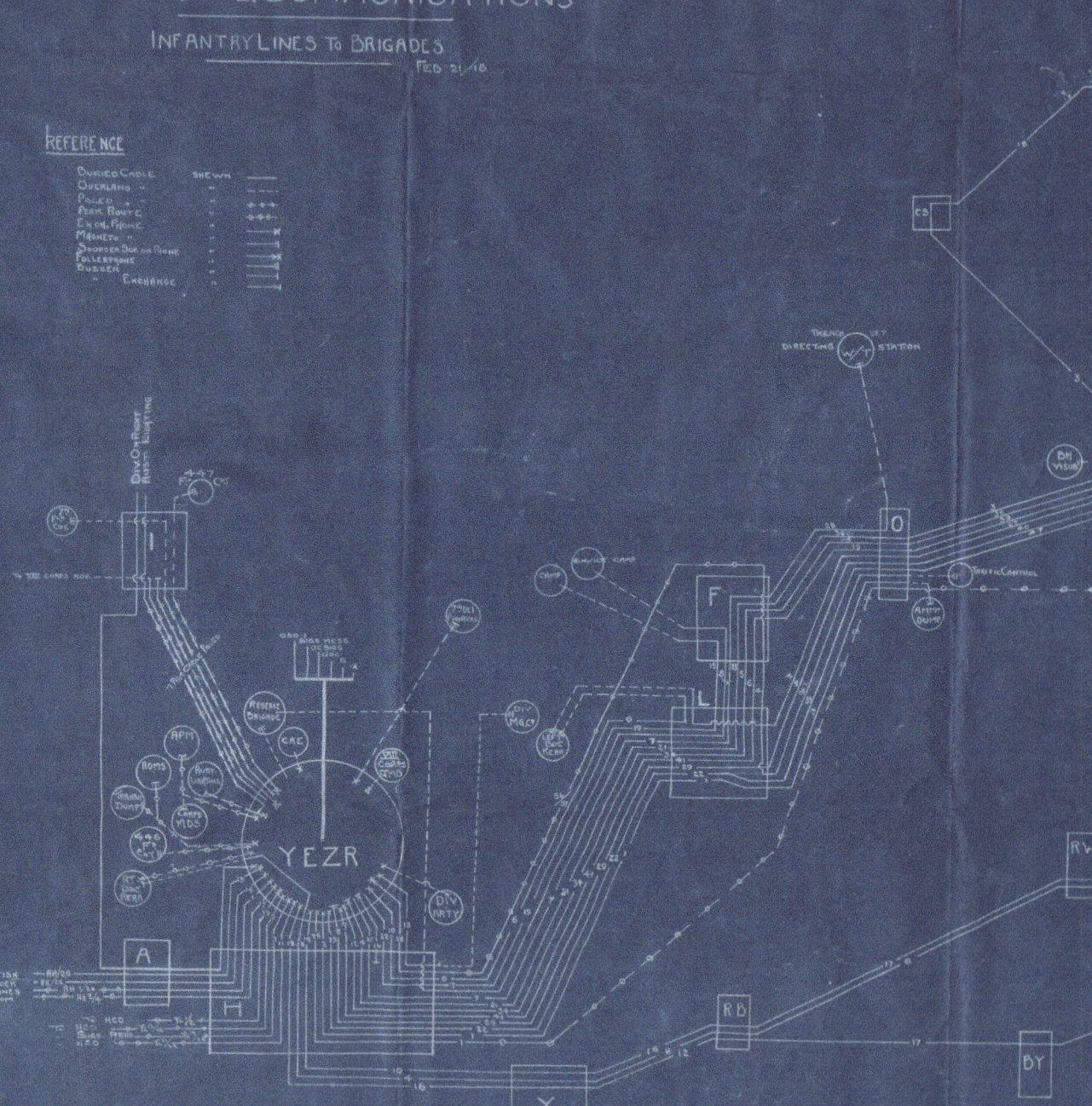

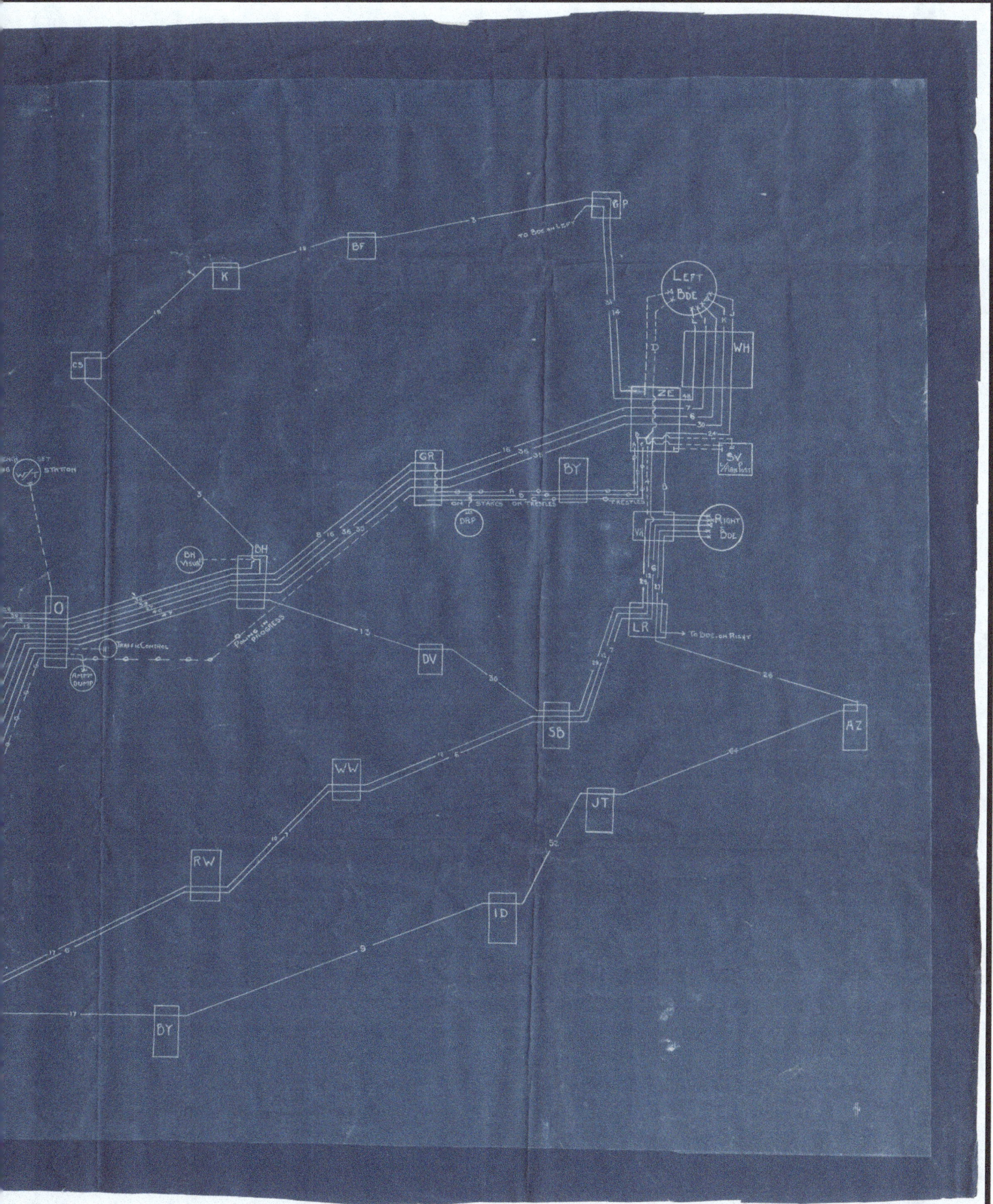

SECRET.

WAR DIARY

OF

50TH (NORTHUMBRIAN) DIVISIONAL SIGNAL COMPANY,
ROYAL ENGINEERS.

VOLUME XL.

******

JULY, 1918.

VOL. XL.

Army Form C. 2118.

WAR DIARY
50 DIVISIONAL SIGNAL COY RE
INTELLIGENCE SUMMARY.

(Erase heading not required.)

Place	Date	Hour	Summary of Events and Information	Remarks and references to Appendices
	1918			
LA NOUE (MARNE)	JULY 1		Office relief, two DRs left in Box Car for HUPPY (ABBEVILLE AREA). Company moved off at 1pm for CONNANTRE where they remained overnight at ABBEVILLE Sheet 14 / 100,000	
	2 & 3		Entrained commencing at midnight at FERE CHAMPENOISE and left at 3 am for PONT REMY	
HUPPY PONT REMY	4 to 11		Detrained at PONT REMY and proceeded by road to HUPPY. Div. HQ. closed at LA NOUE at 3pm. on 3rd and re-opened at HUPPY at same hour. Administered by XXII Corps in Fourth Army Area. Communication by telephone to Corps, three Infy Bdes and Arty. Sounder autointerfered to XXII Corps. Above party sent on on 11th Office opened at MARTIN EGLISE at 10 am on 12th and office at HUPPY left open till 19th as part of	DIEPPE 16 1 / 100,000
MARTIN EGLISE	12 to 31		Q office remained Division reduced to Cadre and Battalions to Ploury Staff. Company renewed attack Boulvary march. Staying Night 12/13th at GAMACHES and night 13/14th at ARGUENESNIL arriving at MARTIN EGLISE at 11am 14th July	
L of C.				

Army Form C. 2118.

WAR DIARY
or
INTELLIGENCE SUMMARY.
(Erase heading not required.)

Place	Date	Hour	Summary of Events and Information	Remarks and references to Appendices
	1916 JULY			
MARTIN EGLISE & of DIEPPE	12 to 31		Communication established with ten Battalions in Groups DIEPPE and BOUXMESNIL and with three Bde Hqrs. On the 15th Bdes had battalions allotted to them as follows :- 149 Inf Bde 2nd Royal Dublin Fusiliers, 3rd Royal Warwicks 13th (S.H) Black Watch 150 Inf Bde 7th Welch Regt, 2nd Norfolk Yorkshire, 2nd Royal Munster Fus. 151 Inf Bde 1 KOYLI 6 Royal Inniskilling Fus, 4th K.R.R.C. Pioneers 5th R.I.R. On 16th July, Div. HQ. moved to GREGES and an office was opened there with two lines (one underground) to the Branch Signal Office which remained the main office. 149 Inf Bde HQrs at ARCHELLES, 150 Inf Bde in MARTIN EGLISE and 151 Bde in ANCOURT. Sounders in use to DIEPPE and HUCHINNEVILLE, 151 Bde and Div H.Q. from Branch Signal Office. Vibrophones to 149 and 150 Inf Bdes. On the 28th July the Divisional Signal Office was reopened.	DIEPPE and Sheet 10000 DIEPPE 16.

Army Form C. 2118.

WAR DIARY
or
INTELLIGENCE SUMMARY.
(Erase heading not required.)

Instructions regarding War Diaries and Intelligence Summaries are contained in F. S. Regs., Part II. and the Staff Manual respectively. Title pages will be prepared in manuscript.

Place	Date	Hour	Summary of Events and Information	Remarks and references to Appendices
MARTIN EGLISE	JULY 12 to 31		with A.W. Bernard DLI as Commandant, 1 Officer and 20 OR from each battalion, chiefly trained signallers who received instruction in Wilkinson & Lucas Lamps, both of which were new to them. One NCO Instructor from each battalion was attached to the School. The Course included instruction in the care and handling of Pigeons.	Sheet 1/100000 DIEPPE 16
			AWARDS B.(?)/A/L. HMS Ponta. MC Bar to MC. 50 Div RO No 3 and 6/7 No. 538239 6/5 Sgt. Ratcliff, P. MM do No 63167 T/Cpl Shearling MM do 1008 a/CSM Ayers, J.W. MM 50 Div RO No 39 d/8/7 Award of MM to No. 532214 Lcpl. Robertson J.W. was 50 Div. R.O. No 58 d/25/7 amended to read Bar to MM. 50 Div. R.O. d/8/7	
			Battle Casualties — Nil.	

Graham Claus Capt R.E.
Command 50 Div Signal
50 Div Signal

SECRET.

WAR DIARY

OF

50TH (NORTHUMBRIAN) DIVISIONAL SIGNAL COMPANY

ROYAL ENGINEERS.

Volume XI.

AUGUST, 1918.

VOL XLI

Army Form C. 2118.

WAR DIARY
OR
INTELLIGENCE SUMMARY. 50th Divl Signal Co R.E.

(Erase heading not required.)

Place	Date	Hour	Summary of Events and Information	Remarks and references to Appendices
MARTIN EGLISE	1918 Aug 1		Wireless Section at Central Wireless School. Power Buzzer Squad being trained under special instructors from Central Wireless School.	DIEPPE SHEET
	Aug 31		Cable Sections continued training in Buzzer Buzz instruments and theory of Telegraphy and Telephony. Working Parties daily for work in Camp. Mats and floor boards for making baths. Digging in tents &c. Fires for making baths.	
			Battle Casualties (with Artillery Sections)	
			16 Aug 1918 463026 2nd Bd[r] Rawson T.J. Wounded fire
			532214 Cpl. Roberts F.W.J. "
			20 Aug 1918 57166 Sapr Bertwch E.E. Wounded
				Graham Adair Capt.
			50th Divl Signal Co R.E. 1st Sept 1918.
			Commg 50th Divl Signal Co R.E.	

Vol XLI

Army Form C. 2118.

WAR DIARY

INTELLIGENCE SUMMARY. 50th Div¹ Signal Co R.E.

(Erase heading not required.)

Instructions regarding War Diaries and Intelligence Summaries are contained in F.S. Regs., Part II. and the Staff Manual respectively. Title pages will be prepared in manuscript.

Place	Date	Hour	Summary of Events and Information	Remarks and references to Appendices
MARTIN EGLISE	1918 Aug 1 to Aug 31		Wireless Section at Central Wireless School. Power Buzzer Squad being trained under special instructors from Central Wireless School. Rest of Sections continued training in Ball Drill, instruments and theory of Telegraphy and Telephony. Working parties daily for work in Bandstand No. 10 and stove lines for making baths, digging in tents &c. Battle Casualties:- (with Artillery Sections) 16 Aug 1918. 463026 2nd Bgd Harrison T.J. Wounded, gas 532214 L/Cpl Roberts L.W. 20th Aug 1918. 57166 2/Cpl Bentinck G.E. Wounded	DIEPPE SHEET 1/100000

Graham Adams
Capt.
Comm'g. 50th Div¹ Signal Co R.E.
1st Sept. 1918.

ROUTE DIAGRAM
Reference Sheets 28 NW³ & 20 SW⁴
Scale 1/20 000

Aerial System shown thus
Buried Routes
Test Dugout   O. OF MF etc.

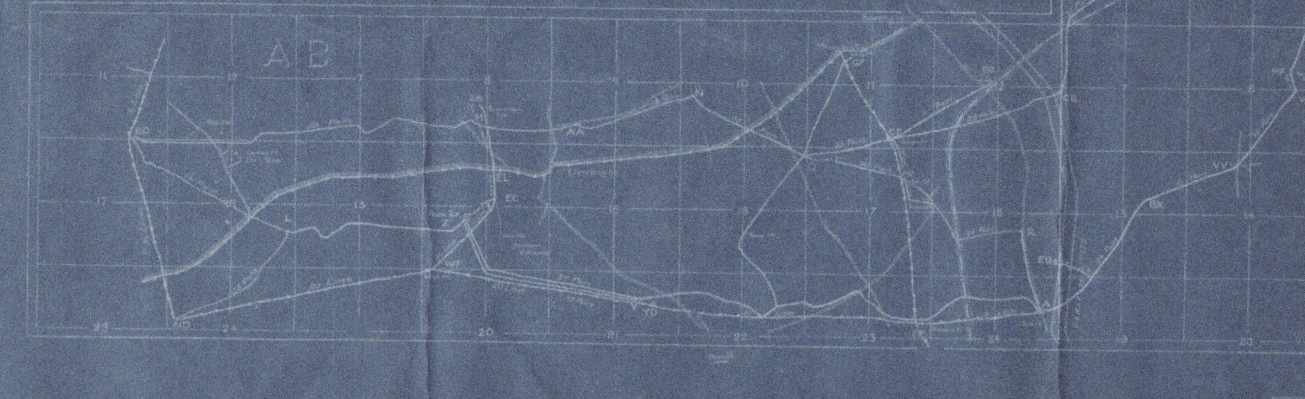

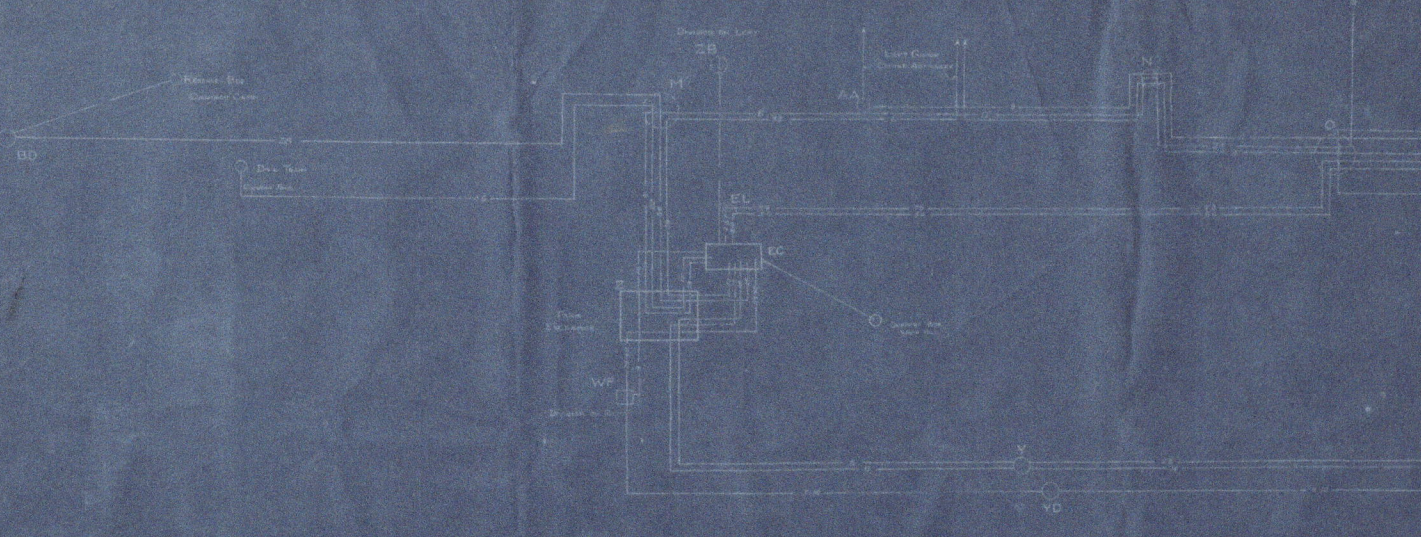

50

50 D Signals
April 1st 33
Pic

ROUTE DIAGRAM

Reference Sheets 28 NW & 20 SW
Scale - 1/20,000

Aerial System shown thus
Buried Routes
Test Dugout   O. CF MF etc

CIRCUIT DIAGRAM OF COMMUNICATIONS

50th (Northumbrian) Divisional Signal Coy. R.E.

October 1917

On His Majesty's Service.

SECRET.

WAR DIARY

OF

50th (NORTHUMBRIAN) DIVISIONAL SIGNAL COMPANY
ROYAL ENGINEERS.

** VOLUME XLII. **

September, 1918.

Vol XL-11

Army Form C. 2118.

WAR DIARY
50TH DIVL. SIGNAL COY R.E.
INTELLIGENCE SUMMARY
(Erase heading not required.)

Instructions regarding War Diaries and Intelligence Summaries are contained in F. S. Regs. Part II. and the Staff Manual respectively. Title pages will be prepared in manuscript.

Place	Date	Hour	Summary of Events and Information	Remarks and references to Appendices
MARTIN EGLISE	1918 Feb 1 to Feb 12		Training continued for all sections. Wireless section returned from course at Wireless School, ABBEVILLE on 7th and continued training. Sound scheme undertaken both with and without troops. Work on Buzz continued.	Topo Sheet 16 DIEPPE
LUCHEUX	Feb 13 to Feb 25		On 13th inst., Advance Party with stores proceeded by lorry to TOUTENCOURT. Bonfire Area but the move was cancelled and another Advance Party sent to LUCHEUX and DOULLENS the first party being recalled and arriving at LUCHEUX on the 16th inst. Div. JHQ opened at LUCHEUX at 10 am 16 inst. closing at MARTIN EGLISE at the same time. Also WG Bn HQrs., HRay Bde and 1st & 2nd Bdes moved to XVII Bonks who were administering Div. Some and to XVII Bonks. Advance Party by box car to MONTIGNY on arrival	1/100000 Sheet 11 LENS
MONTIGNY	Feb 26/28		of 26 inst. Div H.Q. opened at LUCHEUX at noon 26th inst. and opened at MONTIGNY CHATEAU at noon from Lines AMIENS	1/100000 Sheet 17 AMIENS

WAR DIARY
INTELLIGENCE SUMMARY.

50 Divl. SIGNAL COY. R.E.

Army Form C. 2118.

(Erase heading not required.)

Place	Date	Hour	Summary of Events and Information	Remarks and references to Appendices
	1918			
MONTIGNY	Sept 28		to GUERRIEU. XIII Corps who were administering since 18.151 Bde at CONTAY and through GUERRIEU, and 149 and 150 Inf Bde at CONTAY and ALLONVILLE that Div direct to H.Q.Rn at ST. GRATIEN	(MOLIENS-AU-BOIS) Sept 17 AMIENS
COMBLES	Sept 28/29		Div HA closed at MONTIGNY at 2 p.m & 28th and transport having moved to MEAULTE via ALBERT on 27 inst. Work on H.Q. proceeded by 18th Divn. and had line to TIL [Loupe?] who were now administering Divn. and to 150 Inf Bde at IEUZE WOOD. Out lines only to 149 and 151 Bde at MURLU. Preparations made on evening of 29 inst. for establishing Advanced Signal Office at 151 Bde HQ. in MURLU. At ten hours when the move was carried up to end of month.	10.00 Shortin LINE

Graham Adams
Capt for Major
Commg 50 Divl Signal Co R.E.
6th October 1918

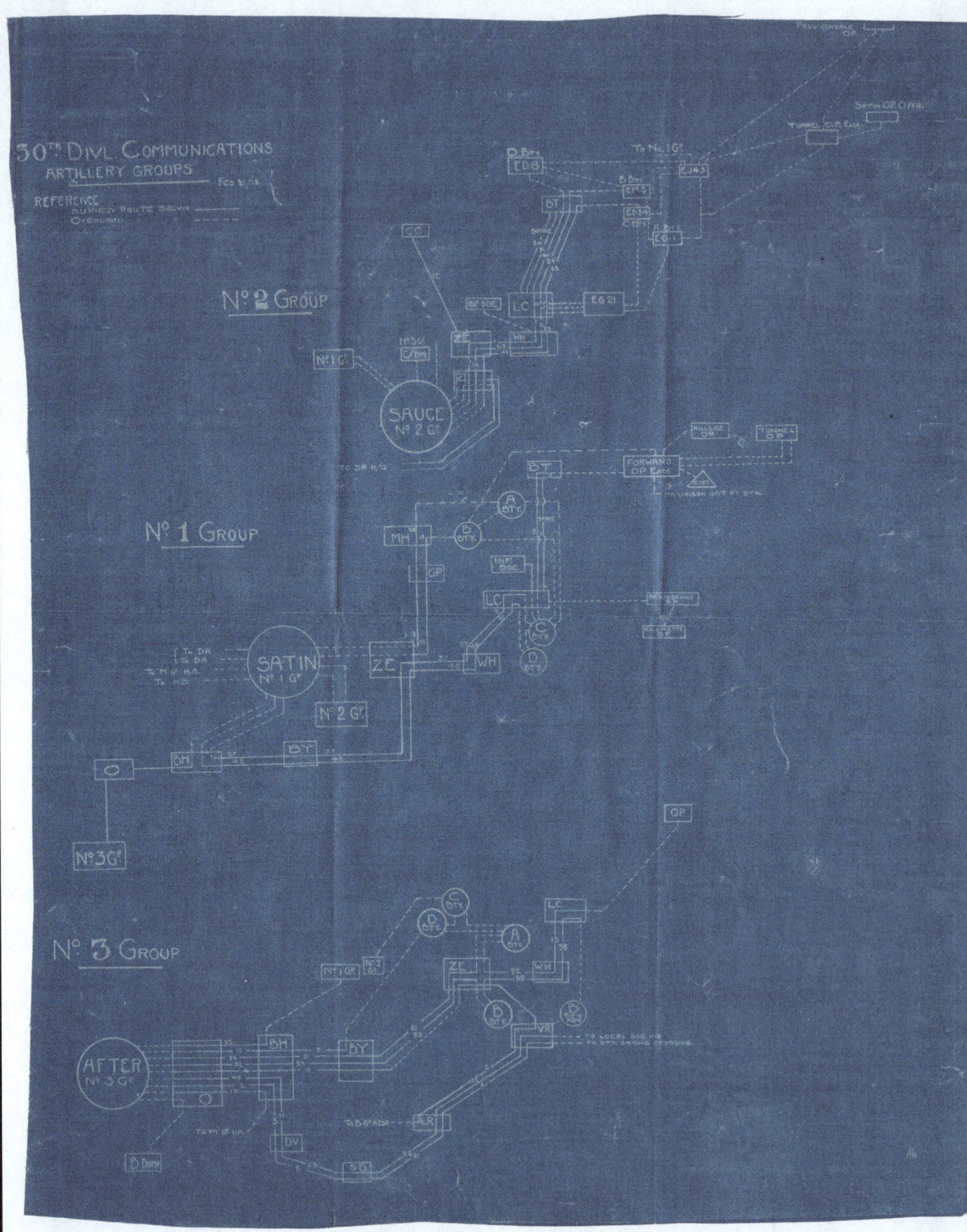

ORIGINAL. SECRET.

WAR DIARY

of

50TH (NORTHUMBRIAN) DIVISIONAL SIGNAL COMPANY R.E.

VOLUME XLIII.

OCTOBER, 1918.

Army Form C. 2118.

Vol. XVIII

WAR DIARY 50 DIVISIONAL SIGNAL COMPANY R.E.
INTELLIGENCE-SUMMARY.
(Erase heading not required.)

Instructions regarding War Diaries and Intelligence Summaries are contained in F. S. Regs., Part II. and the Staff Manual respectively. Title pages will be prepared in manuscript.

Place	Date	Hour	Summary of Events and Information	Remarks and references to Appendices
COMBLES	1918 Oct 1st and Oct 2 Oct 11		Division moved from COMBLES to LIERAMONT on the morning of 1st Oct and took over from 18th Division at 10 a.m. on 2nd October. For detail of diary from 2nd to 11th October 1918 see APPENDIX 1.	1/100000 LENS 11 APPENDIX 1.
LE TROU AUX SOLDATS	Oct 12		At 8am on 12 Oct Divnl relieved 25th Divn at LE TROU AUX SOLDATS. Sans existed to 13th Corps at RONSSOY, CORPS EXCHANGE at MARETZ, 150 Inf Bde at HONNECHY STATION (our line of cable); the north circuit formerly in use from GUISANCOURT FARM to 151, 149, BDE at HONNECHY was brought into office at MARETZ and 149 Inf Bde. at HONNECHY was broght into office at LE TROU AUX SOLDATS. 25 Divl Arty was in the west house and a line existed to them. On the 13th October, a second cable line was laid to HONNECHY STATION by the same route as the existing one and on the 14th a third one was laid by a different route, 149 Inf Bde also being tapped on to these one. Adv new hqrs was also put out to 151 Inf Bde who had changed their Hqrs in MARETZ. See APPENDIX 2	1/100000 Sheet 51B
	Oct 16 Oct 19			

Army Form C. 2118.

WAR DIARY
or
INTELLIGENCE SUMMARY.
(Erase heading not required.)

Instructions regarding War Diaries and Intelligence Summaries are contained in F. S. Regs., Part II. and the Staff Manual respectively. Title pages will be prepared in manuscript.

Place	Date	Hour	Summary of Events and Information	Remarks and references to Appendices
LE TROU AUX SOLDATS 31B	1918 Oct 20	12.00	At 12.00 on the 19th October 25th Division relieved 50th Division, taking over Div. HQ at HONNECHY and 50 Div. returned to H.Q. at LE TROU AUX SOLDATS. 151 Bde was in LE TROU AUX SOLDATS and 150 Bde facing in MARETZ. A line was returned to 149 Bde and 150 Bde, M.G. Bn and Engineers were put in that exchange. A definite line was run from 151st Bde HQ. 50 Div. Arty arrived at LE TROU AUX SOLDATS on the 20 October and Bdes, 250 and 251 came under orders of 16th Div. On the 29 inst., 149 Inf. Bde moved to REYMONT and got a line from CORPS SIGNALS to HONNECHY Exchange, 150 Bde to LE CATEAU where they had a line to NRC, the Boche Exchange just west of the town on the BUSIGNY road, and 151st Inf Bde to MAUROIS. The latter were along put on HONNECHY Exchange the latter Having a direct line from LE TROU AUX SOLDATS. At 4 p.m. on the 20th October, Div H.Q. moved to CHATEAU SEYDOUX, LE CATEAU. Two call pins were laid to LE FAYT	1 /wwo SHEET 57B.

Army Form C. 2118.

WAR DIARY
or
INTELLIGENCE SUMMARY.
(Erase heading not required.)

Instructions regarding War Diaries and Intelligence Summaries are contained in F. S. Regs., Part II. and the Staff Manual respectively. Title pages will be prepared in manuscript.

Place	Date	Hour	Summary of Events and Information	Remarks and references to Appendices
LE CATEAU	1918 Oct 30	3¹⁵	FARM from CHATEAU SEYDOUX on the 29th October, and on the 30th October, when it became known that 50 Divl Artillery would be crossing 50 Divl front, a 2nd line to LE FAYT FARM this afternoon being tapped in also to 149 Infy Bde who had moved to POMMEREUIL, other communication with the latter thus lines on the CORPS permanent route were all(?) established TY Exchange in POMMEREUIL. One of these was extended to 149 Bde & the other on TY Exchange thus giving also a line between TY Exchange and 149 Bde Hd Qrs. Two lines were laid from LE FAYT FARM (150 Bde H.Q. Arty H.Q. Divl Divl (Arty HQ) to TY Exchange. Of these one was put through direct to 149 Bde and the other put on TY Exchange. A line was also laid from LE FAYT FARM to 13 Divl Arty H.Q. 151st Infy Bde H.Q. was established at the west end of LE CATEAU and is all Divl HQ offices except G and Q were now there, the following was put through the Bde Exchange. Divl Train, DADOS, CRE.	1 Appx 5/B

A6915 Wt. W14422/M1160 35,000 12/16 D.D.&I. Forms/C./2118/14.

Army Form C. 2118.

WAR DIARY
or
INTELLIGENCE SUMMARY.
(Erase heading not required.)

Place	Date	Hour	Summary of Events and Information	Remarks and references to Appendices
LE CATEAU	1918 Oct 20		150 Bde Bd Rear HQ, 5 BIR (Reserve). A line was obtained direct to	
	31		151 Bde HQ and another from NRC to 151 Bde HQ. about 57 B.	
			From Bde HQ, a supervisory line was run to 13 Corps	
			and a second line to NRC (13 Corps Advd Exchange). Corps also	
			laid a line from Bde HQ to 18th Bde in LE CATEAU and 25th Div	
			laid a line from their HQ at LE CATEAU STATION to CHATEAU	
			SEYDOUX.	
			Div Arty Signal Office was established in advancing	
			cellar of CHATEAU and on W. of the direct lines forward were	
			used as these exchanges. All messages work for Artillery was	
			dealt with in Div Signal Office. Div Arty Rear lines to 50 DAC	
			and 85 Bde R.G.A. from CHATEAU SEYDOUX and to 250, 251 and	
			104 Arty Bdes from LE FAYT FARM, also 18th Div Arty Advd HQ.	

Army Form C. 2118.

WAR DIARY
or
INTELLIGENCE SUMMARY.
(Erase heading not required.)

Instructions regarding War Diaries and Intelligence Summaries are contained in F. S. Regs., Part II. and the Staff Manual respectively. Title pages will be prepared in manuscript.

Place	Date	Hour	Summary of Events and Information	Remarks and references to Appendices
	1918 Oct.			
LE CATEAU	31		Battle Casualties	
			3/10/18 161606 Bgd Whalley, W. Man.R. 6/10/18 47915 Spr Bryan J. Gased.	
			4/10/18 463136 Sgt Smith, H. 17/10/18 463155 Bmlr P.J. Wounded	
			538254 Bgd Harper, Q.J. Gased 463141 Dvr. Martin, M. Gased	
			293474 Cpl Bagnall, H. 19/10/18 463167 Cpl Chestney, G.H. Gased	
			322186 Knowles, A.H. 21/10/18 500263 Cpl Hayward, A.E. Wounded	
			Honours and Awards	
			93594 Sch. O'Brien, J. Bar to M.M. DRO. 4306 22/10/15	
			463100 Bgl. Dutty, J. M.M.	
			47599 Sgt. Waltham, P. M.M. DRO 4336 29/10/18	
			241810 Pte Meacon, A. M.M.	
			2nd N.F. (attached)	
				Graham Adams Capt. Adjt
				Browning 50 Divl Signal Co. R.E.

A6945. Wt. W14427/M1160 35,000 12/16 D. D. & L. Forms/C/2118/14.

APPENDIX I

Operations of 3rd to 11th October 1918
South West of LE CATEAU

Communications

1. Telegraph and Telephone.

50 Division took over from the 18th Division on the 2nd October /18, with Headquarters at LIERAMONT, and lines existed from Div. HQ to 149 Inf. Bde. at MAY COPSE (F9c.5.7), 151 Inf. Bde. at EPEHY (F1.D98) and 150 Inf. Bde. in reserve at NURLU. The Advanced Divisional Report Centre was fixed at LEMPIRE (F1cc.1.2), to which place two lines existed from LIERAMONT, these being part on a buried system and the remainder overland cable. On the evening of the 2nd October, 151 Inf. Bde. relieved the 10th Australian Inf. Bde. with H.Q. at DUNCAN POST (F.7.D.9.4). A line was laid from LEMPIRE to DUNCAN POST and later the same day another line was laid by a different route. The Division attacked on the morning of the 3rd October and about noon Advd. Divl. Report Centre moved to DUNCAN POST, two lines having been laid in the meantime from there to GOUY (R1.5C.9.0) to which place 151 had moved. A third line was also laid from LEMPIRE to DUNCAN POST by a circuitous route. 150 Bde. H.Q. moved to EPEHY (F1.D.9.8) and later to DUNCAN POST and BONY. On the 4th October 149 Inf. Bde. moved to GOUY (R.11.d.4.5), and a line was laid to them from BONY, and the Advd. Divl. Report Centre moved to BONY. A second line was laid to 149 Inf. Bde. via Prospect Hill with a view to opening an Advd. Report Centre on the hill if necessary. 151 Inf. Bde. Advd. H.Q. had moved to PIENNE (S.23a.7.2) on the 5th October, and a line was put out to that point from BONY. 38th Division, on the left at S.21 Central were also linked up with BONY on the 6th October and an alternative line laid to PIENNE. On the evening of the 7th October, 151 Inf. Bde. Advd. H.Qrs. was established at VAUXHALL QUARRY (T.25.b.2.5), one of the PIENNE lines being extended there. The line to Prospect Hill was also extended to VAUXHALL QUARRY. Div. Rear Hdqrs. moved from LIERAMONT to EPEHY on the morning of 8th October. At 01.00 on 8th, 151 Bde. attacked and captured VILLERS FARM (T.20.b.9.6) and later the same day, Divisions on left and right met on final objective and 50th Division was squeezed out. By the 9th inst. Div. Rear H.Q. was at EPEHY, Advd. Div. H.Q. at BONY, 149 Inf. Bde. H.Q. remained at GOUY, 150 Inf. Bde. in BONY and 151 Inf. Bde. in a trench just west of VAUXHALL QUARRY. Divl. H.Q. closed at EPEHY on the 10th October, and opened at GUISANCOURT FARM (T.26.d.9.2). In preparation for this, and the moves of Inf. Bdes. and M.G. Bn., the Prospect Hill line from BONY was diverted from VAUXHALL QUARRY to GUISANCOURT FARM and an earth circuit laid from to butter place from MARETZ with a tap off to 150 Inf. Bde., on to MAUROIS, with a tap off to 149 Inf. Bde. and on to BEAUMONT for 151 Inf. Bde. M.G. Bn. at HONNECHY were also tapped on to this line.

II. Wireless.

Oct 3rd. DUNCAN POST. At dawn a wireless station was here established on a derelict tank and maintained communication throughout the operations with Corps & 149 and 151 Inf. Bdes. A certain amount of jamming was experienced, but in spite of this all traffic was successfully dealt with.

(2)

II. Wireless (conto.)

Oct. 4th. BONY. Divisional Wireless Directing station was erected and worked successfully throughout the operations to Corps, 149 and 151 Inf. Bdes. About 9 p.m. hostile aircraft bombed the station with the result that instruments were thrown to the ground by concussion, and slightly damaged. A spare French set was at once brought into use and communication by Wireless again restored. Wilson set was sent to Corps for repair.

Oct. 5th & 6th BONY. Wireless communication maintained without incident worthy of mention.

Oct. 7th & 8th BONY. Wireless communication maintained between 151 Bde. at VAUXHALL QUARRY and Div. Wireless Directing Station, thence to Corps.

Oct. 9th/10th. GOISANCOURT FARM. Divl. Wireless Directing Station erected in a dugout, subsequently found to be mined. Set was dismantled and re-erected some distance away in consequence. Jamming again experienced, but communication with Corps and 149 Bde was maintained.

III. Visual.

Oct. 3rd. DUNCAN POST. At dawn a visual station was established on high ground near Wireless station and maintained communication via two transmitting stations to 149, 150 and 151 Inf Bdes. The success of visual on this day lay in the lamps marked. One transmitting station was shelled for a short period, but no casualties resulted. Good use was made of disabled tanks both for cover and working, and their presence greatly facilitated the work of our signallers.

Oct. 4th. BONY. Visual was opened from high ground close to the Hindenburg Line and worked via one transmitting station to 149 and 151 Bdes. About midnight the station was attacked by hostile aircraft with bombs and machine guns, but with no result.

Oct. 5/6/7th BONY. Visual maintained with incident worthy of mention.

Oct. 9-10th GOISANCOURT FARM. No visual employed.

APPENDIX 2

Operations from 16th to 19th October 1918

South West of LE CATEAU

Communications

1. ### Telegraph and Telephone.

On the 16th October Divl. H.Q. was established at LE TROU AUX SOLDATS, 149 Inf. Bde at Northern end of HONNECHY, 150 Inf. Bde at HONNECHY STATION and 151 Inf. Bde in MARETZ. M.G. Battn. H.Q. was in HONNECHY. A line was laid from Div. H.Q. to the east end of MARETZ and the single line which had been laid from GUISANCOURT FARM was split there, 151 Bde coming on the rear portion and 149 & 150 Bdes on the forward portion. M.G. Battn. laid a line to 149 Bde Exchange. In addition to this one cable line to HONNECHY STATION was taken over from the 25th Div. on relief. A second cable line was laid by the same route and both pairs poled as far as the railway. 149 Bde. also laid a line to 150 Bde at the Station. As this latter district was shelled considerably, an alternative line was thought advisable and a cable line was run by a different route, chiefly on Boche permanent routes as far as HONNECHY village, from the outskirts of which to the Station it was laid in a sunken road and a shallow ditch. 149 Bde tapped on to this line west of the village and ran to their own H.Q. west of the houses. Thus three good lines were available to Div. H.Q. from HONNECHY Station which had been fixed as Advanced Divl. Report Centre. Corps put in lines direct from Corps H.Q. and from the 66th Divn on the left. The 108th American Inf. Bde. on the right also laid a line to the Station.

Before ZERO on the 17th inst., at which hour the Advd. Divl. Report Centre opened at HONNECHY STATION, two lines were laid by different routes to the farm in Q.19 Central and two pairs forward from there, also by different routes to the Culvert at Q.20.b.8.5 which was to be the Advd. Report Centre for 149 and 151 Inf. Bdes. In addition, 149 Bde. laid a line from the farm in Q.19 Central to this report Centre. Before ZERO 149 and 151 Advd. Hdqrs were established at Q.19 Central, 150 Bde. remaining at HONNECHY STATION.

At ZERO on the 17th October, one cable detachment was held in readiness at Q.20.b.8.5 to lay lines forward to advanced headquarters of Brigades in the event of their moving, and, 150 Bde having opened a report centre at Q.28 Central, a line was laid there from the exchange at Q.20.b.8.5. This remained as a report centre during the day, and the Bde. H.Q. moved to Q.27.a.6.3, tapping in on the line to Q.28 Central.

Telegraph and Telephone (Contd)

On the morning of the 18th October, the attack was resumed and two lines were laid from Q.20.b.8.5 to the HQ of 151 Bde which had moved to Q.22.a.6.3, two lines also being laid between these HQ and those of the 7th Inf. Bde. 25 Divn, which was then under orders of G.O.C. 50 Divn. Later in the day, a line was laid to LE QUENNELET FARM in Q.24.a, which was to be the report centre of 151 Inf. Bde. On the night of the 18th October, however, all three Bde HQ. returned to the farm in Q.19 Central, and the forward lines were taken over on the morning of the 19th October, 75 Bde. continuing at Q.22.a and using one line back, the second line back and that forward to LE QUENNELET FM being taken into use by the 7th Inf. Bde. 25th Divn with HQ. in Q.22.a, and report centre at LE QUENNELET FM.

On the afternoon of the 18th October, orders were issued for the move of 150 Bde HQ. to ST. BENIN, Q.18.c.4.2, with advd report centre at Q.10.d.8.8, and a line was laid from Q.20.b.8.5 to ST. BENIN and from ST. BENIN to Q.10.d.8.8, but these were never used by that Bde, different orders having been issued while they were being laid.

II Wireless.

LE TROU AUX SOLDATS. Oct. 12th Took over from 25th Div and worked without incident to Corps, 150 & 151 Inf. Bdes. Trench set from 149 Bde. withdrawn.

LE TROU AUX SOLDATS Oct 13/14th Divl. Directing Station worked without incident. Trench set at 149 Bde. replaced.

HONNECHY Oct 15th. ~~Special Wireless Officer arrived here to supervise 150 Bde Wireless communication~~. Trench set erected near Honnechy Station and worked successfully to Div. Directing Station, Corps, and 151 Inf. Bde.

HONNECHY Oct 16th. Divl. Wireless Directing Station took over from 150 Bde. and worked to Corps, 149, and 151 Inf. Bdes.

HONNECHY Oct 17th At ZERO hour 150 Bde. Trench set went forward to Q.20.b.8.5, but very heavy shell fire prevented erection of mast and station. A loop set worked successfully at this point however and maintained communication a little later in the day with Report Centre at Q.28 Central. Trench set of 149 Bde. worked back from Q.19 Central to Div. Wireless Station at P.29.d.3.4 and dealt successfully with all traffic. Some jambing experienced.

(3).

Wireless. (Cont'd)

Oct. 18th Loop sets maintained communication from Bde. H.Q. at Q.19 Central to Advd. Bde. at Q.27a, and thence to Report Centre at Q.28 Central. During the day this line of communication proved its worth by getting messages through during a period when the buzzer line was smashed by shell fire. Normal working effected to Corps from Divisional Wireless Directing Station at Q.29d.3.4. during the day.

Oct. 19th Acting upon special orders the 50 Div Wireless Officer proceeded to 7 Inf. Bde. H.Q. and took their Trench set forward to 75 Inf. Bde. Advd H.Q. at Q.14d.3.8. A change in plans prevented the erection of the advanced station which was intended to work back to 75 Bde. H.Q. and 25 Div. Directing Station. At noon the Wireless stations of the 50 Div withdrew according to orders received.

During the whole of the period Oct 3/19th Loop sets were employed by 149, 150, & 151 Bdes. with good results and quite justified their presence with the respective Bdes.

III. Visual

LE TROU AUX SOLDATS Oct. 12th. No visual employed.

Oct. 13/14/15th. Visual established via one transmitting station to 150 Inf. Bde. H.Q. at HONNECHY. P.29d.3.4 from Div H.Q. at LE TROU
× ~~Please~~ AUX SOLDATS & worked without interruption up to dawn Oct 16th

Oct. 17th Visual communication extended to Bde. H.Q. Q.19 central via C.V.S and later to Bde. Report Centre at Q.28 central via one transmitting station. Some shelling experienced but communication continued without interruption.

Oct. 18th. Visual maintained as on previous day. Exceedingly clear weather experienced and signals were in consequence particularly good.

Oct. 19th At dawn attempts were made to establish a direct visual line from Div. H.Q. at P.29d.3.4 to the road at Q.23 b.5.2. Special long range lamps were employed, but an exceedingly heavy mist defeated the project.

At noon stations were withdrawn according to orders.

× **Oct. 16 HONNECHY.** Visual established at P.29d.3.4 working to C.V.S at Q.26.a.8.8

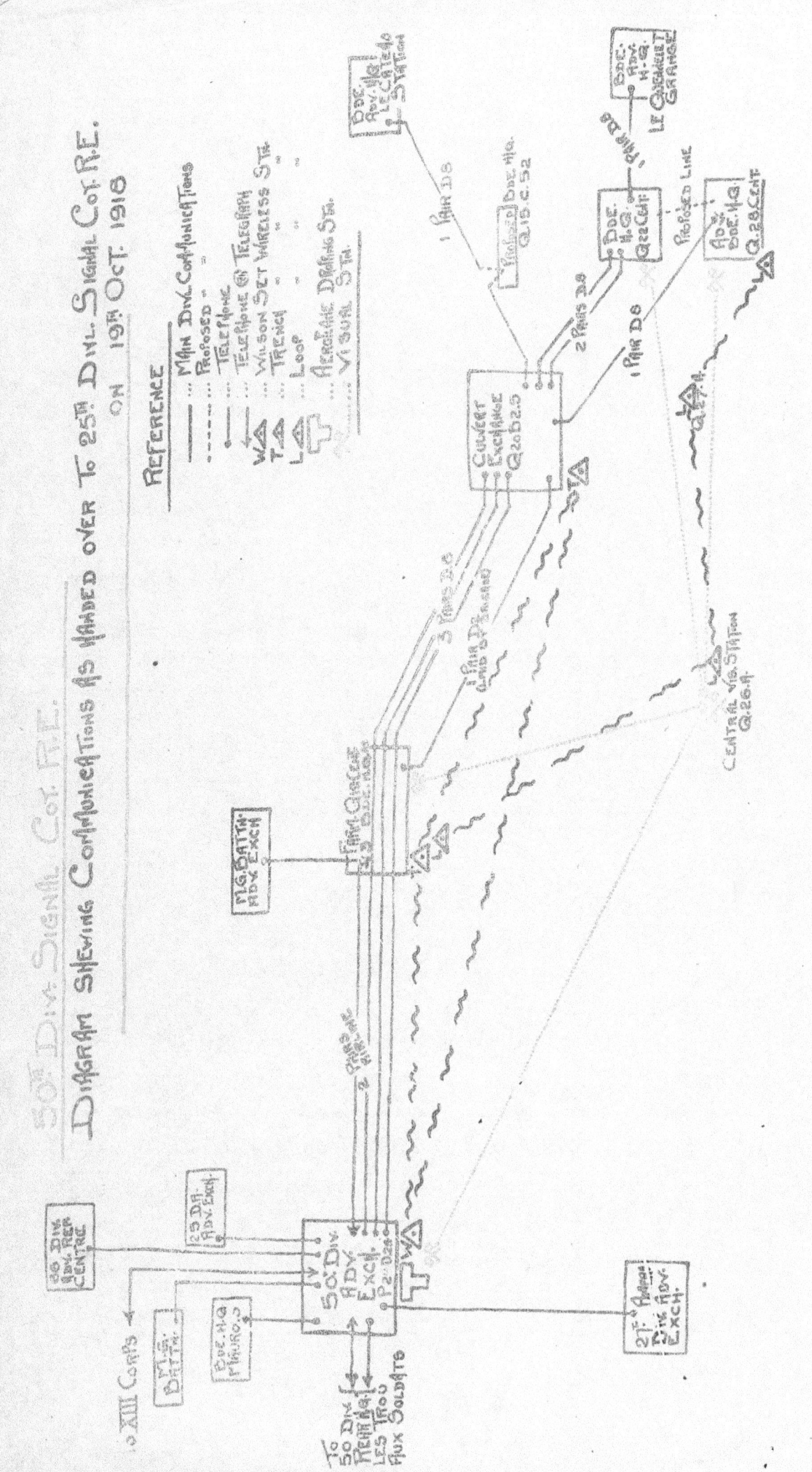

SECRET.
Copy No. _____

50th. DIVISION INSTRUCTIONS No. 3.

16th. October, 1918.

1. The following methods of communications will be available :-

        A. Telegraph.
        B. Wireless.
        C. Visual.
        D. Despatch Riders.
        E. Contact Patrols.

2. The diagram attached shows communications in operation at ZERO hour.

3. The forward chain of communications from HONNECHY will be along the HONNECHY - LE CATEAU ROAD to about Q.20.a. thence via Q.20.b.8.5. and FASSIAUX to LE QUENNELET GRANGE.

4.   A. <u>TELEGRAPH and TELEPHONE.</u>
Before ZERO hour 2 or 3 forward cables will be laid as far as Q.20.b.8.5.
As soon after ZERO hour as the situation permits these cables will be extended to Q.22.a.8.2. and LE QUENNELET FARM. One cable detachment thereafter being placed at the disposal of the 150th Infantry Brigade.

  B. <u>WIRELESS.</u>
At ZERO hour Wireless communications will be as follows :-
Wilson Set at HONNECHY STATION working to Trench Set at Q.19.central and in communication with Corps Directing Set.

P.T.O.-

- 2 -

After the Red Line is taken the communications will be as follows :-

Wilson Set at HONNECHY STATION working forward to Q.20.b.8.5. (Trench) also to Trench Set at Div. Report Centre Q.22.a.8.2. Loop Set communications will be established between Q.22.a.8.2. and LE QUENNELET GRANGE Q.24.a. and Q.20.b.8.5.

A Third Loop Wireless Set will be with the 150th Infantry Brigade to maintain communications forward of LE QUENNELET GRANGE.

C. VISUAL.

At ZERO hour communications will exist between HONNECHY STATION and Brigades via Central Visual Station near Cross Roads in 26.a.

150th Infantry Brigade when advancing will keep communication with Central Visual Station.

A Terminal Station will later be provided near Q.20.b.8.5. (H.Q. 149th & 151st Brigades.)

D. DESPATCH RIDERS.

(1) Motor Cyclists.

At ZERO hour there will be 2 Divisional and 2 Brigade D.R's at the Farm in Q.19.central. 1 Brigade and 2 Divisional D.R's at Advanced Div. Report Centre, the remainder being at Divisional Headquarters.

Forward Divisional D.R's will reconnoitre as early as possible the roads through BENIN in the direction of LE QUENNELET FARM and report thereon.

P.T.O.-

- 3 -

(ii) Mounted D.R's.

At ZERO hour 6 Mounted Despatch Riders from the Northumberland Hussars I.Y. will report to Capt. ADAM, M.C., R.E. at HONNECHY STATION.

Two will be retained at Advanced Report Centre, four being sent forward to Farm in Q.19.central.

These four Mounted D.R's, together with 2 Div. M.C.D.R's will move to Div. Advanced Report Centre when it opens at Q.22.a.6.2.

H. **CONTACT PATROLS.**

Dropping Station is established at V.8.a. near Divisional Headquarters.

A forward station will be established at P.29.d. South of Railway, on receipt of orders.

ACKNOWLEDGE.

Issued at

16th October, 1918.

Major for Lt.-Col,
General Staff,
50th. Division.

```
Copy No. 1.    149th. Inf. Bdo.
         2.    150th. Inf. Bdo.
         3.    151st. Inf. Bdo.
         4.    C.R.A.
         5.    1st. Bn. Tanks.
         6.    35th Squadron R.A.F.
         7.    66th. Division.
         8.    27th. American Division.
         9.    XIII CORPS.
```

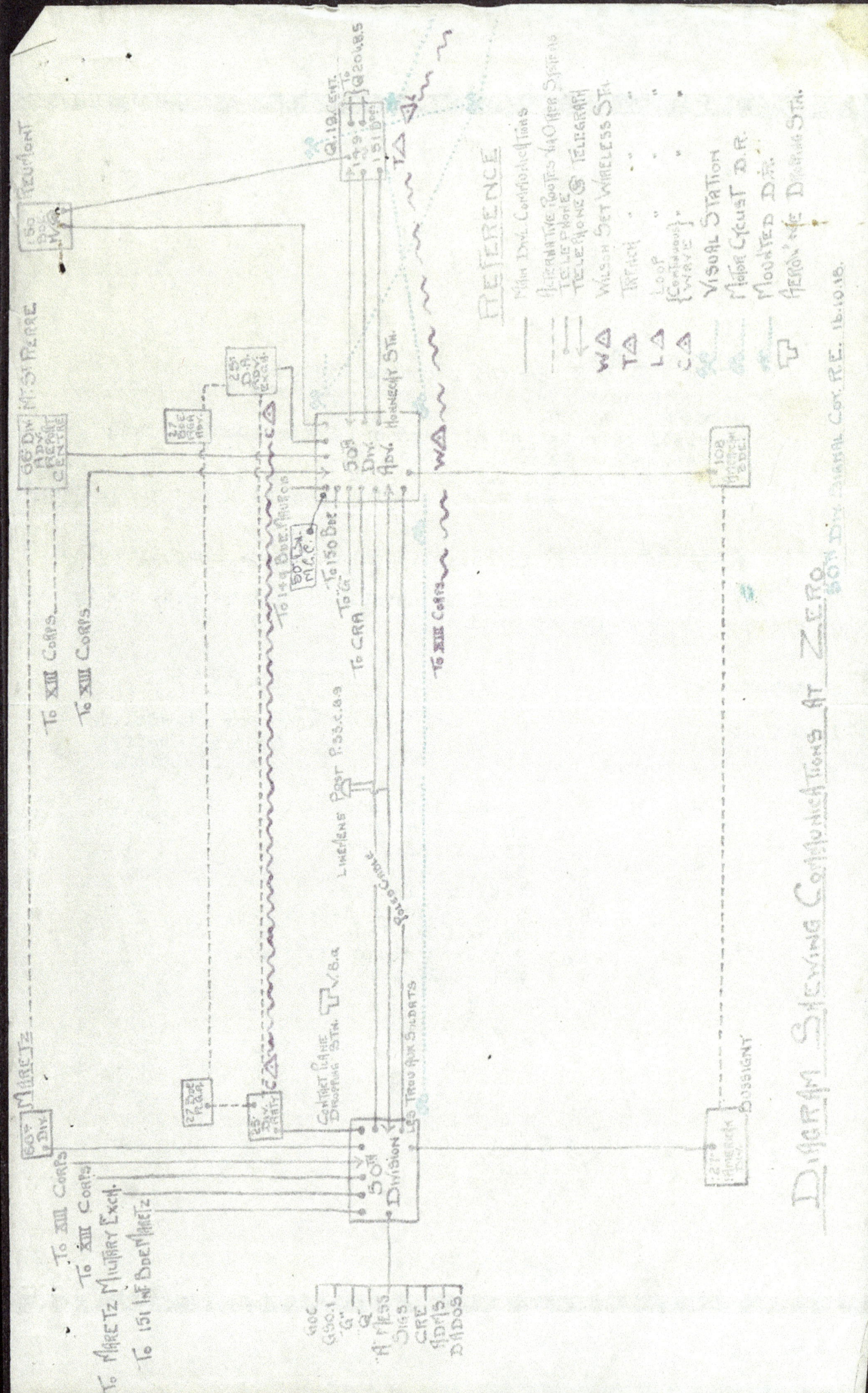

SECRET.
Copy No. 13

50th. DIVISION INSTRUCTIONS No. 5. - SERIES "E".

COMMUNICATIONS.

2nd November, 1918.

1. Diagram I attached shows methods of Communication in existence on November 3rd 1918.
Diagram II attached shows main Communications as they will be at ZERO hour.

2. The following means of Communication will be available during forthcoming operations :-

   A. Telegraph and Telephone.
   B. Wireless.
   C. Visual.
   D. Despatch Riders.
   E. Contact Patrols.

3. The forward chain of Communications from LE FAYT Farm will be via Brigade Headquarters in G.1.d.2.3. - ROSIMBOIS - ROUTE de LANDRECIES - BUTT OF RIFLE RANGE in G.6.a.

4. (a) Telegraph and Telephone.
Before ZERO hour three pairs will be laid as far forward as possible from Brigade Headquarters in G.1.d.2.3.
As soon as situation permits lines will be extended to ROSIMBOIS, two Cable Detachments and one Tank, being held in readiness for this purpose. After leaving ROSIMBOIS the Tank will proceed along the ROUTE de LANDRECIES and will endeavour to keep in touch with battalions of 151st Infantry Brigade; two pairs of cable will be laid from tank.
A Signal Officer will accompany the Tank.

P.T.O.

(b) **Wireless.**
At ZERO hour Wireless Communication will be as follows :-

Directing Station at LE FAYT Farm in communication with Brigade Headquarters in G.1.d.2.3. and Flanking Divisions and Corps.

As soon as the situation permits, a Trench Wireless Set will be erected at DRILL GROUND CORNER. Another set will be at the disposal of 151st Infantry Brigade for opening communication from the Rifle Range BUTT.

Loop Set Wireless Stations will be attached to each Brigade for forward communications.

A charging set for accumulators will be established at LE FAYT Farm.

4. (c) **Visual.**
At ZERO hour there will be visual communication between LE FAYT Farm and Brigades in G.1.d.2.3.

The country is difficult for visual signalling. Visual, however, will be established wherever possible.

(d) **Despatch Riders.**
(i) **Motor Cyclists.** At ZERO hour there will be two Divisional and two Brigade M.C.D.R's. at Brigade Headquarters in G.1.d.2.3.

One D.R. will remain at Rear Headquarters, the remainder being at Advanced Divisional Headquarters.

Forward Div. D.R's will reconnoitre the roads to ROSIGBOIS as early as possible.

(ii) **Mounted D.R's.** Mounted D.R's will be attached to Divisional Headquarters and the three Brigade Headquarters.

A mounted D.R. should be sent in by Brigades on completion of moves. This D.R. on returning will be accompanied by one or more Div. Mounted D.R's in order that they may know the way.

P.T.O.-

(c) Contact Patrols.

A Dropping Station will be established in the vicinity of LE FAYT Farm, L.9.b.3.2.

5. Cable Supplies.

The Cable laying Tank mentioned in Para. 4 (a) will carry 50 miles of cable and supply of poles.

Supplies of Cable will be dumped at ROSIMBOIS and in ROUTE de LANDRECIES at junction of LAIE des LIEVRES.

Instructions will be given to Signal Officer i/c. of Tank, who will have authority to issue cable to Brigades and Battalions.

There will also be an advanced Cable Dump near LE FAYT Farm from where cable may be drawn under authority from O.C.Signals.

6. Pigeons.

It is improbable that Pigeons will be available for the first day's operations. Should supplies be ready for the 2nd. and subsequent days' operations, arrangements will be made.

7. ACKNOWLEDGE.

C. R. Hill Maj.
for Lt.-Col,
General Staff,
50th. Division.

Issued at 19.00 hrs.

Distribution:-

XIII Corps. (2 copies).
18th. Divn.
25th. Divn.
66th. Divn.
35.Sqdn.R.A.F.
9th. Bn. Tank Corps.
149th. Infantry Bde.
150th. Infantry Bde.
151st. Infantry Bde.

C. R. E.
C. R. A.
A.D.M.S.
"Q".
Div. Sig. Coy.
50th. Bn. M.G.Corps.
"C" Sqdn., Northumberland Hussars.
O.C., "C" Coy., XIII Corps Cyclists.

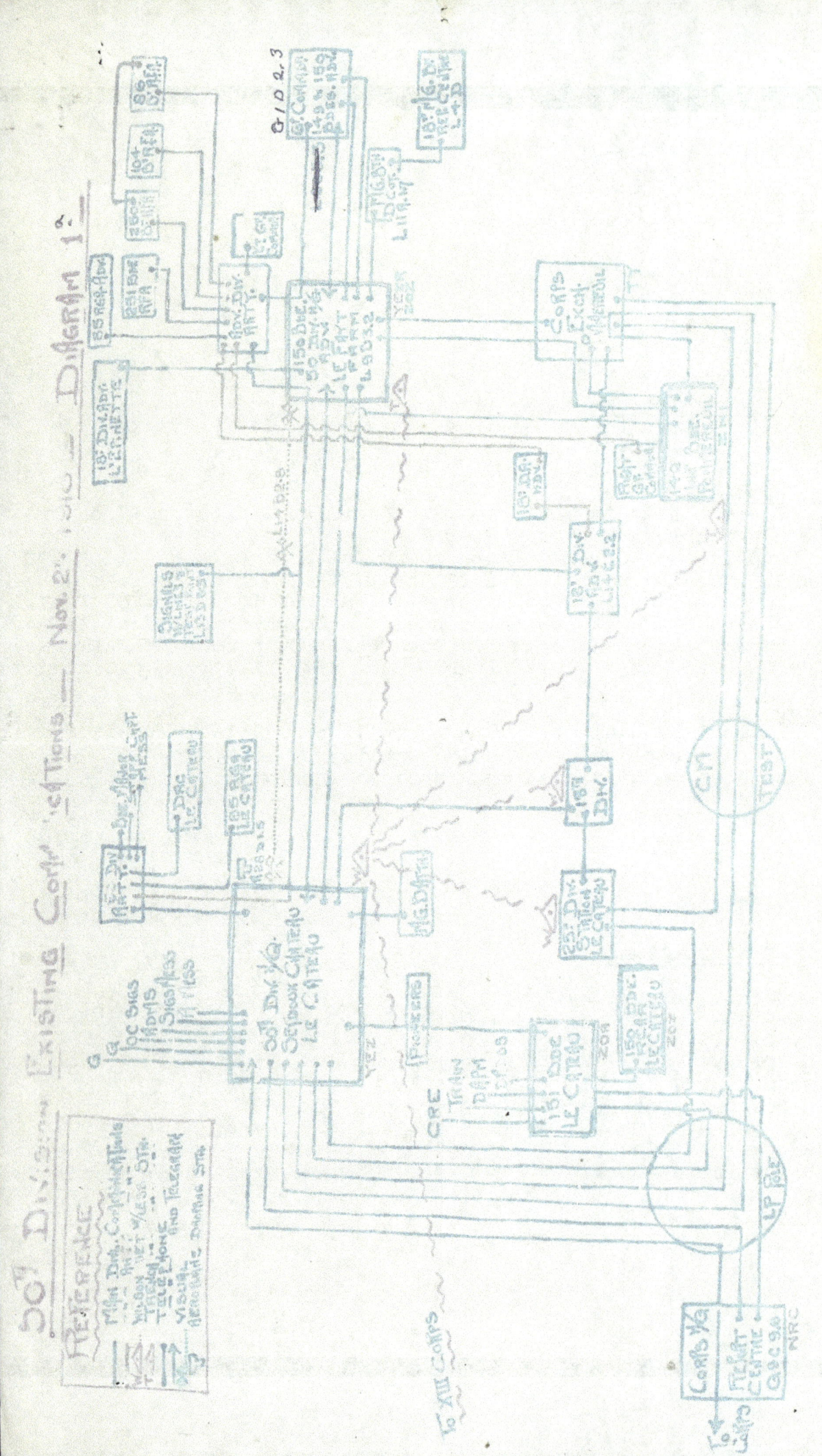

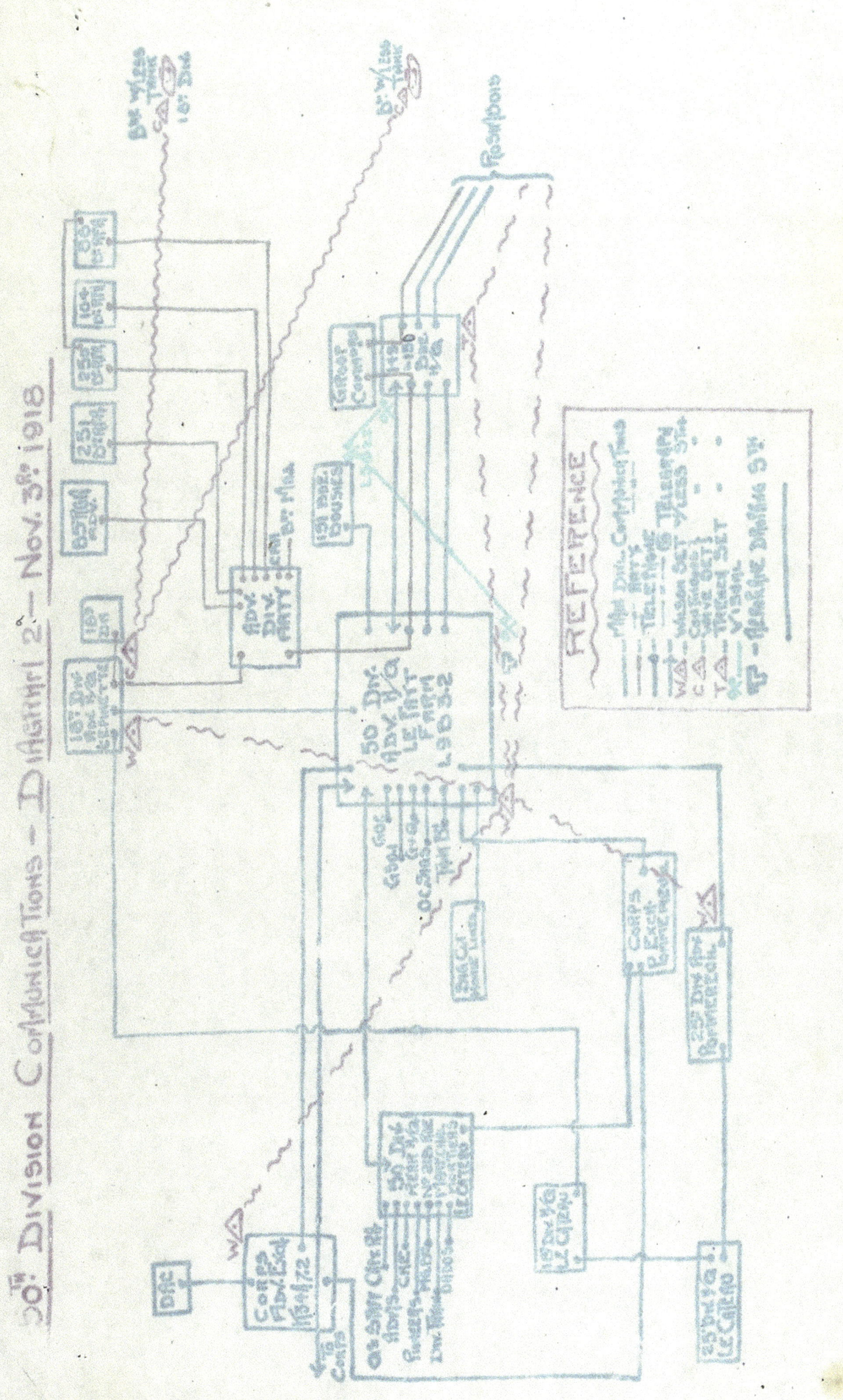

31. Oct. 1918. — 50. Division took over command of sector from elements of 18. and 25. Divisions. As no forward communications were taken over, a considerable amount of preliminary work had to be done.

Description and diagrams of communications established before Zero day are given in 50. Div. Instructions No. 5 series 'E' of Nov. 2/18.

Nov. 1st to 3rd — On the 1st Nov/18 the Div. H/Qrs was still at SEYDOUX CHATEAU, LE CATEAU, with advanced signal office at LA FAIT FARM. Lines were this day laid to FONTAINE-AU-BOIS to Headquarters occupied the next day (2nd Nov.), by the 150 Sig. Bde, who moved forward from LE FAIT FARM.

To improve communication to this point, two more pairs were laid from LE FAIT FARM to FONTAINE-AU-BOIS by a different route; the attached diagram — with detailed particulars of means of signalling — shewing the communications on this day.

3. Nov. 1918 — On the morning of the 3rd a pair was laid from LA FAIT FARM to 151 Sig. Bde., who established their headquarters at BOUSIES.

4 Nov. — Zero hour was at 0615, Headquarters being disposed as follows:

Div. Headquarters : LE FAIT FARM
149 Sig. Bde. : Q.1.D.2.3
150 " " : Q.1.D.2.3
151 " " : BOUSIES

Owing to long lengths having been cut out of two forward pairs, Signal Tank laid a pair from LE FAIT FARM to 149 and 150 Bde H/Qrs in FONTAINE-AU-BOIS Q.1.D.2.3, thence laying 2 pairs to ROSIMBOIS where an exchange was established. At the same time, two cable detachments laid 2 more pairs between FONTAINE-AU-BOIS and ROSIMBOIS (149 Sig. Bde.)

The Signal Tank, still laying 2 pairs and 1 cable detachment, going by different routes followed up the infantry as they advanced through the FORÊT DE MORMAL. Owing to difficult country and failure of cigar, the tank was compelled to stop at R.4.D.4.3, detachment with cable wagon pushing on to cross-roads B.25.A.3.9, this point being the H/Qrs. of the 151st Inf. Bde. for the night.

Communication by telephone was established to all three Infantry Bdes. and Arty. Group Commander before dusk of the 4th. their positions being

149 Inf. Bde.: R.10.A.3.4
150   "   " : A.29
151   "   " : B.25.A.3.9

ROSIMBOIS was used as an advanced exchange. Divl. H/Qrs. moved to FONTAINE-AU-BOIS.

— See Diagram I —

5th. Nov. 1918 — Commencing at dawn, the Signal Tank pushed forward, completing two pairs to 151 Bde. H/Qrs. at cross-roads B.25.A.3.9 via A.30.C.2.4.

Divisional Report Centre opened at RUE DE LIEVRES A.30.C.2.4. at 8 AM. Mobile Signal Office having been moved forward at dawn and utilized.

Cable detachment and Tank then laid lines forward by different routes to HACHETTE FARM where Divl. H/Qrs. was established at 17.00.

At this point the Tank dumped remainder of cable and returned to Tankodrome, as it was unable to proceed further, due to bridge over the SAMBRE being blown up.

The Signal Tank proved of inestimable value, carrying nearly four tons of cable and laying cable over very difficult country.

Headquarters were: { Division: HACHETTE FARM
149 & } Vicinity of
150 BDES. } HACHETTE FARM
151 BDE.: { Cross roads
B.25.A.3.9

— See Diagram II —

Nov. 6th) — The detachments on No. 6 Paid lines in
1918) the morning to BASSEE NOYELLE (H/Qrs.
150 Inf. Bde.) The Bde. H/Qrs. moved on to
HAUTE NOYELLE, cable detachments extending
the two pairs to this point which became
Divisional Advanced Signals in the evening
of the 6th, with a line to 150 Inf. Bde.
at BOUT DU DIABLE, and local lines to
H/Qrs. of the 149 and 151 Inf. Bdes. in the
village of HAUTE NOYELLE.
— See Diagram 3 —

Nov. 7th) — At dawn on the 7th a line was Paid to
1918) LEVAL, where advanced Divl. H/Qrs. was
established in accordance with Operation
Order No. 265, a line also being laid to
point C.17.A.6.6 for a Staff O.P.
Division moved to HAUTE NOYELLE as
Rear H/Qrs on 7th. Lines were extended from
LEVAL to MONCEAU by mid-day of the 7th, with
a tap off for 149 Inf. Bde. at C.18.C.1.1 up to
CHATEAU ROMBISE C.18.A.9.5 which became
Adv. Divl. H/Qrs. with lines to 149 and 150 Inf. Bde.
H/Qrs. at MONCEAU ST. WAAST, and a line to 151
Inf. Bde. at ST. REMY - CHAUSSEE.
— See Diagram 4 —

Nov. 8th) — On the 8th, Divl. H/Qrs. was established at
1918) CHATEAU ROMBISE, MONCEAU - ST - WAAST in accordance
with warning order. Two pairs of lines were poled
forward to ST. REMY - CHAUSEE for use of 149 and
151 Inf. Bdes. and 250 Arty. Bde. R.F.A., also a
lateral was Paid to 38th Divn. at AULNOYE
U.29.A.2.8. In the afternoon, the lines to
ST. REMY - CHAUSSEE were extended to ST. AUBIN
(150 Inf. Bde. H/Qrs.) and beyond this to H/Qrs.
149 Inf. Bde. at DOURLERS.
— See Diagram 5 —

Nov. 9th) — It was decided on the evening of the 8th,
1918) to make 150 Inf. Bde., a mobile brigade,
Signal Company moving forward with
skeleton Divl. H/Qrs.
Divl. H/Qrs. opened on the 9th at DOURLERS
CHATEAU. (c/o Telegram RA.102) at 9.00 hrs. The 150 Inf. Bde.
moved forward, a detachment following with telephone
line, and a Staff O.P. was opened at LA SAHTE at
12.00 hrs. This line was extended to CARS POTERIES
where H/Qrs. 150 Inf. Bde. opened Signal Office and
Bde. H/Qrs. at F.19.B.1.9 at 13.00 hours.
— See Diagram 6 —

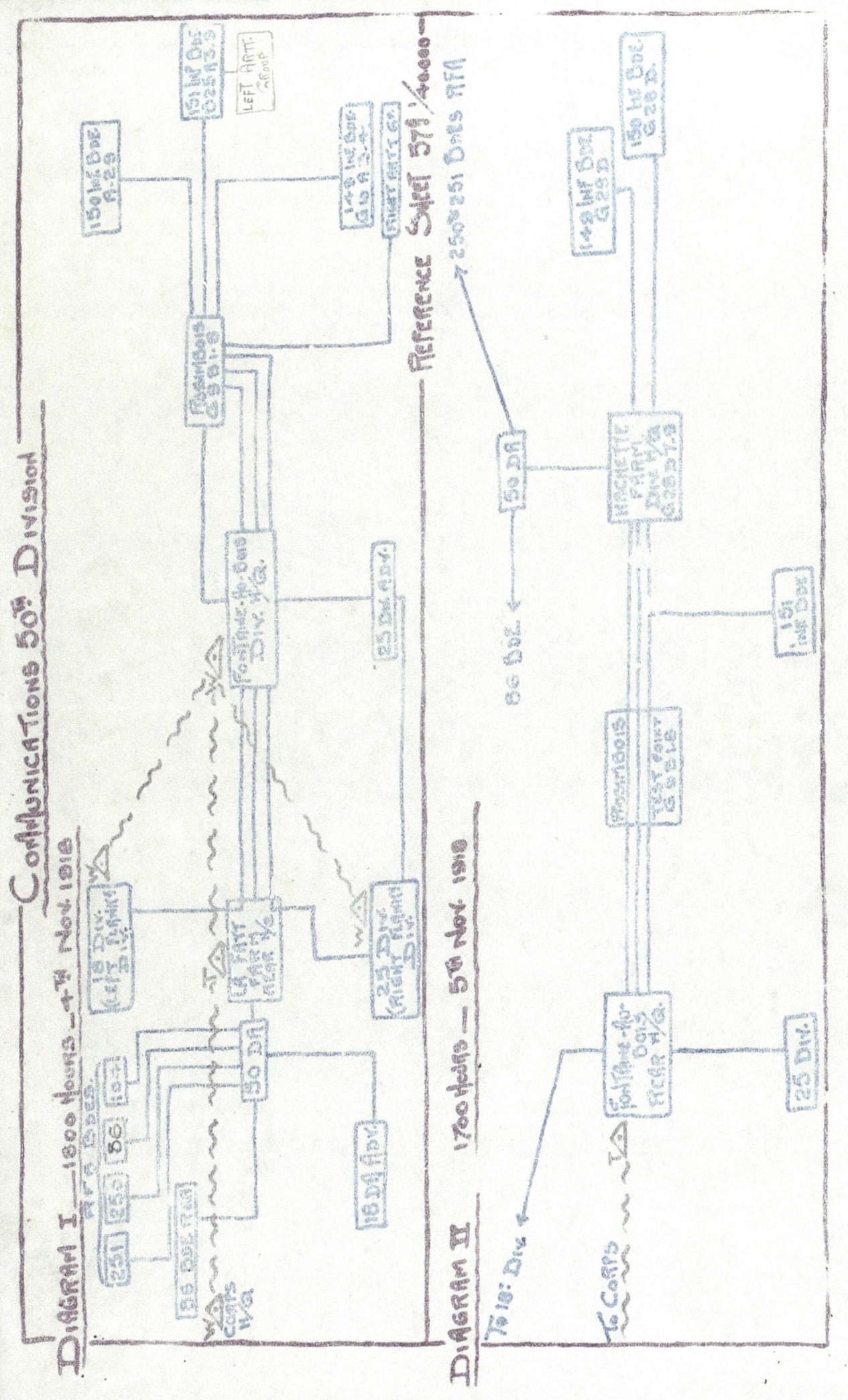

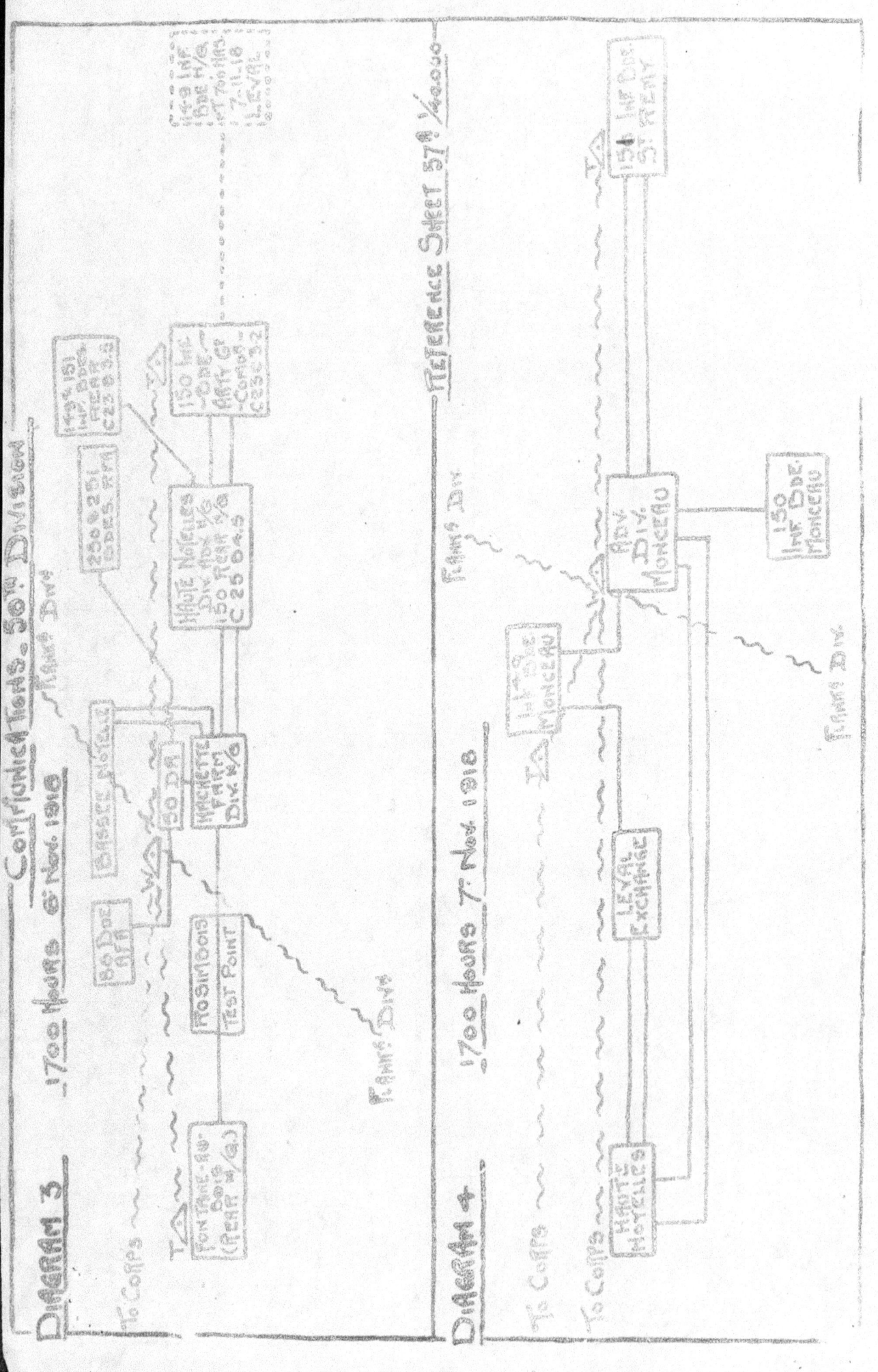

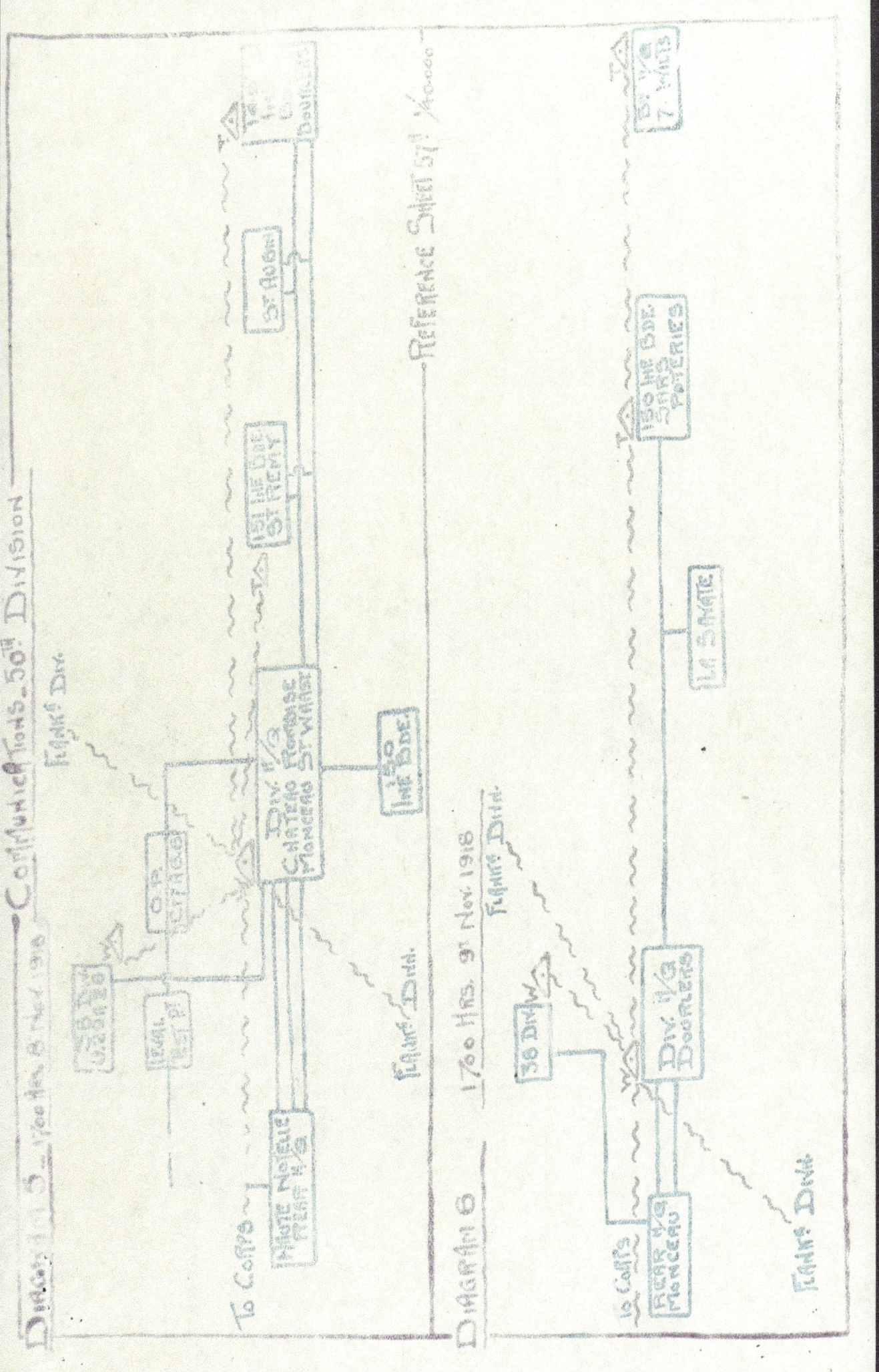

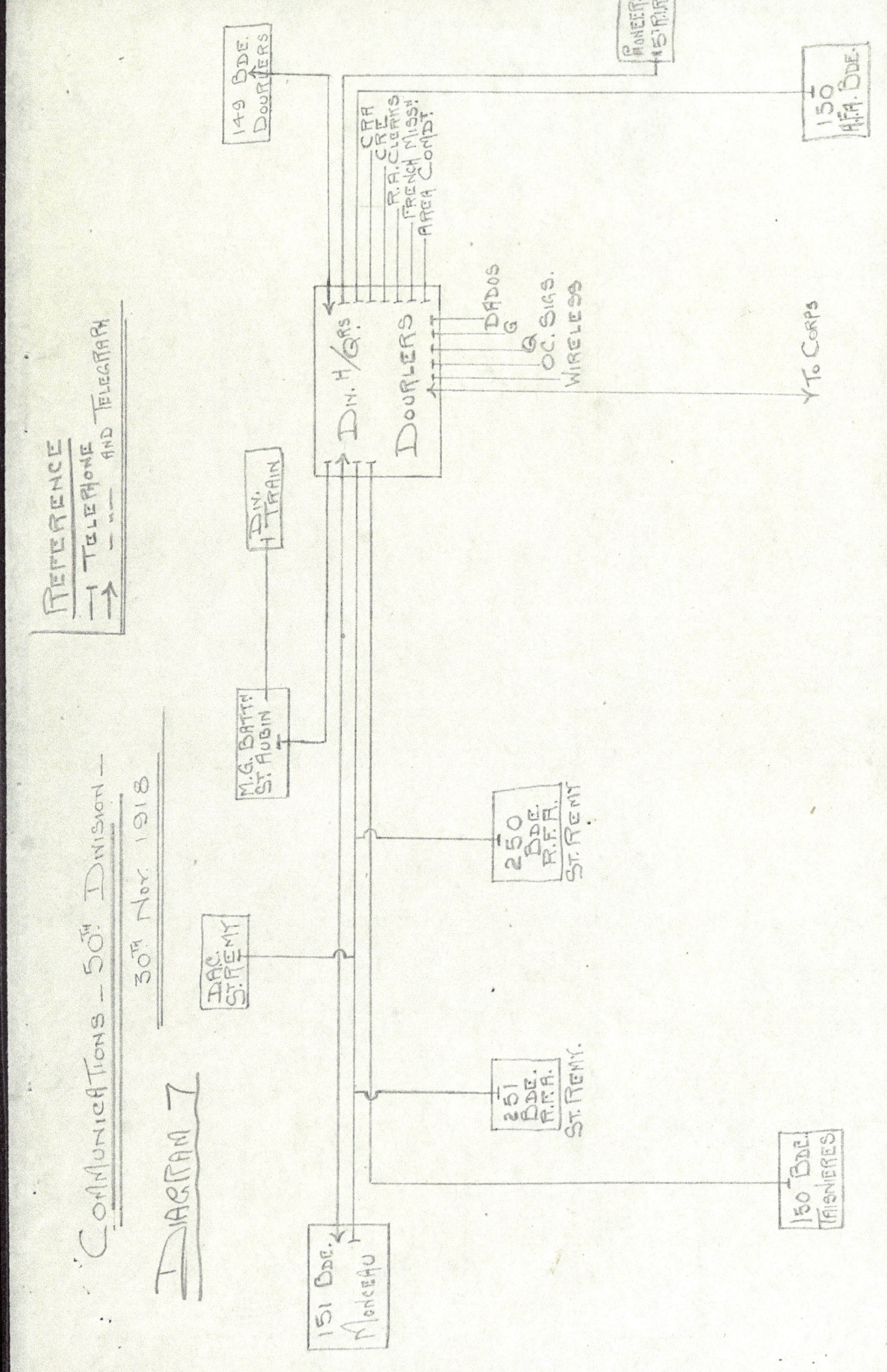

50th Divn.   **Wireless Communications**
1918

Nov. 3rd — The 149 and 150 Inf. Bdes. moved to FONTAINE-AU-BOIS and there erected a joint Wireless Station. The 151 Inf Bde. moved from LE CATEAU to BOUSIES and erected Wireless Station at 1600 hours. The Divl. H/Qrs. moved to LA FAYT FARM and established communication with Corps, flanking Divs. and three Inf Bdes. — SEE DIAGRAM 2.

Nov. 4th — At ZERO hour communications were as above. A little later, other communications with the 149 and 150 Inf Bdes. having temporarily broken down, opportunity was given to the Wireless Stations to dispose of a number of messages. This was satisfactorily done. At noon, these two brigades moved forward, and owing to continuous moves, did not again this day, erect Wireless Stations.

The 151 Bde. moved from BOUSIES without wireless instruments and personnel, and did not recover same until 1200 hours, on Nov. 6th. At LA FAYT FARM at 1300 hrs. a trench set was substituted for the Wilson set, which was sent forward to FONTAINE-AU-BOIS and there established communication with Corps, flanking divisions, and rear Divl. H/Qrs. at 1600 hrs. — SEE DIAGRAM I

Nov. 5th — At 1000 hours the Wireless Station at LA FAYT FARM was ordered to move to FONTAINE-AU-BOIS when the rear Divl. H/Qrs. moved: the Wilson set was dismantled and taken forward to HACHETTE FARM. Owing to transport difficulties caused by bad weather, the state of the roads through the FORÊT DE MORMAL, and the positions of mine craters, the set was not erected until 2000 hours, when reception of messages only was possible, owing to the accumulators having suffered from exposure and dampness. — SEE DIAGRAM II

Nov. 6th — At 0800 hours Nov. 6th complete communication was again established with the flanking divisions, and later in the day with Corps.

For several hours during this day, the Corps Wireless Station seemed to be completely

Wireless Communications (Cont'd)

Nov. 6th (Cont'd)
"dio", as signals were not received from there, by any of these divisions.

SHEET 57A (1/40,000)
The 149 and 150 Inf. Bdes, which were situated at HACHETTE FARM on the 5th, moved forward — the 149 Inf. Bde. to NOYELLES, LEVAL, and thence to MONCEAU, where the Wireless Station was erected at C.18.c.1.2 at 1600 hours on Nov. 7th:— the 150 Inf. Bde. to NOYELLES, the Wireless Station being erected at C.25.B.Central at 1400 hours Nov. 6th.

At 1400 hours the 151 Bde. moved forward to NOYELLES and erected Wireless Station at C.25.B.2.6 at 1900 hours. SEE DIAGRAM 3

Nov. 7th — At 0800 hours, the Divl. Station was dismantled and taken forward to NOYELLES and erected at C.25.B.Central at 10.00 hours: before however the instruments were completely connected, the station was dismantled and ~~taken forward to NOYELLES~~ transferred to MONCEAU, C.18.A.7.3, and erected at 1500 hours, communication being established with Corps, flanking divisions, and 149 Inf. Bde.

The 150 Bde., at 1630 hours Nov. 6th moved to MONCEAU, but the Wireless Station was not erected.

The 151 Bde. moved from NOYELLES at 0800 hours Nov. 7th to ST. REMY CHAUSSEE, the Wireless Station being erected at D.13.c.Cent. at 1100 hours; at 1600 hours the office was moved to D.14.c. and communication established with Divl. H/Qrs. SEE DIAGRAM 4

Nov. 8th — Divl. H/Qrs. remained at MONCEAU, communication being maintained with Corps, flanking divisions, and 151 Inf. Bde.

The 149 Bde. moved from MONCEAU, about 1400 hrs., and passing through ST. REMY CHAUSSEE erected the Wireless Station at DOURLERS, D.18.A.7.0 at 1800 hours.

During the evening of this day, arrangements were made by which the 150 Inf. Bde. was made mobile: it was allotted three rear Pook sets, one front Pook set, and two Trench sets. The Wilson and one Trench set were kept for use at Divl. and advanced Divl. H/Qrs. SEE DIAGRAM 5

Wireless Communications Contd.

Nov. 9th — On the morning of this day, the Wireless Personnel and instruments were withdrawn from the 151 Inf Bde. and sent to the 150 Inf Bde. (The front Poop set being exchanged for a rear set at Divl. H/Qrs.)

SHEET 57A (/40,000)

The 149 Bde. was at this time situated at DOURLERS and it was intended to pick up the Wireless personnel for use at Divl. H/Qrs. during the continued advance, as either Wireless or Visual men. DOURLERS was reached by the Signal Transport at 1500 hours, and orders were there received, cancelling the intended advance to LA SAVATE. Consequently, the Wilson set was erected and communication established with Corps, 18th, 25th, 38th, and 66th Divisions, the 150 Bde. H/Qrs., and the Battn. H/Qrs. of the 7th Wilts. Regt. The 150 Bde. was situated at SARS POTERIES, F.13.D.2.5., and the Trench set attached to the 7th Wilts Regt. Battn. H/Qrs. at SOLRE CHATEAU A.13 (SHEET 57)

SEE DIAGRAM 6

The chief difficulties encountered throughout the operations, relate to the transport of instruments. The continued advance, and the long distances between Headquarters, made it impossible for the personnel to carry anything above their necessary kit. Motor transport was long delayed by the blown-up bridges, crossroads etc., and horse transport was badly affected.

The need for small strongly-built and well sprung wagons fitted up properly as W/less Stations, wherein it is unnecessary to disconnect instruments, is imperative to efficient communication by wireless.

The question of re-newing and re-charging accumulators, is an important one: the box-car could only be used behind Divisional H/Qrs. and during such an advance, horse transport for this purpose is essential.

The great distance between Corps and Divl. H/Qrs. caused much inconvenience, and even delay as it necessitated the use of high aerials: these, besides being difficult to erect in the dark, and at any haphazard place, cause much jamming, thus difficulties to operators.

Wireless Communications.

(Sheet 57A.)

Whilst at Le Trou aux Soldats one W/T trench set and two Loop Sets were attached to each Bde. One Wilson Set and one Trench Set were kept for use at Div. H.Q. and Adv. Div. H.Q.

Oct. 28th On the evening of this day the W/T Stn. at Le Trou aux Soldats was moved to Le Cateau, and communication was established from Div. H.Q. at Soydoux Chateau to the Corps H.Q., 18th & 25th Div. H.Q., the 149 Bde. at Pommereuil and the 150 Bde. at La Fayt Fm., by 1800 hours on Oct. 29th 1918.

Nov. 3/18 The 149 & 150 Bdes moved to Fontaine-au-Bois and there erected a joint W/T Stn. The 151 Bde. moved from Le Cateau to Bousies & erected W/T Stn. at 1600 hours. The Div. H.Q. moved to La Fayt Fm. and established communication with Corps, flanking Divs. and three Bdes.

Nov. 4th At zero hour comm⁻ⁿˢ were as above. A little later other communications with the 149 & 150 Bdes. having temporary broken down, opportunity was given to the Wireless Stns. to dispose of a number of msges. This was satisfactory done. At noon these two Bdes. moved forward and owing to continuous moves did not again this day erect W/T Stns. The 151 Bde. moved from Bousies without its W/T instruments and personnel and did not recover same until 1500 hours Nov. 6th. At La Fayt Fm. at 1300 hours a trench set was substituted for the Wilson Set which was sent forward to Fontaine-au-Bois and there established communication with Corps, flanking divisions, and rear Div. H.Q. at 1600 hours.

Nov. 5th. At 1000 hours the W/T Stn. at La Fayt Fm. was ordered to move to Fontaine-au-Bois when the Rear Div. H.Q. moved; the Wilson Set

Wireless Communications (contd.)

Nov. 5th contd. was dismantled and taken forward to Hachette Inn. Owing to difficulties to transport caused by bad weather, the state of the roads through the Forêt de Mormal, and the positions of mine craters, the set was not erected until 2000 hours, when reception of msges. only was possible owing to the accumulators having suffered from exposure & dampness. At 0800

Nov. 6th hours Nov. 6th complete communication was again established with the flanking divisions, and later in the day with Corps. For several hours during this day the Corps W/T Stn. seemed to be completely "dis" as signals were not received from it by any of these divisions. The 149 & 150 Bdes. which were situated at Hachette Inn on the 5th, moved forward — the 149 Bde. to Noyelles, Leval, & thence to Monceau where the W/T Stn. was erected at C 18 c 12 at 1600 hours Nov. 7th.; the 150 Bde. to Noyelles, the W/T Stn. being erected at C 55 b cent. at 1400 hours Nov. 6th. At 1400 hours the 151 Bde. moved forward to Noyelles and erected W/T Stn. at C 55 b S.6 at 1900 hours.

Nov. 7th At 0600 hours the Divisional Stn. was dismantled and taken forward to Noyelles, and erected at C 55 b cent at 1000 hours; before however the instruments were completely connected the Stn. was dismantled and transferred to Monceau, C 18 a 7.3, and erected at 1500 hours communication being established with Corps, flanking divisions & 149 Bde. The 150 Bde. at 1430 hours Nov. 6th moved to Monceau but the W/T Stn. was not erected. The 151 Bde. moved from Noyelles at 0600 hours Nov. 7th to St. Remy Chaussée, the W/T Stn. being erected

Wireless communications (contd.)

3.

Nov. 7th (contd.) at D 13 c cent. at 1100 hours; at 1600 hours the office was moved to D 14 c, & communication established with Div. H.Q.

Nov. 8th Div. H.Q. remained at Honeau communication being maintained with Corps, flanking divisions, & 151 Bde. The 149 Bde. moved from Honeau about 1400 hours & passing through St. Remy Chaussée erected the W/T Stn. at Dourlers D 18 a 7.0 at 1800 hours.
During the evening of this day arrangements were made by which the 150 Bde. was made mobile; it was allotted three rear loop sets, one front loop set, and two Trench sets. The Wilson and one Trench Set being kept for use at Divisional and advanced Div. H.Q.

Nov. 9th On the morning of this day the W/T personnel and instruments were withdrawn from the 151 Bde. and sent to the 150 Bde. (the front loop set being exchanged for a rear set at Div. H.Q.) The 149 Bde. was at this time situated at Dourlers and it was intended to pick up the W/T personnel for use at Div. H.Q. during the continued advance, as either Wireless or Visual men. Dourlers was reached by the Signal transport at 1500 hours and orders were there received cancelling the intended advance to Le Sabate. Consequently the Wilson set was erected and communication established with Corps. 15th 25th 38th & 46th Divisions, the 150 Bde. H.Q. and the Bn. H.Q. of the 7th Wilts Regt. The 150 Bde. was situated at Sars-Poteries F 13 d 2.5 and the Trench set attached to the 7th Wilts Regt. Bn. H.Q. at Sobre Chateau A 13 (Sheet 57).

Wireless communication (contd.)

The chief difficulties encountered throughout the operations relate to the transport of instruments. The continued advance and the long distances between Headquarters made it impossible for the personnel to carry anything above their necessary kit. Motor transport was long delayed by the blown-up bridges, cross-roads, etc; and horse transport was badly effected. The need for small strongly built & well sprung wagons fitted up properly as W/T Buses, wherein it is unnecessary to disconnect instruments, is imperative to efficient communication by Wireless.

The question of re-newing & re-charging accumulators is an important one; the Box-car could only be used behind Divisional H.Q., and during such an advance horse transport for this purpose is essential.

The great distance between Corps. & Divisional Headquarters caused much inconvenience and even delay, as it necessitated the use of high aerials; these besides being difficult to erect in the dark, and at any haphazard place, cause much jamming, thus difficulties to operators.

55"/18.   Vincent Hawes 2/Lt. R.E.
i/c Wireless.
50 Div. Sig. Coy. R.E.

ORIGINAL   SECRET

WAR DIARY

of

50TH (NORTHUMBRIAN) DIVISION SIGNAL COMPANY R.E.

VOLUME XLIV

NOVEMBER, 1918.

Army Form C. 2118.

WAR DIARY
or
INTELLIGENCE SUMMARY.
(Erase heading not required.)

Instructions regarding War Diaries and Intelligence Summaries are contained in F. S. Regs., Part II. and the Staff Manual respectively. Title pages will be prepared in manuscript.

Place	Date 1918	Hour	Summary of Events and Information	Remarks and references to Appendices
LE CATEAU	Nov. 1		Shuel Telephone Lines were laid on Nov. 1st from LA FAIT FARM (150 S/F Bde. S/Qrs. and Divl. Signals Adv.) to 150 S/F Bde. S/Qr. at FONTAINE-AU-BOIS. Due to shelling these lines were frequently broken.	S/SHEET 57A 1/40,000
LA FAIT	2-3		Two wires were laid on 2nd from LA FAIT FARM to S/Qr. 150 S/F SHEET 57A N/W Bde. and Arty. Liaison Officers Exchange at FONTAINE-AU-BOIS. Line (1/25,000) paid from LA FAIT FARM to 151 S/F Bde. S/Qr. at BOUSIES. For details of operations see appendix attached.	S/SHEET 57A N/W (1/25,000)
	4		Divl. S/Qrs. moved to FONTAINE-AU-BOIS. Line paid from S/Qr. 150 S/F Bde. at POSINBOIS, then on to 151 S/F Bde. S/Qr. at B. 25 A 3 9 in FORÊT DE MORMAL. Advanced Divl. S/Qr. opened at RUE AT LEVRES, FORÊT DE MORMAL at 8AM on Nov.5th. Later opening at HACHETTE FARM.	
	5		Lines were paid to HACHETTE FARM.	
	6		On the 6th, lines were paid to BASSEE NOËULE (S/Qr. 150 S/F Bde.) then on to HAUTE NOËULE (Divl. Signals Advd.)	
	7		Line was paid to Bde. Signals Advs. LEVAL, on the 7th (Divl. S/Qrs. being at HAUTE NOËULE) and on to CHATEAU FRAMBISE, MONCEAU, which later in the day became Divl. S/Qrs. Local lines were then laid to	S/SHEET 57A 1/40,000

Army Form C. 2118.

WAR DIARY
or
INTELLIGENCE SUMMARY.
(Erase heading not required.)

Instructions regarding War Diaries and Intelligence Summaries are contained in F. S. Regs., Part II. and the Staff Manual respectively. Title pages will be prepared in manuscript.

Place	Date 1918	Hour	Summary of Events and Information	Remarks and references to Appendices
	Nov. 7		149 & 150 Bde. S/O¹s. were paid on 9o. 8ʳᵈ Bde. S/O.	Sheet 57A 1/40.000.
	8		Sine were paid on 9o. 8ʳᵈ to Bde. of St. REMY CHAUSSEE and St. AUBIN. Sine also paid to	
			and a Patrol Rue to 38ᵗʰ Division at AULNOYE. Sine also paid to S/O. 149 Suf Bde. at DOURLERS	For details of operations see appendix attached.
DOURLERS	9	0900	S/O. 149 Suf Bde. at DOURLERS. At 9 A.M. on Nov. 9ᵗʰ Div. S/O. was established at DOURLERS Sine was paid to 150 Suf Bde S/O. at SARS POTERIES.	
	10		Local Rues paid.	
	12		Thanksgiving and Memorial Service held near Div. S/O. on morning of 12ᵗʰ 11oo, followed by Presentation of Medals by Div. Commander, Maj. General F. G. JACKSON D.S.O. The Parade was attended by Signal Company Commanders, and a number of the men. Div. O.S. whom received decorations.	
	18ᵗʰ-20ᵗʰ		The 150 Suf Bde. moved from DOURLERS to TAISNIERES, on 18ᵗʰ 9/00. and a Rue was paid from MORCETTO (51 Suf Bde. S/O.) to TAISNIERES using the Signal Office at MORCEAU on exchange. The 149 moving, very satisfactory, a Rue was paid on Nov 19ᵗʰ from DOURLERS	
	-30ᵗʰ			

Army Form C. 2118.

WAR DIARY
or
INTELLIGENCE SUMMARY.
(Erase heading not required.)

Instructions regarding War Diaries and Intelligence Summaries are contained in F. S. Regs., Part II. and the Staff Manual respectively. Title pages will be prepared in manuscript.

Place	Date	Hour	Summary of Events and Information	Remarks and references to Appendices
DOUCHIERS	Nov. 1918 18th, 29th – 30th		to MONCEAU and joined the TIRAILLEURS Rue at the Usine Kuneby giving a direct Rue from Div. S/G par to 150 Suf Bde.	SHEET 57A. S/G (1/40,000)
			On Nov. 20th the 159 Suf Bde Rdr TROOPS and went into billets previously occupied by 150 Suf Bde at DOURIERS, linking up the Rue Hot Rod previously been used by 150 Bde.	SEE D.R.R.App. 7 attached.
			From Nov. 3rd onwards throughout operations normal signalling was used. During the movement much cable was talked in the area also a German Signal Wagon Cable wagon Telephones and Telegraphic instruments.	
	1-30		BATTLE CASUALTIES – NIL	
	1-30		HONOURS AND AWARDS	
			463071 Cpl. Richardson. R. M.M. } D.R.O. 4345 1/11/18.	
			463022 „ M. Drake GT. M.M. }	
			463052 Cpl. Hall S.G. M.M. }	
			262265 „ Richdos C.A. M.M. } D.R.O. 4354 2/11/18.	
			463105 „ Hall ON G. M.M. }	

WAR DIARY
INTELLIGENCE SUMMARY

Army Form C. 2118.

Place	Date	Hour	Summary of Events and Information	Remarks and references to Appendices
	Nov. 1918 1-30		Honours & Awards (Cont'd)	
			463167 Sgt. Chestney E.J. Bar to M.M. DRO.4356 4/1/18.	
			463258 L/Cpl. Spinks E.S. M.M.	
			498620 Pte. Golding J. M.M. } DRO.4356 4/1/18.	
			430741 " Brown J.A. M.M.	
			458771 A/Cpl. Johnson J. M.M. DRO.4362 7/11/18.	

Major.
Comdg. 50. Div. Sig. Coy. R.E.

ORIGINAL   SECRET

W A R   D I A R Y

of

50TH (NORTHUMBRIAN) DIVISIONAL SIGNAL COMPANY R.E.

V O L U M E   XLV.

DECEMBER, 1918.

Army Form C. 2118.

VOLUME XLV

WAR DIARY
or
INTELLIGENCE SUMMARY.
(Erase heading not required.)

Instructions regarding War Diaries and Intelligence Summaries are contained in F. S. Regs., Part II. and the Staff Manual respectively. Title pages will be prepared in manuscript.

Place	Date 1918	Hour	Summary of Events and Information	Remarks and references to Appendices
DOURIERS	Dec 1st to 17th		Major C.F. Macon. MB. RE. (Special Reserve) took over command of the Coy. from Lt/Col Major C.F. Bagnall MB at Battn Dur H.Q. afterwards Commanded 3rd Army Signal School from Major C.L. Bagnall MB.	
Mob. Unit Headquarters 102,000.			On 5th Dec the 151 Inf Bde moved from MONCEAU to MECQUIGNIES, communication being established with them at the latter place by Wireless & despatch Riders. On the same day the HQ Inf Bde left DOURIERS for 151 Inf Bde & the O/s Hd qrs at MONCEAU, using the existing telephone & telegraph lines for communication. An advance party left DOURIERS on the 16th Dec. for LE QUESNOY and at 12:00 hrs on 17th Dec opened an advance office.	Rep from O.O. 267 4-10-12-18
LE QUESNOY	Dec 17th to 31st		On 18th Dec Div HQ moved from DOURIERS to LE QUESNOY. The Signal Office at DOURIERS at 12 hrs. & opening at LE QUESNOY at the same time. Telegraphic & telephone communication was established to XIII Corps at CAUDRY, 149 Inf Bde in LE QUESNOY, 150 Inf Bde at WARGNIES (19th Dec), 151 Inf Bde at BAVAI (19th Dec). Telegraphic & telephone communication was established with Div Artillery at CARNOY on 21st Dec. Wireless communication was established with XIII Corps, Flanking Divisions 150 & 151 Inf Bdes.	
Mob. Unit Headquarters 102,000.			The Divisional Signal Class was reassembled at ALLONVILLE on 29th Dec, when all the students returned to their Battalions; the personnel & stores coming by lorry from ALLONVILLE to	

WAR DIARY
INTELLIGENCE SUMMARY.
(Erase heading not required.)

Army Form C. 2118.

Place	Date	Hour	Summary of Events and Information	Remarks and references to Appendices
VILLERS POL			on the 27/29th Dec.	
			Much cable was also sent to the XIII Corps during the month and progress was made with the Education Scheme	
			Sent 20 miners belonging to the Coy were demobilized towards the latter end of the month, their place in the Coy being filled ultimately by reinforcements	
			Honours & Awards	
			321287 Sjt. T.Stoke	2/Lieut R.L.Gelderd, awarded M.B. per 50 Div Routine Order no.6704. 13/7/18
			354847 Sjt. C.Keightley	Awarded Military Medal per 50 Div Routine Order
			463029 L/Cpl. Shannon	no.6613 dated 31st Oct/18.
			77495 Spr. W.J.Hopkins	
			94549 A/C. Gale	
			463025 2/Cpl. Barnes W. D6M.M.M. awarded Bar to D6M per 50 Div RO no.6812 dated 19.12.18
			173424 A/Cpl.Menton J. D6M. Mentioned in Despatches per London Gazette of 23.12.18	 Major RE O.C.[?] 50 Div Signal Co RE

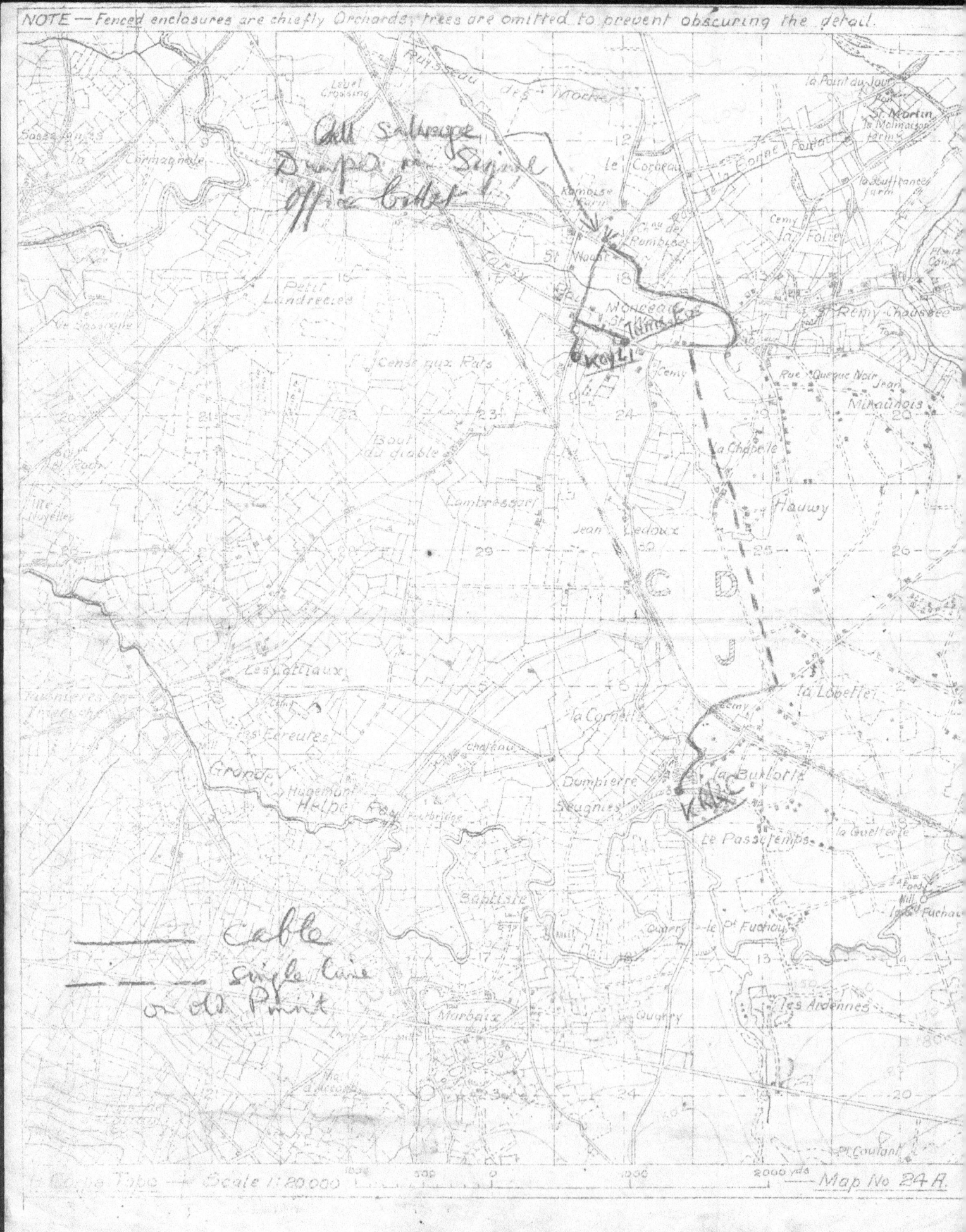

— Message

To _____

I am at _____ and am consolidating.
I am at _____ and am pushing forward
I am temporarily held up at _____
by Rifle. M.G. fire from _____
I want more S.A.A.
My casualties are _____
My strength is _____
Information about my own front is: _____
(mark situation on map)

Situation on my flanks appears to be _____

I intend to — _____

Time _____ Signed _____
Date _____ Regiment _____

ROUTE DIAGRAM

Sheet 57A

ARMY ZNI 4.XII.18 SIGNALS

DOURLERS

D | E
BDE HQRS | ROYAL FUSILIERS
18 | 13

SCOTTISH HORSE
SEMOUSIES

AVESNES + MAUBEUGE ROAD

(R) INZ

J 18 | 13 K
R DUB FUS
BAS LIEU

F. Williams Sgt

CIRCUIT DIAGRAM

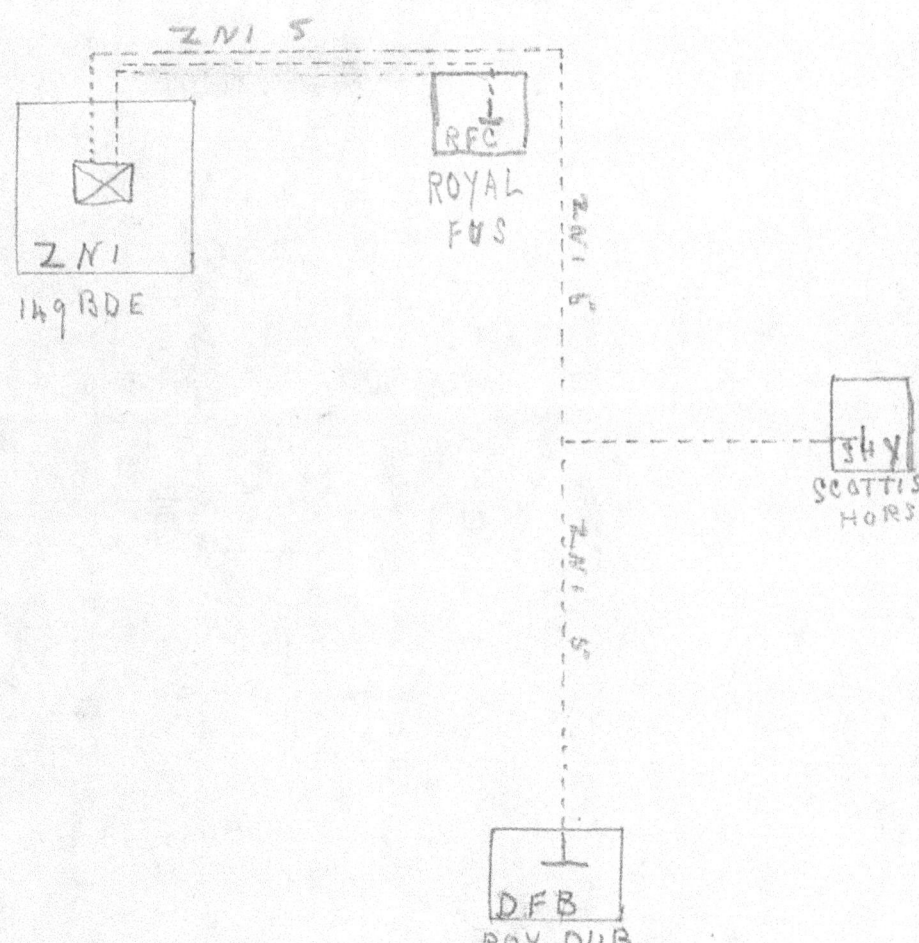

F. Williams Sgt

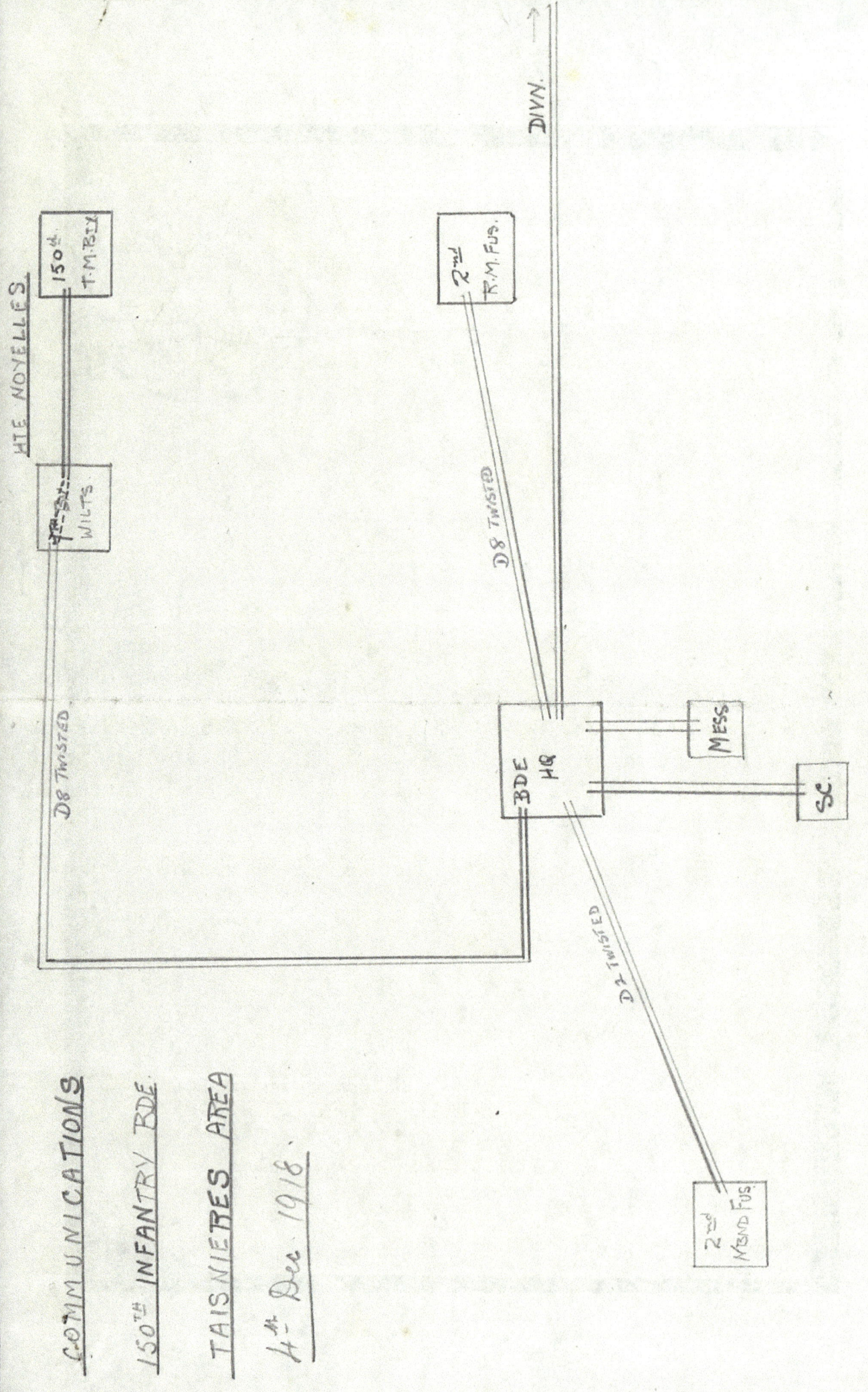

OC Signals
30th Division

Herewith Route Diagram
called for

4/2/18

W Barnard
Lieut
Cmdg No 3 Section

ORIGINAL   SECRET

WAR DIARY

of

50TH (NORTHUMBRIAN) DIVISION SIGNAL COMPANY R.E.

VOLUME XLVI

JANUARY, 1919

WAR DIARY
INTELLIGENCE SUMMARY

Army Form C. 2118.
VOL. XLVI

Place	Date	Hour	Summary of Events and Information	Remarks and references to Appendices
Le Quesnoy (France)	Jan 1st to 31st		Divisional Signal Company all the month remained at Le Quesnoy	
	17th		Entertainment in men's billet, a string being wired in the men's dining room	
	25th		150 S. of Bn. moved from Brig. to Bath, extends the Divisional line Runner Bay to Bath, where telegraphic & telephonic communication was maintained to Division. A Dinner for all Engineer Officers in the Division was held tonight in the Signal Officers Mess. 7 Russian Observing Telemetry at which the O.C. XIII Corps was present. During the month progress was made enlarging the area of cable Ye. two lorry loads of cable being sent to Corps dump. The Educational Scheme was carried out so far as the Signal Coy was concerned by many members of the Coy attending classes also topographs instruction to was given in the Coy to men of other units. Sports were indulged in during the month – namely football – Lewis gun returns fulfils the health of the Coy. remained very good. Several musical divertisements also on hand.	
			Awards	
			463087 Sgt. N. Jenner M.M. 27179 Sgt. Walter	Awarded the M.M.
			463015 " C. Parkam 463022 Bdr McAnlis M.M.	See London Gazette dates 18.1.19.

Forms/C./2118/14.

ORIGINAL　　　　　　　　　　　　　　　　　　　　　　　　　　　　　　SECRET

WAR DIARY

of

50TH (NORTHUMBRIAN) DIVISION SIGNAL COMPANY R.E.

VOLUME XLVII.

FEBRUARY, 1919.

Army Form C. 2118.

WAR DIARY
or
INTELLIGENCE SUMMARY.
(Erase heading not required.)

Vol. XLVII.

Instructions regarding War Diaries and Intelligence Summaries are contained in F. S. Regs., Part II. and the Staff Manual respectively. Title pages will be prepared in manuscript.

Place	Date	Hour	Summary of Events and Information	Remarks and references to Appendices
Le Quesnoy (France) Mob. Valenciennes /10.0.0.0.	Feb ? to 28th		Divisional Signal Company remained all the month at LE QUESNOY. 151 Inf Bde moved from BAVAI to POIX DU NORD, a new line being laid from LE QUESNOY to the latter village, where telegraphic & telephonic communication was maintained to Division. During the month salvage work was carried out in the Divisional Area. The Education Scheme was carried out so far as the Signal Company was concerned by many members of the Company attending classes also telegraph instruction &c was given in the Company to men of other units. A number of men and a few horses were demobilized during the month. The mens billets were improved and the health of the men in the Company was exceptionally good.	

Roland Stewart
Lt-Adjt-for Major R.E.
Comdg 50th (Nor) Div Signal Coy RE

ORIGINAL
****

SECRET
****

WAR DIARY

OF

50TH (NORTHUMBRIAN) DIVISION SIGNAL COMPANY R.E.

VOLUME XLVIII.

MARCH 1919.
****

VOL XLVIII

WAR DIARY

INTELLIGENCE SUMMARY.

(Erase heading not required.) 50 Divisional Signal Coy. R.E.

Army Form C. 2118.

Instructions regarding War Diaries and Intelligence Summaries are contained in F. S. Regs., Part II. and the Staff Manual respectively. Title pages will be prepared in manuscript.

Place	Date	Hour	Summary of Events and Information	Remarks and references to Appendices
	1919			
LE QUESNOY (FRANCE)	Mar 1 to Mar 31		Company remained in LE QUESNOY throughout the month. Salvage work was continued but owing to duplication it was found impossible to entrain of Education classes	Map Valenciennes Sheet 1/2 1/100,000
Wet. Valenciennes 1/100,000			Though Lewd men were sent away on leaves at R/ph and Army Schools During the month, the health of the men continued to be very good. 8 oft R.W. Grange and Lieut B.J. Sny Lewis was demobilised in March 1919, and 42 other ranks & 64 horses were also sent away. All stand-out actually in use were withdrawn from the outlying Divisions, as also all surplus men. Telephonic work was reduced to messages of a priority nature and the Local Deleute Pole Totoa Lines to local villages was reduced considerably. On 31st March R.A. HQ moved into Le Quesnoy and 150 Inf Bde. H.Q. to WARGNIES-LE-PETIT. Latter used the same line for telephone	

Army Form C. 2118.

WAR DIARY
or
INTELLIGENCE SUMMARY.
(Erase heading not required.)

Place	Date	Hour	Summary of Events and Information	Remarks and references to Appendices
LE QUESNOY (FRANCE)	1919 Mar 1 to Mar 31		Communication tapping at near WARGNIES-LE-PETIT. Casualties — Nil. Awards — Nil.	

Graham Adams
Capt. R.E.
OC 50 Dvl Signal Co R.E.
Conny, 50 Divl Signal Co R.E.
1st April 1919

Abey File

50th Division G.

N1265
13.3.19

In about a week's time this unit will be reduced to Cadre establishment, with addition of such retainable men as I have. I will continue the present communications as long as possible, but it will be necessary shortly to make some reduction. It is suggested that the D.R. service be reduced to one run a day, and the telegraph service to priority messages. Ordinary messages will be sent as far as possible by wire during slacks in the traffic, and the balance will be sent by D.R.L.S. Signal offices will probably be closed at night.
The use of Special D.R. to be discontinued. The text of such messages as would be sent by Special D.R. to be wired priority, followed by the full text by next ordinary D.R. I am reducing the staff at Bdes. and Div. Arty. at once, and it will soon be necessary to discontinue the lines to Battalions and Batteries, following which the switchboards at Bdes. will be withdrawn and a telephone put in the Bde. Staff Office connected directly to the Divisional Exchange. It will simplify matters considerably if such units can be concentrated as near as possible to Divl. H.Q.

Cadre demobilised 18 June 1919
Equipment guard proceeded to UK
for Final Demob 12th July 19
13. 3. 19.

Major R.E.
Cmdg 50 Divl. Signal Coy R.E.

War Diary

of

50th. (Northb'n.) Div'l. Signal Coy., R.E.

for Month of

April, 1919.

Volume XCIX.

Vol XLIX

WAR DIARY

INTELLIGENCE SUMMARY.
(Erase heading not required.) 50. Divisional Signal Coy. R.E.

Army Form C. 2118.

Instructions regarding War Diaries and Intelligence Summaries are contained in F. S. Regs., Part II. and the Staff Manual respectively. Title pages will be prepared in manuscript.

Place	Date	Hour	Summary of Events and Information	Remarks and references to Appendices
	1919			
LeQuesnoy (FRANCE)	Apl 1 to Apl 30		The Cadre of the Company was reduced this month by 30% making 3 Officers & 82 O.R's instead of the original Cadre of 3 Offrs & 72 O.R's. The bulk of the retainable men were drafted to various units and as the consequence of losing nearly all the DR's the DR.L.S was reduced to one delivery per day. The communications were rearranged so as to give two alternative routes to Infantry Brigades, Artillery and Div. train, to compensate for the slowness in getting faults repaired owing to reduced personnel. Our mobilization stores were loaded up expeditiously in the usual way, by Vocabulary Sections, so as to make out a fresh loading table, each load being replaced in the Stores in separate heaps, each heap being marked with the number of the wagon it was to be loaded in & each wagon having a corresponding number printed on it. Messages had become considerably reduced in number owing to the Divisional Staff being reduced to "Packet" Codes - average number of Telegrams per day. 49. Average number of DRLS packets per day. 123	VALENCIENNES Sheet 12 Map $\frac{1}{100,000}$

C.Ranson
Major R.E.
Cmdg 50th Divn Signal Coy R.E. 1st May 1919

www.ingramcontent.com/pod-product-compliance
Lightning Source LLC
Chambersburg PA
CBHW080806010526
44113CB00013B/2334